Dark World

Discover the hidden depths of the digital underworld in this comprehensive, interdisciplinary exploration of the dark web.

Ideal for security agencies, professionals, counter-terrorism experts, and policy-makers alike, this work offers invaluable insights that will enhance understanding and fortify strategies. By shedding particular light on the nuances of the 'dark market,' this book provides readers with a detailed understanding of the dark web, encompassing both its sinister underbelly and unexpected potential.

This book also uncovers the latest trends and cutting-edge mitigation techniques. From illicit transactions to thriving business ventures, it examines the key domains and sectors that thrive within this clandestine environment. This book consolidates myriad perspectives on security and threats on the dark web.

Dr. Atif Ali – Postdoctoral Researcher at RMC|MMU Cyberjaya Malaysia. He has a PhD in Computer Science (Artificial Intelligence-Based Software Engineering) and is certified by OS Forensics. His research contributions are in the Dark Web, Artificial Intelligence, and Software Engineering. He has more than 40 research articles to his credit that are internationally recognized. He has received more than 47 National/Provincial awards in different co-curricular activities. He is working hard to make the cyberworld safe.

Muhammad Qasim – MS Security Technology, from the University of Wales, Cardiff (UK). He holds multiple international publications and certifications in Cyber Security, Cloud Networks, and Information Technology. Currently he has CyberSec First Responder, CompTIA|CEH|CHFI|Security +, SixSigma, and Microsoft–Azure.

Dark World
A Book on the Deep Dark Web

Atif Ali and Muhammad Qasim

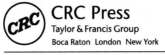

CRC Press
Taylor & Francis Group
Boca Raton London New York

CRC Press is an imprint of the
Taylor & Francis Group, an **informa** business

Designed cover image: shutterstock

First edition published 2024
by CRC Press
6000 Broken Sound Parkway NW, Suite 300, Boca Raton, FL 33487-2742

and by CRC Press
4 Park Square, Milton Park, Abingdon, Oxon, OX14 4RN

© 2024 Atif Ali and Muhammad Qasim

CRC Press is an imprint of Taylor & Francis Group, LLC

Reasonable efforts have been made to publish reliable data and information, but the author and publisher cannot assume responsibility for the validity of all materials or the consequences of their use. The authors and publishers have attempted to trace the copyright holders of all material reproduced in this publication and apologize to copyright holders if permission to publish in this form has not been obtained. If any copyright material has not been acknowledged please write and let us know so we may rectify in any future reprint.

Except as permitted under U.S. Copyright Law, no part of this book may be reprinted, reproduced, transmitted, or utilized in any form by any electronic, mechanical, or other means, now known or hereafter invented, including photocopying, microfilming, and recording, or in any information storage or retrieval system, without written permission from the publishers.

For permission to photocopy or use material electronically from this work, access www.copyright. com or contact the Copyright Clearance Center, Inc. (CCC), 222 Rosewood Drive, Danvers, MA 01923, 978-750-8400. For works that are not available on CCC please contact mpkbookspermissions@ tandf.co.uk

Trademark notice: Product or corporate names may be trademarks or registered trademarks and are used only for identification and explanation without intent to infringe.

ISBN: 9781032518879 (hbk)
ISBN: 9781032518893 (pbk)
ISBN: 9781003404330 (ebk)

DOI: 10.1201/9781003404330

Typeset in Times
by codeMantra

I want to thank my family for their support and love and express special gratitude to my parents, who helped me become who I am. I would also like to thank my leader, Dr. Yasir Hafeez, for his help whenever I need it.

Atif Ali

First, I would like to thank God for allowing me to write another book. I would also like to thank my family for their unconditional support. My thanks go to my co-author and friend, Dr. Atif Ali, for the great partnership and my wife's amazing support throughout this project.

Muhammad Qasim

Contents

Aim

When it comes to terrorist organizations' web content, we mean "ALL" of it. That includes everything from blogs to websites, forums, chat rooms, videos, virtual worlds, and everything in between. The East Valley Tribune, the BBC, Discover Magazine, Fox News, Information Outlook, Wired Magazine, and Arizona have all covered Dark Web research extensively. This unique effort will help educate the next generation of future cyber/internet-savvy intelligence, justice, and defense professionals.

Audience

This book's objective is to present an interdisciplinary and easily understandable book on the Dark Web. This research will benefit security agencies, security professionals, counter-terrorism experts, and policymakers. The proposed work could be incorporated as a textbook or reference in my graduation degree on terrorism, policy-making, criminology, and data security.

The proposed monograph's target audience includes the people listed below.

- **IT Academic Audience:** Choose juniors and seniors from universities interested in computer science or related IT fields like information systems, computer science, digital forensics analysis, information security, information systems, or information science educators.
- **Government Audience:** Managers, analysts, and public policymakers from all levels of government are interested in knowing more about the Dark Web and its impact on society and its security.
- **Security Industry Audience:** Think tanks and research institutes in the security and defense industries, as well as analysts and researchers, conduct IT-related security research and development, notably employing open-source web materials.
- **Security Academic Audience:** The general public, as well as academics, researchers, and graduate students interested in learning about the Dark Web's impact on society, including political science, terror studies, and criminology.

Contributors

Dr. Abdul Razzaque - Postdoc UK
(Cyber Security & AI)

Prof. Ghulam Ali Mallah - Postdoc
Glasgow

Zulqarnain Freed Khan
(Criminologist)

Dr. Muhammad Adnan Khan
(Computational Intelligence)

Dr. Muhammad Sharreh Qazi
(Information Warfare Expert)

Muhammad Shahid Iqbal
(Cyber Threat Intelligence Expert)

Syed Abdul Haseb Shah
(Criminologist)

Prof. Dato' Dr Mazliham Bin Mohd
Su'ud
(President at Multimedia University
Malaysia)

Bilal Ahmed Khan
(IT/Cyber Security Expert)

Ali Raza
(AI/ML Expert)

Syed Asim Raza
(Anti-Money Laundering Specialist)

Khushbu Khan Ghori
(Cyberspace Analyst)

Muhaamd Islam Satti (Data Scientist)

Prof Dr. M Mansoor Alam
(IT Expert)

Qurat ul Ain Haider (Blockchain
Expert)

Hina Naseem (Crypto Analyst)

Haroon Akhtar (Recruitment Head
Cyber Security)

Usama Nazir (Artificial Intelligence
Expert)

Khurram Shehzad (Machine
Learning/AI)

Acknowledgments

Please accept our sincere gratitude for your unwavering support and love. We understand that pursuing a career means spending a lot of time away from you, so we are sorry and speechless at how appreciative we are because of your unwavering support. We are motivated to do more.

Because of this, neither our parents received higher education nor were they allowed to read or write. Our parents sacrificed a great deal throughout their lives to allow us to pursue higher education. We are speechless at how appreciative we are of everything you've done for us.

We want to thank Prof. Dato' Dr Mazliham Bin Mohd Su'ud (President at Multimedia University Malaysia) and Prof. Munawar Hussain Ch (MD Robox. ai www.robx.ai) for providing us with the research opportunity and for all of their encouragement from the bottom of our hearts. Your perseverance, inspiration, and guidance were invaluable as we researched and wrote the book.

1 Cybersecurity and the Dark Web

INTRODUCTION

Internet and World Wide Web (WWW) are far more extensive than we see when we're just browsing in the digital environment. New information technology (IT) applications are causing the internet and its users to increase, which is expected to continue. Although the internet has overgrown, its vulnerability to misuse and abuse has increased, creating a severe risk and a problem in cyberspace that affects everyone. Every day, many cybercriminals attempt to illegally access unauthorized data on the web. Apple Safari, Mozilla Firefox, Microsoft Internet Explorer, and Google Chrome are most popular web browsers among internet users. When using a standard web browser, you access what is known as the surface web. However, much of the content on the deep websites is hidden. Recent studies show that most major search engines crawl a small portion of the web. According to the literature, many website contents are concealed on a deep website. There is a sector of the deep web referred to as the dark web (DW) where most cybercriminals conduct their illegal activities, also called the darknet. The following will be discussed in detail in this chapter:

- Cybercrime and cybersecurity.
- Web and its levels.
- Cyberspace malware challenges.
- The DW and emerging criminal threats.

CYBERCRIME AND CYBERSECURITY

The expansion of the internet has given users in various sectors, including academia, government, business, and industry, a significant opportunity. Although this growing development has created new opportunities for cyberwarfare, it has also created new vulnerabilities that can be exploited to attack critical infrastructure and systems. Users' privacy and safety in the cyber world must be protected in cyberspace. For example, governments and businesses use the term "cybersecurity," which refers to safeguarding critical computer networks and national databases, such as those belonging to the military, government agencies, civil society, large corporations, and law enforcement agencies.

CYBERCRIME

The following are examples of cybercrime as defined by Interpol:

> The area of cybercrime is rapidly expanding. To commit various crimes with no boundaries, physical and virtual criminals increasingly use the internet speed, convenience, and anonymity.

DOI: 10.1201/9781003404330-1

Most social scientists use the term "cybercrime," which means committing a crime using a computer or other electronic device. It means a thorough examination of criminal activity and the people who commit it, such as romance scams and online fraud schemes. It also means an assessment of cyberbullying and online extremism. The focus is on both the perpetrator and the victim in this story.

Cybercrime includes computer-related offenses and offenses against the privacy, validity, and accessibility of digital information and services. For example, consider computer-related forgery, unauthorized access to computers, unlawful interception of computer data transfer, and tampering with data without authorization. Businesses might expect to pay hundreds of millions or even billions of dollars in damages if they are the target of a cyberattack.

As a result of the financial loss and disruption, there are increased attempts to keep the attacks under control. Since more of our customers live online and there are many undetectable attacks, our efforts are becoming more focused. Rather than being broad in scope, cybercrime attempts have honed in on the time and expense of carrying out an attack compared to its monetary value in recent years.

According to the Australian Cybercrime Online Report, cybercrime refers to "crimes against computers or other devices and where computers or other devices are crucial to the crime." This definition encompasses a wide range of cybercriminal activities. Malicious software (such as viruses) is either developed and deployed against specific computer networks, or these networks are exploited to further criminal agendas like identity fraud. As cyberattacks grow, security experts work around the clock to keep cyberspace safe from accidental and intentional attacks. As a result, cybersecurity is a critical area for protecting online users' personal information. Types of cybercrimes are elaborated in Figure 1.1.

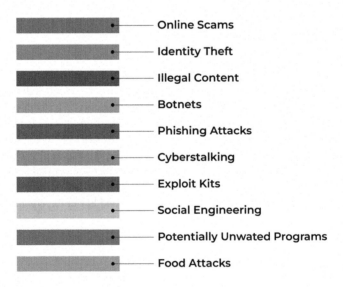

FIGURE 1.1   Types of cybercrime.

CYBERSECURITY

Security in cybercrime refers to measures taken to prevent online criminals' unauthorized access to computer software, hardware, data, programs, and intellectual property. Physical access to hardware and/or cyberphysical infrastructure can be controlled. Many code injection attacks (CIA) like SQL injection, cross-site scripts (XSS), or service disruption. Cybersecurity is defined by the International Telecommunications Union as

> The term "cybersecurity" refers to a wide variety of actions and technology that can be utilized to safeguard a company's digital assets and its customers. A company's or individual's assets in the cyber environment include anything from computing machines to users to applications, services to telecommunications infrastructure, and everything in between. Cybersecurity is the achievement and maintenance of an organization's and its users' security attributes to protect assets from relevant cybersecurity dangers. Accessibility, integrity, and confidentiality are all possible security features.

Because of these three CIA principles, cyber security is a need. Only people with access to classified or sensitive information should have such access. Availability means that information and systems must be easily available to people who need them. Integrity means that originality and trustworthiness are retained while any adjustments are prevented.

Cybersecurity has grown in relevance due to the rising use of computer systems, intelligent gadgets, wireless networks like Bluetooth and Wi-Fi, and the spread of the internet. Protecting information and systems is part of cybersecurity at home, work, or business.

Cybersecurity encompasses many concepts, including application and data security, network security, and disaster recovery. When it comes to cyberspace security, various activities and operations are included. These include threat reduction and vulnerability prevention policies for protecting systems and networks. Provide response in the event of an incident and data recovery policies to ensure data security. This software guards against malware and hacker attacks. The cybersecurity landscape is shown in Figure 1.2.

One of the goals of cybersecurity is to keep people safe from becoming victims of cybercrime. It is impossible for legal and regulatory organizations to fully benefit from the IT revolution because there is no cyberspace security. As a result, extra care must be taken to keep cyberspace from becoming a source of danger for governments and citizens and from becoming a haven for cybercrime.

There are numerous opportunities to improve human development and better integrate into the information society provided by cybersecurity. It affects nearly all activities and almost all citizens around the world. It also aids in formulating policies and strategies and disseminating information and education.

Malicious activities in cyberspace have increased dramatically. The release of thousands of new sophisticated malware and spam aimed at damaging computer systems or stealing or destroying their data is a major cause for concern, as shown in Table 1.1.

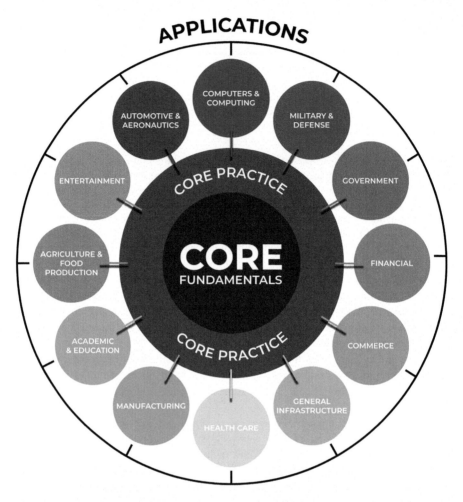

FIGURE 1.2 Cybersecurity landscape.

TABLE 1.1
Differences Exist Between Cybercrime and Cybercrime Prevention and Detection

Sr.	Cybercrime	Cybersecurity
1	There are purely scientific explanations for why and how criminals commit crimes; no further assumptions are made.	Applied science, coding, and engineering of networks to increase their security.
2	Sociology, criminology, and psychology are all branches of social science.	STEM (Science, Technology, Engineering, and Mathematics) includes computer science, engineering, and IT.
3	The principal sources of law enforcement are state and local governments.	Federal authorities are in charge of law enforcement.

(Continued)

TABLE 1.1 (*Continued*)
Differences Exist Between Cybercrime and Cybercrime Prevention and Detection

4	Special interest groups have ordinary people as their targets.	Networks in government and business are particularly vulnerable to conflicts of interest.
5	A growing number of criminals are turning to computers as a tool (cyberbullying, romance scams, fraud, and identity theft).	Network crimes involving computers are the most common, with software or hardware being the most frequently targeted victims (code injection, malicious software, DoS attacks, and XSS).
6	Individuals, families.	Governments, corporations.

DoS, denial-of-service; IT, information technology; XSS, cross-site scripts.

WEB AND ITS LEVELS

The invisible or hidden web and the DW describe the WWW. The DW's content is inaccessible via traditional search engines because it is hidden. Search engines like Google do not have access to this content because it exists exclusively on private encrypted networks or peer-to-peer configurations. The deep web is referred to because traditional search engines cannot reach large portions of it (the invisible web). Virtually everyone who uses the internet daily makes unintentional trips to what might be considered deep websites. Hackers, spies, and government agencies will have difficulty tracking deep web users and seeing what sites they visit or how they use the deep web. Pictorial views of all levels are shown in Figure 1.3.

WEB LEVELS

Even though the deep web is divided into several levels, the "open to public" portion is the lowest (known as level 1). In contrast, the "dark" portion (known as level 5) cannot be accessed with a standard web browser and necessitates using Tor or another private network. Table 1.2 summarizes the DW's maturity level.

WEB CATEGORIES

Here are the distinct types of webs, each with a different level of security.

Dark Web: Only specific software, configurations, or authorizations can access this part of the WWW or deep web, and it frequently uses nonstandard communication protocols and ports. It is necessary to use the Onion Router to access the Tor network, a DW service.

Deep Web: An internet resource that isn't found on the main page of a search engine. As a result, you can no longer search to find locations; you must go to each one manually. If you have an address, they'll be waiting, but there aren't any instructions for getting there. Because search engines can't cover the

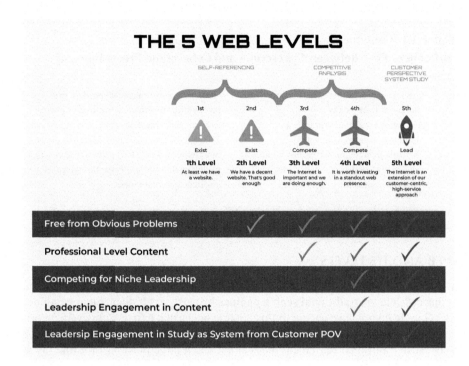

FIGURE 1.3 Levels of web.

TABLE 1.2
Levels of Dark Web

L-1	Websites/Purpose
L-2	Temp email services.
	Web 2.0.
L-3	Honey ports.
	Bergie Web.
	Freehive, Bunny Tube, etc.
	Google locked results.
L-4	Shelling Networking AI theorist.
	Charter Web Hacking Groups.
	Banned videos, books, etc.
L-5	Exploits, black markets, drugs.
	Onion sites.
	Questionable materials.
	Human trafficking, bounty hunters, rare animal trade.

---

entire internet, there is a lot of content on the deep web. Most of the deep web comprises pages that can't be located using standard search engine techniques.

Public Web: Unencrypted or non-darknet is the most common usage. When using the conventional WWW's low-base anonymity, most websites frequently identify individuals by their IP address.

Darknet: The darknet, a subset of the deep web, includes a variety of networks and technologies for sharing digital content. Users of standard browsers can't see the website address or find the servers they're visiting when using the darknet. It also keeps users from accessing the DW. The surface, deep, DWs, and darknet are compared below.

Figure 1.4 emphasizes the significant diversity between the internet, deep web, and DW (Table 1.3).

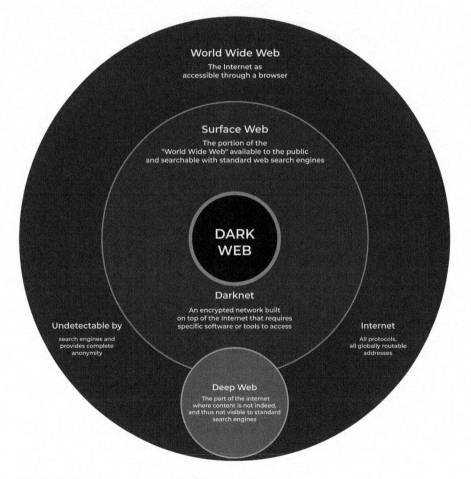

FIGURE 1.4 Internet, deep web, and dark web distinctions.

TABLE 1.3

Deep Web, Darknet, Dark Web and Surface Web Distinctions

Explanation	Darknet	Dark Web	Deep Web	Surface Web
	–	Intentionally omitted information	Search engines can't find this content	Easily indexable material for search engines
Referred as	Underbelly of internet	–	Deep net, Invisible web, hidden web	Lightnet, Visible web, indexable web, indexed web
Comprises	Network	Web	Web	Web
Matters	Illegal	Illegal	Legal + illegal	Legal
Reliable Sources of Data	–	–	96%	4%
Browser	RetroShare, Freenet, I2P, GNUnet, Tor, OneSwarm,	Tor Browser	–	Opera, Google, Mozilla, Chrome, Firefox, etc.

THE CONSEQUENCES OF CRIMINAL ACTIVITY ON THE DW

Trust and security must be built using IT to thrive on the DW. Cyberspace's lack of security erodes public trust in the information age. It is important to remember this primarily when cyberattacks lose money, assets, and highly sensitive information concerning military, economic, and commercial operations worldwide. As information travels across legal systems and networks worldwide, it is increasingly important to safeguard personal information, financial assets, and national security. As a result, both the public and private sectors are becoming more interested in cybersecurity. Types of crimes on the DW are shown in Figure 1.5.

Because of the increasing number of computers and IT-related applications, cybercrime has become a significant problem worldwide. Every day, tens of thousands of cybercriminals attempt attacks on computer systems to gain unauthorized access to them via the internet. Hundreds of new computer viruses and spam are released each month to steal or destroy data. Threats of this nature are prohibitively expensive, both in quantity and quality. Many security experts are concerned about securing communication and computer systems from expanding cyberattacks, including deliberate attempts by unauthorized persons to gain system-level access to steal crucial data, make illegal financial transfers, disrupt or damage systems' operations, or engage in any other illegal activity.

Network stability has become more challenging to maintain as computer security improves. It was discovered by the Australian Cyber Security Centre (ACSC) that the culture has shifted to emphasize low-risk, high-reward aims to achieve their objectives, with a focus on social engineering tactics to launch new assaults in particular.

In addition, because the internet is so widely available, criminals have developed increasingly detailed portraits of their victims by exploiting and analyzing their digital footprints. Spear-phishing attacks, identity theft, and fraud have increased, and specialized malware tools have emerged.

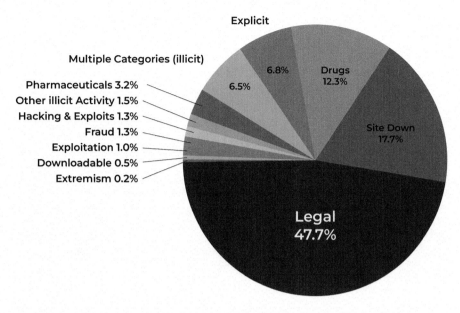

FIGURE 1.5 Types of crimes on the dark web.

A cybersecurity incident can severely compromise computer and network systems due to numerous dangers and pitfalls. Malicious users, disasters caused by human activity, or inadequate cybersecurity controls are all possibilities.

TROJAN HORSES, WORMS, AND MALWARE

There are various ways to distribute malware, including email, instant messaging, malicious websites, and even non-malicious websites that have been infected with it. Some websites let users download malware without their knowledge or agreement, and other strategies call for people to click on a website's link or button. Major types of malware are shown in Figure 1.6.

RANSOMWARE

According to the ACSC, ransomware is a post-exploitation denial-of-service (DoS) attack that uses malware to prevent legitimate network users from accessing their devices or system content. The hacker will typically issue a ransom demand by unlocking the infected computer. Requesting payment from the victim data on infected devices is encrypted using modern versions of ransomware, which demand a payment to decrypt. The victim must pay a ransom to obtain the decryption key. The evolution of ransomware is shown in Figure 1.7.

Because of the anonymity of using cryptocurrencies, most people prefer to pay with Bitcoin or another cryptocurrency. You must receive a "ransom message" explaining how to pay the ransom in question to receive the instructions. A common tactic is to demand money from the victim, usually large sums. The scanning phase of the compromise is where this data is gleaned. Additionally, ransomware can

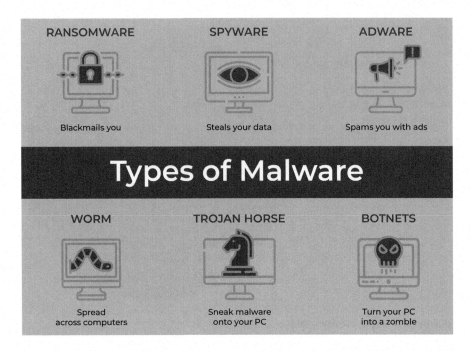

FIGURE 1.6 Types of malware.

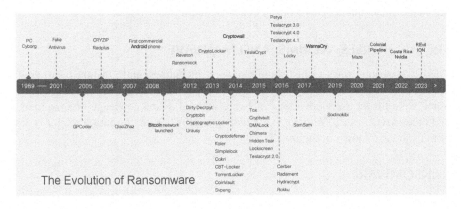

FIGURE 1.7 Evolution of ransomware.

increase the amount of money demanded in exchange for faster delivery of the funds into victims' accounts. Even if you pay the ransom, your data may not be unlocked immediately. A list of ransomware is listed in Table 1.4.

DISTRIBUTED DoS ATTACK

An assault that successfully prohibits or affects the authorized operation of networks, systems, or applications by draining resources is known as a distributed DoS. The pictorial view is shown in Figure 1.8.

TABLE 1.4

Ransomware

Ransomware	Summary
Crysis	If a compromised device is still on the network, the virus can infect the victim's machine. ESET, an antivirus company, has developed a decryption algorithm to allow victims of the Crysis ransomware to regain access to their files.
WannaCry	It can spread throughout a network by exploiting flaws in Windows-based operating systems (released by the Shadow Brokers). One hundred seventy-six file types of ransomware encrypt and append the extension WCRY to the file name. Once it's finished, a ransom note is sent to the victim, requesting Bitcoin payment.
PETYA	It has the same vulnerability as WannaCry, but it's a software update for M.E. Doc that allows it to get past the firewall and spread. The Ukrainian government uses this software. By overriding the system's master boot record, PETYA provided an attack vector for the adversary to seize control of the device.
SAMSAM	Healthcare-related ransomware has been targeted. It uses vulnerable servers to spread throughout the network, compromising each one. SAMSAM secures the compromised system by encrypting all data.
Locky	As a macro attachment, it's been widely distributed via spam. Spam emails are the primary method by which this ransomware is spread. The emails contain either a malware Microsoft Office file or a ZIP attachment. In the latest releases, file extensions have been renamed to ".diablo6" or ".lukitis".

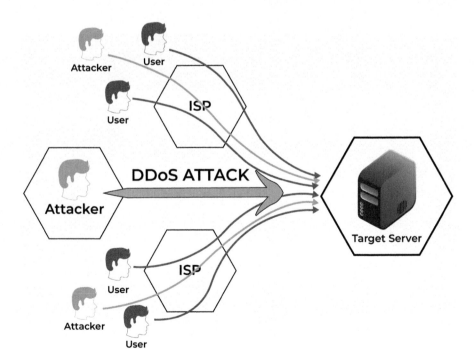

FIGURE 1.8 Distributed denial-of-service attack.

SOCIAL NETWORK (SN) ATTACKS

Because of the sheer number of people using social media and personal information, attacks on SNs are common. Internet SNs are a prime target because users trust their virtual friends. For example, a malicious website may invite users to click on a link to someone else's page.

SCAREWARE

False security software warnings says, "It's not important, so don't worry about it." Because many people believe the pop-up alerts that their system is infected and are tempted to download and pay for special software to "guard" their system, fraudsters can benefit significantly from this scam. Scareware warning signs are shown in Figure 1.9.

BOTNETS AND ZOMBIES

When we say botnet, we're talking about a network of infected computers linked to a single "controller." Computers that have been infected are referred to as "zombies" in the press. Threats will also grow as attack techniques improve and become more widely available. This is because fewer people with specialized technical understanding may launch successful attacks. Botnets that steal data and encrypt it are becoming increasingly difficult to detect. The working of a botnet is shown in Figure 1.10.

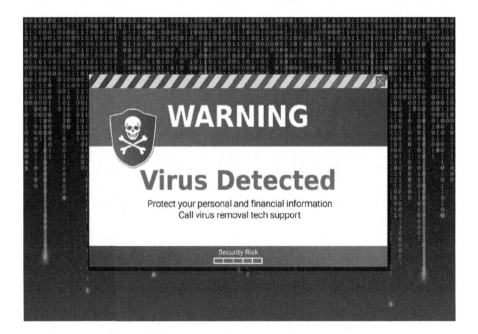

FIGURE 1.9   Scareware warning signs.

How a Botnet Works

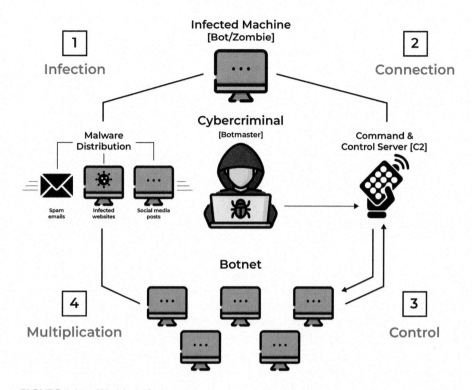

FIGURE 1.10 Working of a botnet.

KEY HITCHES

The Key Hitches are one of the most challenging hazards in cyberspace because security concerns are constantly changing and evolving. Additionally, it imposes new economic, professional, and social paradigms, resulting in a wide range of legal and technological difficulties that must be addressed while considering the industry's specific characteristics and needs. As a result, a new strategy and set of methodologies are required.

It's never been easy to maintain a secure online presence. Excellent cybersecurity is crucial because attacks change daily as attackers improve their inventiveness.

CATEGORIES OF CRIME

An overview of various cybercrimes and their attack patterns is provided in the following categories of cybercrime:

- **Individual Level:** Cyberstalking, pornography distribution, human trafficking, and "grooming" are all examples of cybercrime.

- **Government Level:** Cyberterrorism refers to crimes against a less common government than the other two. Criminals who hack into government and military websites or disseminate false information fall. They can wreak havoc and spread fear throughout the civilian populace if they are successful. Terrorist organizations or hostile governments in other countries can be the perpetrators.
- **Property Level:** When someone's bank account information is stolen, money is siphoned off, credit card information is misused to make a slew of purchases online, a scam is run to fool unsuspecting victims into parting with their money, malicious software is used to access a company's website, or the organization's systems are disrupted.
- **Cybercriminals through SN:** The use of social media has permeated every aspect of our lives. This platform is used by cybercriminals, who take advantage of it to steal user credentials, identities, and other sensitive data. This technology may appeal to cybercriminals because it provides a convenient means of committing crimes. Cyberattacks on SNs can handle some different forms.

  - **Target:** Using a social media outlet, the cybercriminal gets in touch with the victim. When sent through SN, the message includes an attachment that directs the recipient to a malicious website or starts an installation file on their computer. Facebook, Twitter, and LinkedIn are the most frequently targeted social media networks.
  - **Infect:** Malware payloads are used in cyberattacks to infect a computer or a network. Malware can come in many forms, such as a Trojan horse, a BotNet, or a fake antivirus program. The malware was primarily distributed via pop-up advertising and malicious attachments in the past. Hackers are now employing advanced tactics to hijack legitimate websites and transmit malware through security weaknesses in a user's operating system.
  - **Attack:** Perpetrators can launch massive attacks on a broad scale or zero in on a specific individual using a network of "zombie" machines. Anyone with internet access could theoretically be the target of an attack, including employees of companies, governments, and online merchants. The attacks can also last for a long time because they constantly change their proxy connections and IPs.
  - **Control:** Zombie computers are known as such because they communicate with an attacker's control plane, which is typically a public server. When a machine is infected, the infection spreads by scanning for vulnerabilities in other machines.

DW MALICIOUS ACTIVITIES

As malware has grown and increased, it has become a crucial challenge for computer system security. Malware has also presented significant challenges in combating it due to increasingly sophisticated evasion methods. Furthermore, an antimalware strategy that worked in the past will no longer work in the future due to the constant evolution of malware design.

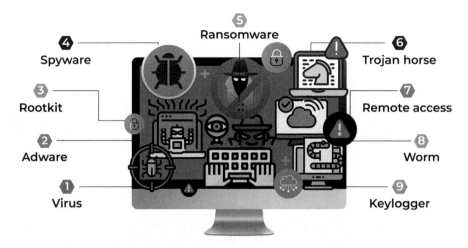

FIGURE 1.11   Malware classification.

Malicious activity on the DW is considered a severe concern. By participating in these nefarious behaviors, the intruder is either trying to disrupt normal computer operations or obtaining sensitive information from private computer systems. AV vendors receive thousands of new malware samples every day.

MALWARE CLASSIFICATION

Malware has become increasingly complex and diverse as the internet has grown more popular. From the first viruses and worms to Trojans and now infamous rootkits. To help you better understand what these terms mean and the dangers they pose, I've attempted to define them here. The malware classification is depicted in Figure 1.11.

CYBERSPACE MALWARE CHALLENGES

Because of their unpredictable and sophisticated attack patterns, malware has emerged as the greatest threat to the cyber community. Cybermalware challenges are illustrated below:

- **Email:** A piece of executable code is delivered to the host via email-based malware, replicating itself throughout the network. Social engineering techniques like encrypting zip files, sending the password via email, or presenting a fake PDF attachment in place of an executable file are popular today.
- **Mobile Malware:** In general, mobile malware attacks steal information by tracking what you do, gaining access to your credentials, or hijacking transactions. Because mobile devices are easily connected to the internet, third-party cloud services, and PCs whose security posture is unknown and not controlled by the firm, accessing company resources via mobile devices raises security vulnerabilities.
- **Cloud Network:** As a technical matter, cloud networks combine wide-area networks and internet-oriented access mechanisms to allow users to obtain

network tools and technology resources from a third-party provider. These networks are referred to as cloud-based ones. Computers and resources are connected and shared among all parties in the cloud, including cloud computing. Because of the hyper-connectivity of the cloud system, malicious activities are a growing source of concern.

- **Insecure Interfaces and APIs:** Customers can use software interfaces or APIs exposed by cloud computing providers to manage and interact with potential services. Cloud service security and accessibility depend on API security, which sets off the complexity of new layered APIs. Now that malware on one VM can access code or data on another VM, it is more challenging to identify malware that uses the new layer APIs.
- **Compact Network Topology:** Because of clouds' densely packed network structure and the chance that homogeneous software would be exploited, malware could spread much faster in a cloud computing environment. As a result, malware detection is complicated than in a non-cloud environment.
- **Virtualization:** It has increased software complexity, and, as a result, the potential for exploits and the sharing of hardware are challenges in the cloud. There is always the chance that complex software will be implemented or misconfigured, leaving users more vulnerable to malicious software.

- **Enterprise Networks:** The growing sophistication and obfuscation of malware with unknown threats puts enterprise networks at risk.
- **Financially Motivated Attacks:** Malware infecting web browsers, plug-ins, and document readers frequently leads to end-user infection with Remote Access Trojans (RATs). Using RATs, hackers can access a victim's accounts while remaining undetected. By using ransomware, all your files are encrypted. The victim must pay a ransom to get the decryption key needed to get their data back. Given their current success level, ransomware attacks are likely to become more prevalent in the future as well.

MALWARE ANALYSIS

Both features are widely used in the malware detection method taxonomy.

1. **Static features:** Extracted from executables.
2. **Dynamic features:** Derived from the way executables behave during their runtimes.
3. **Hybrid features:** Includes both techniques above.

Malware characteristic analysis is shown in Figure 1.12 as a general summary of traditional malware analysis.

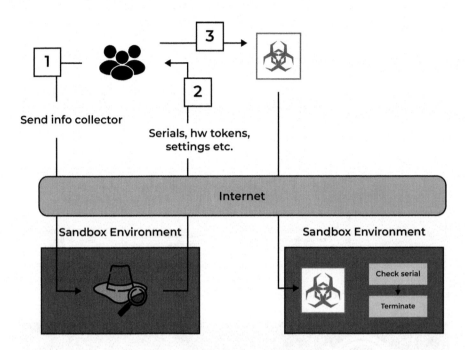

FIGURE 1.12   Classical malware analysis.

STATIC ANALYSIS

Static features from executables are used in traditional malware detection and classification systems. These four features are used to extract static information from images:

- String characters
- Portable exes
- Function length
- Evaluation

An overview of static malware analysis is shown in Figure 1.13. Classification and evaluation are carried out using the WEKA interface, a well-known classification technique. (https://cs.waikato.ac.nz/ml/weka/).

DYNAMIC ANALYSIS

The dynamic analysis takes time. Because each malware sample must be executed for a certain period of time and its behaviors must be logged in a controlled environment to verify that it cannot infect a live platform, performing dynamic analysis takes a long time. As a result of the differences between a controlled virtual environment and a natural run-time environment, malware may behave differently, leading to an inaccurate log picture. The process of dynamic analysis is depicted in Figure 1.14.

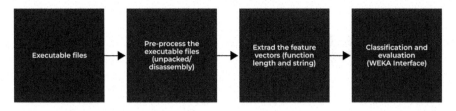

FIGURE 1.13   Static malware analysis overview.

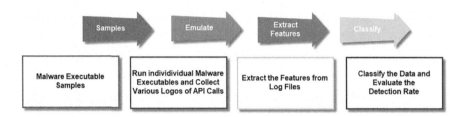

FIGURE 1.14   Dynamic analysis.

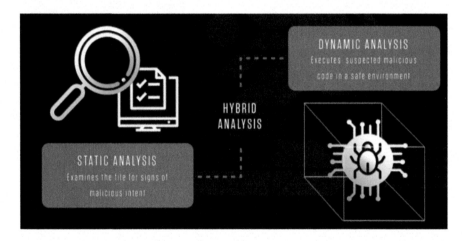

FIGURE 1.15   Hybrid malware analysis.

Virus behaviors may be triggered in certain situations (through specific commands or human interaction), which cannot be detected in a virtual setting. Dynamic extraction is preferred as it is less vulnerable to code obfuscation alterations, even though static approaches are more secure in the long run (Figure 1.15).

HYBRID ANALYSIS (INCLUDES BOTH TECHNIQUES ABOVE)

Hybrid analysis helps detect unknown threats, even those from the most sophisticated malware. Fundamental static analysis is not a reliable way to detect sophisticated malicious code, and sophisticated malware can sometimes hide in the presence of sandbox technology. Combining basic and dynamic analysis techniques, the hybrid analysis

provides the security team with the best of both approaches, primarily because it can detect malicious code that is trying to hide and extract many more indicators of compromise (IOCs) by statically and previously unseen code.

For example, hybrid analysis applies static analysis to data generated by behavioral analysis, like when a piece of malicious code runs and causes some changes in memory. The dynamic analysis would detect that, and analysts would be alerted to reevaluate and perform fundamental static analysis on that memory dump. As a result, more IOCs would be generated, and zero-day exploits would be exposed.

MALWARE DEFENSIVE MEASURE

Numerous strategies that use static and dynamic analysis to identify malware have been examined. Still, the current malware propagation technique with dynamic nature has piqued the interest of malware researchers and vendors. Successful antivirus strategies will no longer work if malware has developed new capabilities in the interim. Antivirus software designed to detect known varieties of malware will miss a new malware that evolves and loses its similarity to its original form or because a completely new malware is produced, unlike any other known malware.

The current body of literature makes it abundantly clear that current malware detection methods will fail miserably in the face of emerging threats. Researchers have proposed cumulative timeline analysis to solve this issue because it has a long track record of exceptional accuracy. Static and dynamic features are both needed in malware detection, and these features can be chosen to produce better results while functioning independently and complementarily, as demonstrated by this method. An executable can have both static and dynamic information extracted using this method, resulting in the same detection accuracy over 10 years.

THE DW AND EMERGING CRIMINAL THREATS

New forms of crime and menace are being developed on the shady side of the internet. Internet users have access to 3% of the internet's free content via search engines like Google, according to a study by Kristin (2017). On the other hand, the deep web is vast and can only be accessed with an anonymous browser like Tor. According to Kristin, the deep web is four to five times larger than the surface web.

Some of the criminal activities on the deep web include drug trade (selling and purchasing), people trafficking, child pornography, assassination contracts, sales of human body organs, and sex trafficking. Other criminal activities include illegal shipments of weapons, the sale of stolen goods, stolen cyber identity information, and terrorism. Using a hidden wiki and a deep search engine is the most efficient browsing method. These web pages provide access to a large number of deep web links. Figures 1.16 and 1.17 depict screenshots of the deep search interface in action (Tor access only).

TRAFFICKING IN HUMAN BEINGS AND SEXUAL SERVICES

As a result of online forums, chat services, and deep web anonymity, sex trafficking and human trafficking now constitute a considerable component of the country's crime. To recruit their victims as enslaved people or sex slaves, human traffickers

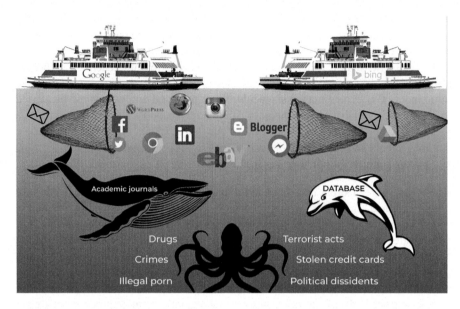

FIGURE 1.16   DW interests.

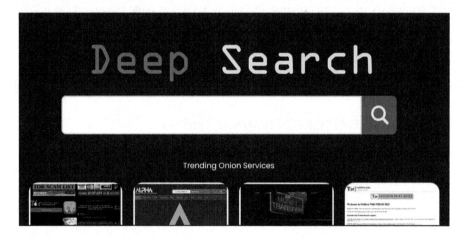

FIGURE 1.17   Deep search user interface.

negotiate and form contracts with them. Because of the deep web and Tor network, governments and anti-human trafficking organization can easily avoid detection, censorship, and surveillance.

ASSASSINATIONS AND ITS MARKETING

Criminals are selling their assassin skills on the deep web, according to a 2013 report from the Daily Mail. In addition to MailOnline and White Wolves, several other websites advertise criminals who can be hired for $10,000 in the US and $12,000 in Europe. A police officer can expect to earn anywhere from $40,000 to $1.5 million per year, depending on experience and position. Figure 1.18 shows the Silk Road website screenshot.

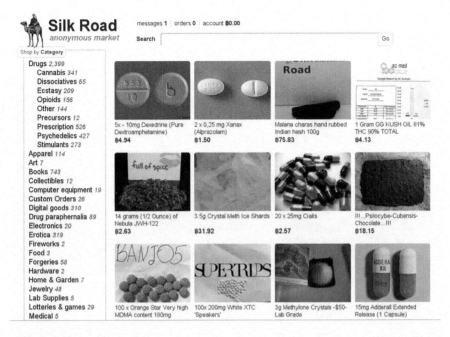

FIGURE 1.18 Silk Road.

TERRORIST AND DW

ISIS broadcasts and films killings in real-time, using the DW as a terrorist tool. As a broadcast medium, the DW serves as a platform to post short video clips. According to Singer and Brooking's research to discover and recruit potential warriors worldwide, released on June 20, 2017.

DRUG TRANSACTIONS

Drug transactions on the deep web have expanded dramatically due to anonymity, establishing a digital black market for drugs. Due to the lack of face-to-face communication essential for the transactions to be successful, criminals turn to the deep web to transact drugs.

The Silk Road website, where the drug was sold for almost $1 billion, is an excellent example. DHL (Dalsey, Hillblom, and Lynn) International courier and drop shipping are the delivery methods; as you can see in Figure 1.19, there is some data to consider.

PORNOGRAPHY INDUSTRY

The pornographic industry preys on trafficking victims, particularly women. Following Peak, traffickers force people to conduct sexual actions after signing agreements because they are afraid of being slain to generate pornography. Without the victims' permission, the sex traffickers record videos. After that, the pornography industry makes them available to anyone who wants them. According

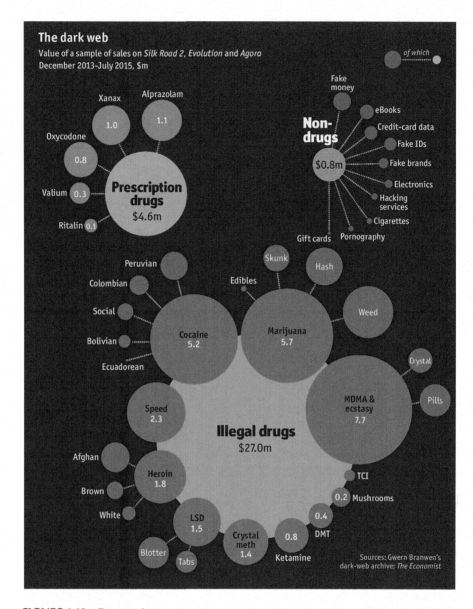

FIGURE 1.19 Drug trades.

to Covenant Eyes (2011), traffickers also post these recordings and images on their websites. Numerous websites are housed on the deep web for security reasons. Human traffickers recruit and kidnap their victims while masking their identities on the deep web, social media, and online forums. It's the same in the pornographic business.

CHILD PORNOGRAPHY

Children use social media and numerous applications to keep in touch with their peers, friends, and loved ones. Most of the time, parents are unaware that their children meet many strangers. *"Omegle and other services hide their users' identities well" (CyberSafetyCop)*. Pederasts can now interact with children more quickly. When sharing child pornography, the DW is a go-to place for pedophiles and other felons. Several well-known companies offer free web hosting for children's pornography, including Freedom Hosting, which runs 550 servers across Europe (the US mulls). According to Federal Bureau of Investigation (FBI) figures, Operation Pacifier arrested many pedophiles from the United States and other nations, with 2,000,000 users, 23,000 explicit images, and 9,000 video clips containing graphic sexuality (FBI report from 2017).

METHODS AND CHALLENGES FOR TRACKING CRIMINALS ON THE DW

Criminals use both the deep web and social media to hide their tracks. Suspects can be identified using various media, including YouTube and Facebook. US law enforcement agencies index deeply hidden websites with the Metasploit Decloaking Engine and Memex systems to find criminals on the deep web, especially human traffickers. The deep web's virtual currency is cryptocurrency. Bitcoin is used as a transaction currency for all payments. To track down offenders on the deep web, police enforcement and policing agencies use Bitcoin traffic. The websites of criminals are tracked, as are purchases of illegal goods by the agencies. The Silk Road server is an excellent example of successfully identifying criminals on the deep web. The FBI was able to track down the server's physical location in an Icelandic data center. Even though Tor is anonymized, it was determined that the server IP addresses and physical location were exposed because of an error on the Silk Road login page. The underground discussion board Dark Mode, where criminals meet daily to exchange information and discuss their illicit activities, was a gold mine of data for the FBI.

Even though some progress has been made in identifying criminals, there are still many obstacles to overcome. International borders pose a significant barrier as they slow down and complicate further investigation. The surveillance and information-gathering operations have been halted thanks to privacy legislation. The deep web's anonymity makes it difficult to track money and criminals. Criminals on the deep web frequently change their IP addresses and usernames, making it difficult to track their activities.

More researchers are needed to correctly identify criminals on the deep web in cyber black-market economics and logistics, antianonymity technologies, and cyber threat vectors that can describe and analyze crime. Finally, the methods used to gather digital evidence should be done to avoid local law problems in court. Dark market statistics for 2018 are shown in Figure 1.20.

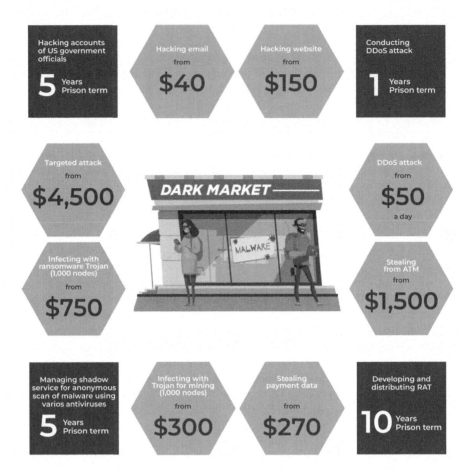

FIGURE 1.20   Dark web market 2018.

SUMMARY

This chapter introduces cybersecurity and DW in more detail. Chapter 1 included a high-level introduction to cybersecurity and covered how criminal activity is becoming more targeted and what can be found on the deep DW. The chapter goes into greater detail about the WWW, including its various categories and web levels. This article discusses some of the basic terms and consequences of the DW and the darknet. The chapter goes deeper into DW's threat landscape and how to get into the deep web. This chapter covers the fundamentals of malicious software (malware), taxonomy, and malware analysis using static and dynamic methods.

2 A Guide to the Dark and Deep Web

It does not matter if it is from a movie, a television show, the news, or even a friend or neighbor telling us about them. We have all heard of them. According to the general public's perception, these sites are depraved and illegal places on the internet where sex dealers, drug dealers, weapons dealers, and other criminals wait to prey on unsuspecting customers. Contrary to popular belief, this is not the case. After reading this book, readers will better understand the Dark Net, Dark Web, and Deep Web. They will be able to use these resources for their own good while also knowing where they are, who uses them, and how to access them safely. However, to fully comprehend them, we must first comprehend the history and workings of the internet. In this chapter, we'll go over the following topics:

- The origin of the internet.
- The dark web.
- The deep web.

THE BEGINNING OF THE INTERNET

Developing new military technology, including the internet, is the Defense Advanced Research Projects Agency (DARPA), a US Department of Defense (DoD) component. However, this is not the first time the internet has appeared. Before, it was more of an intranet because every computer was connected. Whatever your definition of the internet is, there is no right or wrong answer here. Since TCP/IP is now a part of the internet, it allows communication and information to flow between nodes in the network. A brief history in pictorial form is shown in Figure 2.1.

Some believe the internet began with the development of packet-switching technology, while others believe it began with the introduction of TCP/IP. Still, others believe the internet originated in the United Kingdom, not the United States. The internet (or ARPANET, as it was dubbed at the time) also has a shady beginning date. Although most people agree that it was launched in 1969, there is concrete evidence that it originated even earlier.

The following Figure 2.2 shows a model of ARPANET.

To a large number of web users, it's like seeing the internet as an underwater island or glacier that's partially submerged, as shown in Figure 2.3.

As seen in the diagram above, the Surface Web is the portion of the internet that can be seen above the water's surface.

An attacker, for example, might aim to harm a company's reputation. Recon Mission uncovers a vulnerability that an attacker can use – the business backs up its customer database to its public website for 24 hours before moving it to a secure

DOI: 10.1201/9781003404330-2

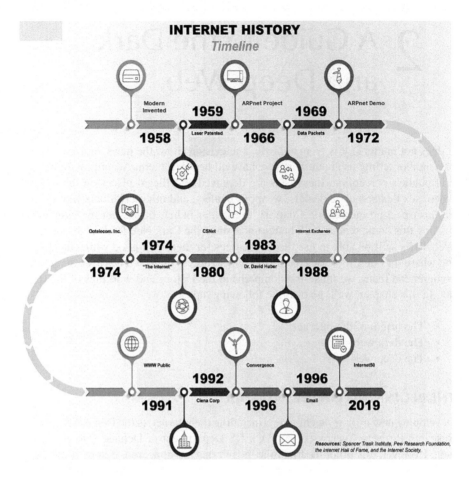

FIGURE 2.1   Internet history.

storage location. Search engines can now crawl the backup as a result of this. The database file on the company's website can be located by an attacker using a search engine. Because the website has been indexed, the search engine can provide the attacker with relevant results. The attacker only needs to download the file(s) and then use them for their own gain.

Search engines can index information, documents, and content in this area. It's unfortunate that many people, including companies, who aren't tech-savvy or aren't aware, let their data be indexed, which gives hackers valuable information that they can use to break into systems and steal data.

THE DEEP WEB

Everything that isn't indexable on the Surface Web is included in the Deep Web. There is no index for the Deep Web because it is either hard to crawl or not currently crawled at all. It's also a lot bigger now. The internet isn't just the World Wide Web (WWW, Surface Web); it's the network infrastructure used to access the Surface

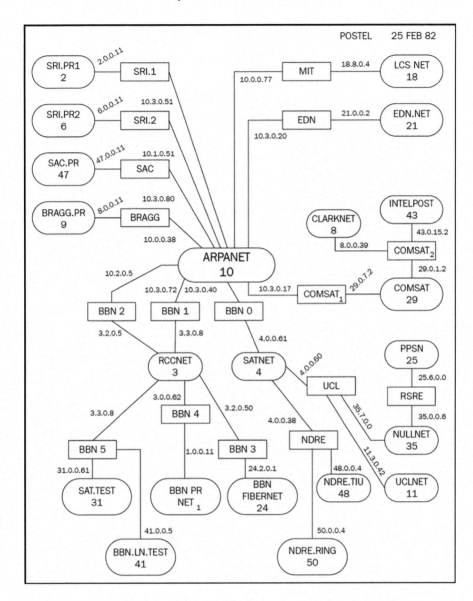

FIGURE 2.2   ARPANET model.

Web. As a result, the Deep Web (or at least the majority of it; we will get to that in a minute) exists on the internet. The Deep Web includes any website or system that necessitates the entry of login credentials.

Additionally, the Deep Web includes intranets of businesses, academic institutions, government departments, and other organizations and websites that prevent search engines like Google Scholar and Amazon from indexing certain parts of the site. Figure 2.4 shows how to conduct a Google Scholar search for terms related to the deep web:

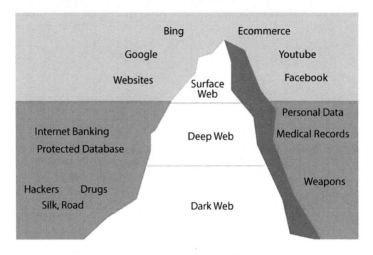

FIGURE 2.3 Dark net, deep web, and surface web.

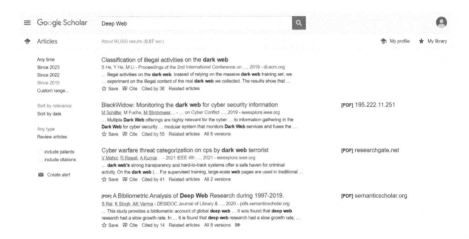

FIGURE 2.4 Deep web searches.

It turns out there are outcomes, as you can see. Figure 2.5 shows what happens after accessing the deep web after clicking the link.

In the end, we have reached the login screen. Even though the article is on the Deep Web, Google returned it as a search result since the title and metadata were indexed. To access the Deep Web, you must use a nonstandard browser and be on a network that is not indexable by search engines such as Google, Yahoo, and Bing.

THE DARK WEB

Like how the WWW exists on the internet, the Dark Web does as well (or rather, multiple darknets). Note that the Dark Web and Dark Net are not interchangeable terms. Networks isolated from ARPANET, such as compartmentalization, were referred to as the "Dark Net" in the 1970s. Aside from not being visible in the ARPANET

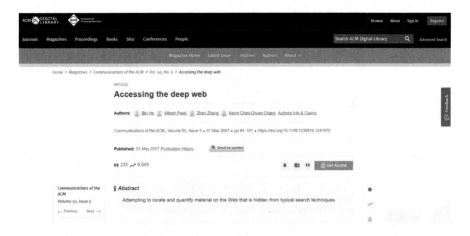

FIGURE 2.5   Deep web access.

network listings and not responding to networking inquiries like ping requests, they were configured to receive external data.

A network overlay is a layer placed on top of a primary network. It is only accessible through specialized browsers or software, such as those that aren't globally routable (hence the term "overlay"). As the term evolved, it came to be used for overlay networks, which use software and hardware to create multiple abstraction layers. Overlay networks include Tor, the Invisible Internet Project, and FreeNet, to name a few.

Consider the Dark Net as a sub-structure of the Dark Web, with restricted content and websites that can only be accessed through the previously mentioned software. I'll use Tor, or The Onion Router, as an example of the Dark Net. Because it's decentralized, users' traffic is bouncing between different routers all over the place. Figure 2.6, taken from the Argonne National Laboratory website, graphically illustrates what I just said.

The internet includes the Deep Web and the Dark Web, as you can see. The Deep Web resides inside the Surface Web (another part of that magnificent network known as the internet).

CRIMINALS

Because of the anonymity and security that the Dark Web provides, criminals frequently use it to shield their identities and evade detection. Even though law enforcement agencies are active on the Dark Web, this does not mean they have complete control over criminals.

LAW ENFORCEMENT

Since the Dark Web is widely believed to be unlawful in some form. We started working with the authorities. So let us reassure you: law enforcement on the Dark Web exists, too, just like in the real world. The Dark Web is popular with criminals because of its secrecy and anonymity. Because of the anonymity, criminals can set

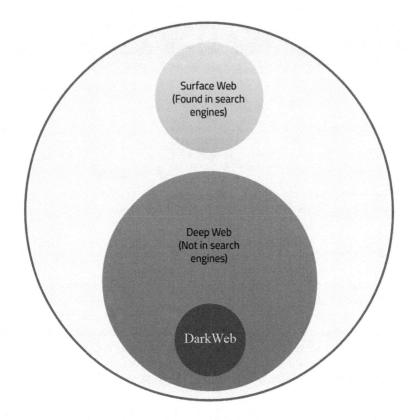

FIGURE 2.6   Anatomy of the internet.

up online markets for drugs, weapons, and other illegal goods. Law enforcement agencies like the Federal Bureau of Investigation and others use the dark net to conduct sting operations and apprehend criminals. Law enforcement agencies take down illegal marketplaces as one of their many tasks. To stop the sale of illegal materials, many agencies try to take over illegal marketplaces and track down both buyers and sellers. They use the Dark Web to their advantage, ensuring their anonymity on the Dark Web while reducing the exposure of governmental IP addresses.

PRIVACY

Many people today are concerned about their right to privacy. As the number of interconnected devices increases and more data is stored in the cloud, there is growing public concern about privacy. A website can perform numerous tracking actions when you visit it regularly. The following are some examples of how a website might make use of them:

- Fingerprinting of the browser
- Tracking cookies
- Referral links
- Tracking scripts
- IP addresses

JOURNALISM

Journalists are frequently compelled to break a story, even if it puts them in danger. Journalists can report and share information anonymously and securely using the Dark Web. Secure Drop, for example, enables organizations to receive documents and tips from a variety of sources without fear of detection. Several well-known news organizations use Secure Drop. To keep track of active instances, Secure Drop maintains a directory at https://directory.securedrop.org

Websites can do various things with the collected data, such as targeting advertising. People can ensure their online legal activity remains anonymous by utilizing the Dark Web, and Websites will never track your location or online activity.

DRUGS AND ILLEGAL SUBSTANCES

A wide range of drugs and illegal substances can be found on various dark web marketplaces. Silk Road is a well-known online marketplace. Silk Road was launched in 2011 and initially served as a marketplace for the sale of magic mushrooms. As the market grew, it expanded to include a wider range of goods and services. Now that Silk Road is at version 3.1, it's time to upgrade. Admins or law enforcement removed the previous versions as well.

The Wall Street Market is another well-known market. Figure 2.7 shows the wide range of goods available in this marketplace.

COUNTERFEIT GOODS

There are a lot of fake goods on the Dark Web. As illustrated in Figure 2.8 below, these include everything from counterfeit electronics and currency to fake identification documents.

Figure 2.9 shows an example of a counterfeit document that can be found online.

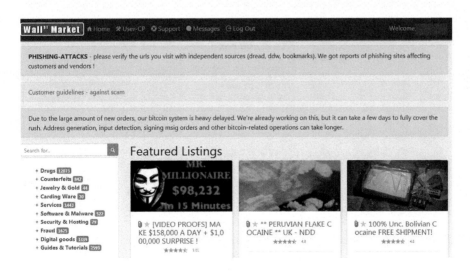

FIGURE 2.7   Wallstreet market categories.

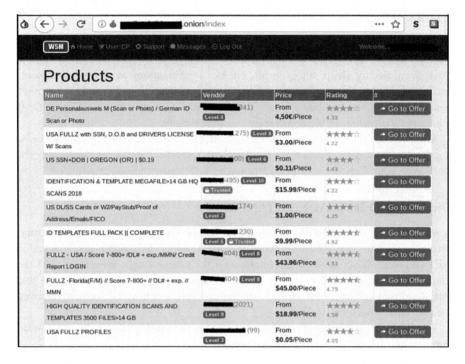

FIGURE 2.8 Product list.

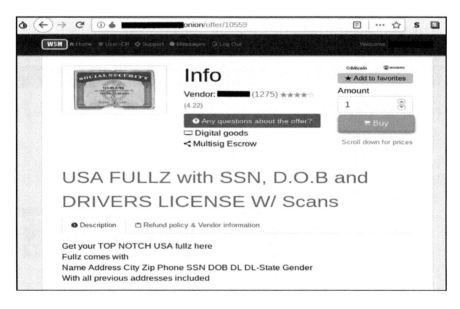

FIGURE 2.9 Counterfeit US identification documents.

STOLEN INFORMATION

More than a few websites have had their data breached and then dumped on the Dark Web, either for free or sold at a premium price to the highest bidder or a specific client. Many stolen data dumps are available today, and hackers are all familiar with the data sources for celebrity photos, videos, and emails. Major stolen data are shown in Figure 2.10.

HACKERS

In the past, hackers were viewed as highly skilled but dangerous individuals who needed to be kept at a distance. Companies and governments alike are now vying for the services of these individuals.

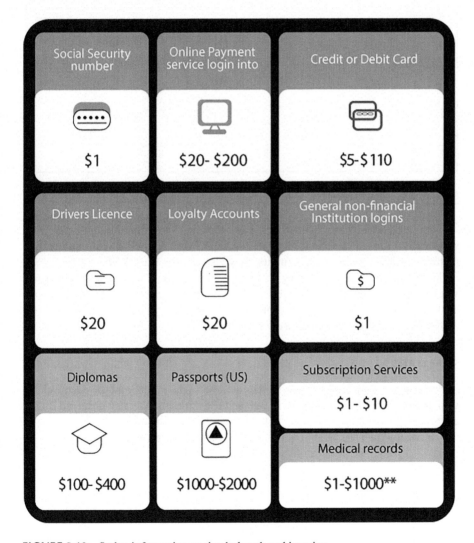

FIGURE 2.10   Stolen information on the dark web and its price.

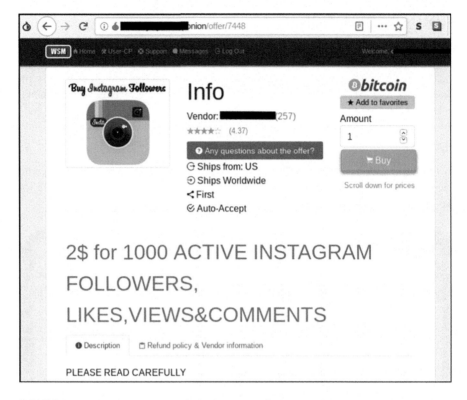

FIGURE 2.11 Hacking service to boost Instagram followers.

The Dark Web is rife with Black Hat Hackers. These people typically offer services, exploits, and tools for sale on the Dark Web. As well as communicating, planning attacks, and sharing exploits, they also use the Dark Web.

The illegal market for hacking services is growing on the Dark Web. Such services are frequently provided at a low cost, making them accessible to many people, as shown in Figure 2.11. As an example, hackers may offer to execute an accurate test of your Facebook account in return for control.

SUMMARY

In this chapter, we learned about the internet, the surface web, and the deep web, as well as what it's like to surf the dark web and use darknets. We also observed different types of Dark Web users and explored how they use the dark web. We found out that accessing the Dark Web requires specialized software and is not indexed.

3 Dark Web Access with Tor Browser

We'll look at installing Tor Browser on Linux using a regular Linux distribution in a few different ways. When I say standard, I'm referring to a desktop distribution that is widely used, not a security-focused distribution like the ones we'll look at in the following chapters. We'll go over how to set up the Tor Browser and use it. In this chapter, we'll study the following topics:

- What is the Tor Browser?
- Installing Tor on Linux
- The Tor Project's recommendations on the safe use of Tor

TOR BROWSER

As described by the Tor website:

> Tor is free software and an open network that aids in the defense against traffic analysis, a type of network surveillance that jeopardizes personal freedom and privacy, private business activities and connections, and state security.
>
> The Tor network is a collection of volunteer-run servers that help people improve their online anonymity and security. Tor users connect to the network via virtual tunnels rather than a direct connection, allowing companies and people to share information across public networks while maintaining their privacy. On the other hand, Tor is an effective censorship circumvention technology, allowing users to access content or destinations that would otherwise be prohibited. Tor may also be a foundation for software developers to construct new communication tools with built-in privacy features.

The Onion Router, or Tor, is a privacy-focused network that hides your online activity by sending it through a slew of different Tor servers. When you communicate with someone (or an organization), your packets will move from server to server before getting to their final destination, making it difficult to track your progress.

Tor Browser is a Firefox-based web browser designed specifically for safely and privately accessing the Tor network. As a result, only the previous server or step from which the packet came and the next one are visible in the Tor network traffic (or communication) packets. This effectively hides the entire route.

Now I'm going to mention something that might catch you off guard. Even if you utilize Tor, you aren't entirely secure. What is the reason for this? Because Tor Browser, like all other browsers, contains software vulnerabilities. Because it's built on top of Firefox, it has some of that browser's drawbacks. Limit or avoid undesirable

DOI: 10.1201/9781003404330-3

behaviors associated with infecting the Tor Browser and the host that runs it by employing common sense and other technologies.

INSTALLING TOR ON LINUX

In most cases, installing applications on Linux is a breeze. There are a few different ways to install Tor Browser, and we'll go over a few of them in this chapter. Start with a standard installation by going to the Tor Project website in a web browser and signing up for an account. We'll use Firefox, as it's the default browser in Ubuntu.

The Tor Project website is continuously attacked by hackers and may have several security or privacy issues. You can install Tor Browser safely: download the file and verify its hash (to make sure it is the correct one) or use another method such as the Terminal, Linux commands, or the Ubuntu Software Center. While this may be the most secure way to install Tor Browser, it is also the least safe.

The first step is to download Tor Browser from the official Tor Project website:

1. Open your browser after your Linux installation has started.
2. Enter the following address into your browser and go to it:
   a. https://www.torproject.org/download/download-easy.html.en#linux
   b. The URL will take you directly to the Tor Project's Linux download page, as you can see. Since Google collects information about users who visit it, we prefer using this technique rather than typing up "Tor" on any search engine and then going to the Tor Project website.
   c. It is because, as you may understand, Google collects information about users who access it. Also, be sure you're viewing the Tor Project website over HTTPS.
3. Click the Download button after selecting either 32-bit or 64-bit as your operating system's architecture.
4. Figure 3.1 shows you how to access or save an archive file in Ubuntu's Archive Manager or on your hard disc.
5. Again, opening the compressed file is the quickest choice, but downloading the file and verifying its hash before proceeding is more secure than using the compressed file.
6. The Tor Project provides GNU Privacy Guard (GPG) signature files with each version of the Tor Browser. If GnuPG isn't already installed on your Linux OS, you'll need to do so to verify the browser package's hash.
7. Open the Terminal and type sudo apt install GnuPG to get started.
8. The installation will begin after you input your password when asked. Figure 3.2 shows that GnuPG is already present in most Linux setups.
9. After GnuPG has been installed, you must import the signed package's key. As stated on the Tor Project website, the import key is 0x4e2C6E8793298290.
10. A new import key is available at https://www.torproject.org/docs/verifying-signatures.html.en if the book doesn't work anymore (updated and changed frequently).
11. To import the key, type gpg -keyserver pool.sks-keyservers.net -recv-keys 0x4e2C6e8793298290.

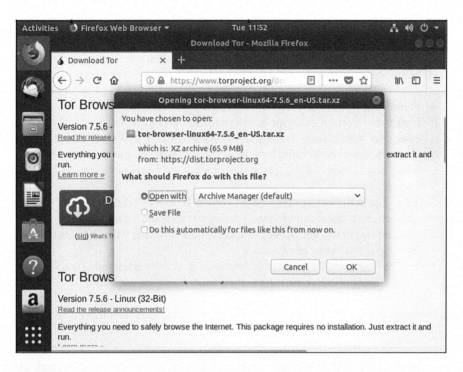

FIGURE 3.1   Downloading the Tor browser.

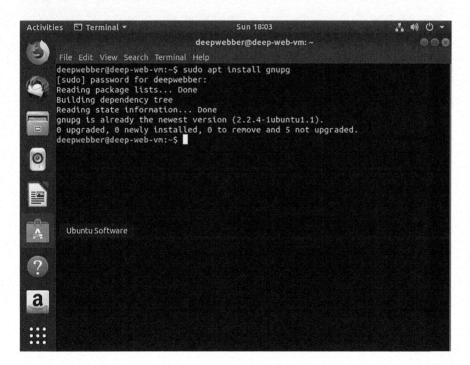

FIGURE 3.2   Installing GnuPG.

12. After that, gpg -fingerprint 0x4e2C6e8793298290.
13. You'll know if the key fingerprint is correct if you get this response. Figure 3.3 will be pretty familiar to you, and it depicts the following:
14. Now, you must download the.asc file, which can be located next to the correct Tor Browser package on the Tor Browser Downloads page, as shown in Figure 3.4.
15. https://www.torproject.org/projects/torbrowser.html is the Tor Browser download page. You can now verify the package's signature using the ASC file.
16. To do so, open the Terminal and type the following command: gpg -verify tor-browser-linux64–7.5.6_en-US.tar.xz.asc   tor-browser-linux64–7.5.6_ en-US.tar.xz
17. Take note of the number 64, which I bolded. If your OS is 32-bit, modify the number to 32. As seen in Figure 3.5, the result should be as follows:
18. You can install the Tor Browser package after verifying its hash (signature). You can do so in one of two ways:
    a. The Tor Browser package is double-clicked to be extracted. Then select the appropriate destination and click OK.
    b. Extract the file to a specific location.
19. In the window that displays, press Trust and Launch, as shown in Figure 3.6.
20. Once Connected, surf using Tor, as shown in Figure 3.7.

```
deepwebber@deep-web-vm:~$ gpg --fingerprint 0x4e2c6e8793298290
pub    rsa4096 2014-12-15 [C] [expires: 2020-08-24]
       EF6E 286D DA85 EA2A 4BA7  DE68 4E2C 6E87 9329 8290
uid            [ unknown] Tor Browser Developers (signing key) <torbrowser@torpr
oject.org>
sub    rsa4096 2016-08-24 [S] [expires: 2018-08-24]
sub    rsa4096 2018-05-26 [S] [expires: 2020-09-12]

deepwebber@deep-web-vm:~$ 
```

FIGURE 3.3   Verify the key fingerprint.

Tor Browser Downloads

To start using Tor Browser, download the file for your preferred language. This file can be saved wherever is convenient, e.g. the Desktop or a USB flash drive.

Stable Tor Browser

Language	Microsoft Windows (7.5.6)	Apple MacOS (7.5.6)	GNU/Linux (7.5.6)
English (en-US)	32/64-bit *(sig)*	64-bit *(sig)*	32-bit *(sig)* • 64-bit *(sig)*
العربية (ar)	32/64-bit *(sig)*	64-bit *(sig)*	32-bit *(sig)* • 64-bit *(sig)*
Deutsch (de)	32/64-bit *(sig)*	64-bit *(sig)*	32-bit *(sig)* • 64-bit *(sig)*
Español (es-ES)	32/64-bit *(sig)*	64-bit *(sig)*	32-bit *(sig)* • 64-bit *(sig)*
فارسی (fa)	32/64-bit *(sig)*	64-bit *(sig)*	32-bit *(sig)* • 64-bit *(sig)*
Français (fr)	32/64-bit *(sig)*	64-bit *(sig)*	32-bit *(sig)* • 64-bit *(sig)*

FIGURE 3.4   ASC file location.

```
deepwebber@deep-web-vm:~/Downloads$ gpg --verify tor-browser-linux64-7.5.6_en-U
S.tar.xz.asc tor-browser-linux64-7.5.6_en-US.tar.xz
gpg: Signature made Sat 23 Jun 2018 22:36:16 IDT
gpg:                using RSA key D1483FA6C3C07136
gpg: Good signature from "Tor Browser Developers (signing key) <torbrowser@torp
roject.org>" [unknown]
gpg: WARNING: This key is not certified with a trusted signature!
gpg:          There is no indication that the signature belongs to the owner.
Primary key fingerprint: EF6E 286D DA85 EA2A 4BA7  DE68 4E2C 6E87 9329 8290
     Subkey fingerprint: A430 0A6B C93C 0877 A445  1486 D148 3FA6 C3C0 7136
deepwebber@deep-web-vm:~/Downloads$ ▊
```

FIGURE 3.5   Verifying the signature.

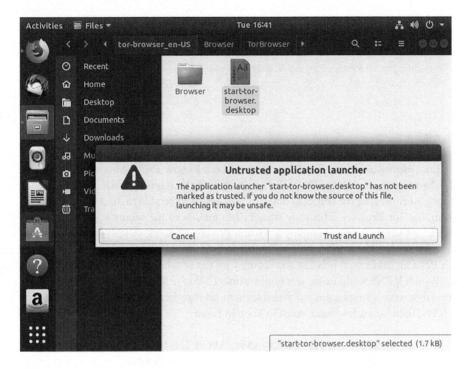

FIGURE 3.6   Launching Tor.

TOR PROJECT RECOMMENDATION

Use the following tips to stay safe when utilizing the Tor network:

1. The Tor Browser should be used.
2. Don't use Tor for torrents.
3. Browser plugins should not be enabled or installed.
4. HTTPS websites should be used.
5. When you're online, don't access documents you've downloaded using Tor.
6. Make use of bridges and/or seek out company.
7. Tor tries to keep attackers from finding out what websites you visit. However, it does not prevent anyone looking at your traffic from noticing that you're using Tor. Instead of connecting directly to the public Tor network.

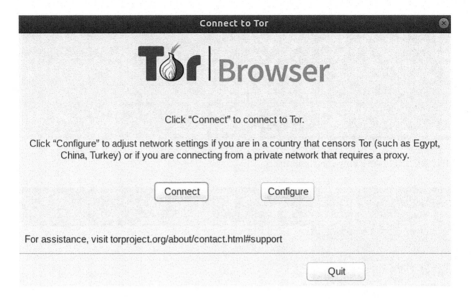

FIGURE 3.7   Tor connection.

But before you fire up Tor Browser, you should know a few things about utilizing Tor Browser to access the Dark Web or even surf the internet. Your ISP (and hence your government or the National Security Agency) will be able to discover that you are using the Tor Browser. This may attract the attention of the security agencies, which we do not want. We must employ a Virtual Private Network (VPN) to avoid this. On your computer, you must install VPN software to use the service. On the other hand, a VPN adds additional privacy and security on top of what the Tor Browser offers.

Which VPN should I use, you might wonder? You're as safe as you can be without resorting to severe measures if you use them all together. When it comes to picking a VPN, there are a few basic rules to keep in mind:

- First, there's the level of encryption. About 128-bit encryption is enough, but 256-bit encryption is superior (much harder to crack).
- Also, look for a VPN that doesn't save logs locally or on the VPN provider's servers.
- Many VPNs have issues with unexpected disconnections, exposing your IP address to your ISP or the rest of the world. So choose one with a kill switch (a mechanism that disconnects the computer's internet connection if the VPN disconnects unexpectedly, for example, Installing a Linux Virtual Machine; it's a mechanism that disconnects the computer's internet connection if the VPN disconnects unexpectedly).
- Select a VPN with anti-IP and anti-DNS leak protection. (If not protected, operating system and browser flaws might leak or reveal your DNS requests and IP address.)
- Select a VPN that offers IP addresses from multiple countries. (When customizing it, select a country other than your own.)

There are numerous free and premium VPNs available. Their setup may differ, but each will come with its own instructions. Just make sure you get one with the features I've listed. Let's get started utilizing Tor Browser now that we've seen how to install it and understand why we need a VPN (and, ideally, picked one).

However, you can remain anonymous online if you utilize a VPN with safeguards. Remember that Tor Browser is a web browser similar to Chrome, Firefox, Edge, and Internet Explorer. Still, it is considerably more private and anonymous, allowing you to accomplish the same essential tasks.

Here's a list of some onion sites to get you started:

- https://www.facebookcorewwwi.onion/ It's Facebook, of course. Facebook provides this for use in places where it is censored (rather than for anonymity).
- http://3g2upl4pq6kufc4m.onion/ an excellent, private Google alternative. Because search behavior and activities aren't logged, the search experience is unique. (This resembles a search experience before Google.)
- https://www.propub3r6espa33w.onion/ The first Pulitzer Prize-winning online publication has a website with an onion extension. Many articles and information, both anonymously and openly published, about various topics can be found there.

Here's a screenshot of the ProPublica website as seen in Figure 3.8 using the Tor Browser:

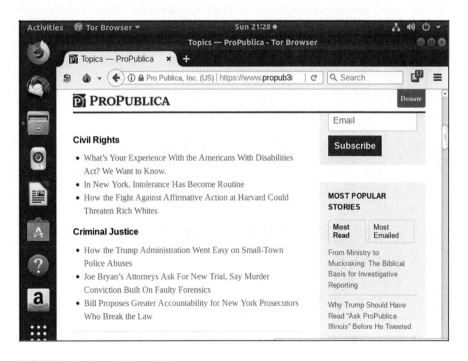

FIGURE 3.8 Propublica website.

THE MYSTERIOUS WIKI

The link to the Wiki is:

http://zqktlwi4fecvo6ri.onion/wiki/index.php/Main_Page contains a wealth of knowledge. There are also search engines on the Dark Web, such as the ones listed below:

- **Torch:** Nearly 500,000 onion services are indexed by this search engine. (http://xmh57jrzrnw6insl.onion/).
- **Haystak:** Performs onion searches and claims to have over 1.5 billion pages from nearly 300,000 domains (many of which have already become obsolete.) (http://haystakvxad7wbk5.onion/).
- **Tor Onionland:** Nearly 60,000.onion websites and about 5 million searchable pages are indexed by this search engine (http://onionlandbakyt3j.onion/).
- **Grams:** Only a market search engine for labor, digital, and physical products you may buy with Bitcoin and other currencies (http://grams7enq-fy4nieo.onion/).
- **Candle:** A simple search engine that ignores operators, parentheses, and quotes, focusing just on words (http://gjobqjj7wyczbqie.onion.link/).
- **Not Evil:** Over 32 million onion URLs are indexed by this search engine (http://hss3uro2hsxfogfq.onion/).

The best way to understand how to use the Dark Web is to use it. When you try many of the sites above, they may not work, and this is because their addresses change regularly. However, I listed them to assist you in getting started with your Deep Web exploration.

4 The Dark Web's Perils

The history of the Dark Web is not rosy. Everyone has heard rumors about what goes on there. Regrettably, the media has exaggerated the stories. So many of the stories you've heard are false or overblown. However, the stories include a kernel of truth, which you must be aware of. As I've discussed multiple times in this book, the primary concerns for the average user are how you access it (in a particular browser) and the anonymity achieved on it. This chapter delves into the risks of the Dark Web.

In this chapter, we'll go over the following topics:

- Online scams
- Avoiding the risks of a dark web market
- The dark web's perils

ONLINE SCAMS

Scams are a real threat on both the public internet and the darknet. There are many different types of scams. Scams on Dark Web markets, as well as those perpetrated by independent sellers, are common. In this chapter, I'll go over a few of them.

Index sites, such as the Hidden Wiki, are dangerous. It's a service that displays links to Dark Web websites. It was created in 2011 and shut down in 2013. However, it was cloned and continues to function. Although most of the links are legitimate (people pay money to have their Dark Web website listed there), those who are solely there to defraud people and steal their money.

Never provide or write your debit or credit card numbers on Dark Web websites; never give out your genuine personal details. Because there's no way to verify someone's identity on the Dark Web, it's best to keep your own hidden. That's what anonymity and being anonymous are all about. Figure 4.1 shows the Hidden Wiki as follows.

You'll probably have a better sense of dangerous and illegal sites after spending some time on the Dark Web. That isn't to say you should relax your vigilance. Even on reputable websites, the stuff you might access can be disturbing.

Many links may also lead to dangerous websites. Also, as a parent, don't give your kids unrestricted access to the Dark Web. On the other side, you're probably out of luck if you want to hire an assassin. Most websites that offer murder-for-hire services are bogus, and Hitmen doesn't advertise their services as openly as this. You can communicate with someone on the Dark Web but cannot see him/her.

There are scary films, numerous services, and products ranging from the repulsive to the bizarre. If you have a sensitive stomach or a weak stomach, be cautious. Don't merely go through the motions of clicking on links; try to learn as much as possible about the website you want to visit.

DOI: 10.1201/9781003404330-4

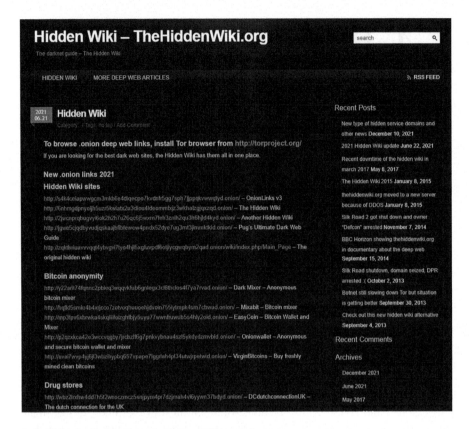

FIGURE 4.1   Screenshot of a hidden Wiki website.

Police enforcement agencies either sponsor these sites to apprehend people plotting murders or scammers who demand between $15,000 and $25,000 in cash, then disappear or blackmail the person who paid them. Fake IDs, social security numbers, credit cards, and other forged credentials are highly demanded. However, not all are genuine, and scammers furnish some of them, delivering phony false IDs that shatter with the smallest examination.

One of the issues is that the websites that sell these forged credentials appear professional and legitimate. We've been conditioned to think of websites as clean and professional. They can, however, be malicious in specific circumstances. The following is Figure 4.2 from a website that sells fake IDs.

Another website that offers false IDs is this one: Figure 4.3).

People's PayPal accounts have been hacked on sites like this, believing that utilizing PayPal would make them safer. You should look for sites where reputable suppliers sell their wares. Another example of a Dark Web website during the Trump election was promising to assassinate President-elect Trump for a large sum of money. The fundraiser accepted Bitcoin, but the precise amount raised is unknown due to the site's closure. Nothing happened, but the administration took advantage of the tsunami of anti-Trump sentiment that swept the country during the election season.

As seen in Figure 4.4, the DeepDotWeb website provides various legal market sites. (Even though reputable websites may include questionable connections.)

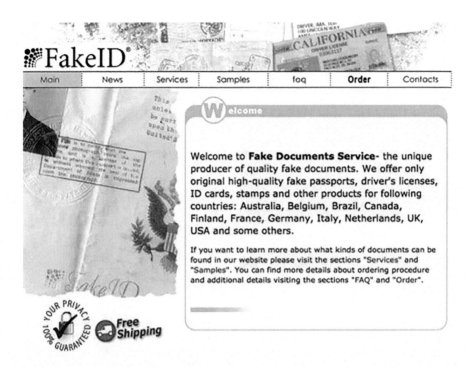

FIGURE 4.2   Website selling fake IDs.

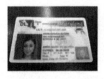

[LIMITED TIME SALE!] - MARYLAND Fake IDs | (Holos, UV, Barcode)
฿0.201288   ☆☆☆☆☆ (320)

ships from: United States
ships to: United States   sold by Ethereal-IDs 94

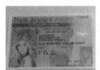

New Jersey Drivers License Holograms UV Scannable Fake ID
฿0.274082   ☆☆☆☆☆ (188)

ships from: United States
ships to: Worldwide   sold by Good-IDs 78

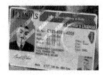

HQ Illinois ID. All Security Features. Great Service.
฿0.345494   ☆☆☆☆☆ (169)

ships from: Undeclared
ships to: Worldwide   sold by ShopWithUs 94

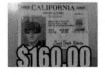

BEST Quality Fake California ID Anywhere – Scan/UV/Bend Test/Holos [TEMPORARY HALF PRICE SALE THIS WEEK ONLY]
฿0.480687   ☆☆☆☆☆ (54)

ships from: United States
ships to: United States   sold by PowderBlue 96

FIGURE 4.3   Fake IDs detail.

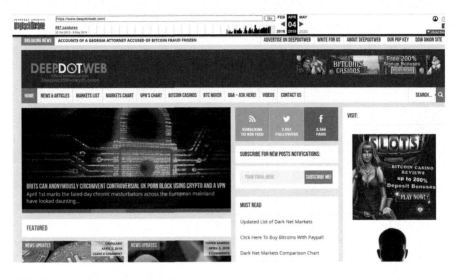

FIGURE 4.4   DeepDotWeb website.

According to its reputation, the Dark Web News website has compiled a list of trustworthy vendor markets. A portion of the list is available here in Figure 4.5.

They also developed a comparison between the two sites, as shown in Figure 4.6 below.

I'm using it as an example to discuss what to look for in a legitimate Dark Web store. I am not endorsing or approving the list or comparison, and this is because I haven't considered all of the possibilities.

AVOIDING THE RISKS OF A DARK WEB MARKET

So, what should you look for in a Dark Web market to limit your risk? You could also look at sites like https://dnstats.net/ or https://www.deepdotweb.com

- **Anonymity and Security:** How secure are you and your account on the market? Is the site protected against phishing, distributed denial-of-service, and PGP? Before signing up, conduct some research on the site and check for this information.
- **Multisig, Escrow, and Finalize Early:** This indicates that the market is serious about safeguarding your funds.
- **Reviews**: Reviews about a market's reputation can be found on various other websites (both on the surface and in the shadows of the internet).
- **Uptime Status:** How long has the site been up? The sites' uptime listed on most Dark Web indexes or search engines is displayed. This is one of the essential metrics and validations you can uncover.
- **Help and Support:** Is there a support team at the market? Is there any response from them? Are they eager to assist with problems that arise between buyers and sellers? On the website, look for Help or Support links. Check to see what level of assistance is available. To check how quickly they respond, send them a message.

Top Markets

Up/ Online : Dream Market - 95.8%

Up/ Online : Wallstreet Market - 89.39%

Up/ Online : Point/Tochka Free Market - 89.77%

Other Markets

Up/ Online : Silk Road 3-87.55%

Up/ Online : Empire market

Down / Offline : Acropolis Market - 99.24%

Down / Offline : Alphabay (ALT) - 91.77%

Down / Offline : Apple Market - 91.74%

Down / Offline : Berlusconi Market - 77.67%

Up/ Online : BitBlender- 98.25%

Up/ Online : BitCloak - 95.12%

Up/ Online : BlockChain info - 85.67%

Up/ Online : CGMC - 97.06%

Up/ Online : CharlieUK - 90.23%

Down / Offline : Dark Rabbit Market - 79.11%

FIGURE 4.5   A list of reliable vendor markets.

THE DARK WEB'S PERILS

Having personal data uploaded and displayed on the Dark Web is one of the hazards. Facebook, British Airways, the Marriott hotel company, and numerous others have all experienced this.

For instance, a well-known financial firm discovered that it saved client information on unprotected servers. The data included PII (Personal Identifiable Information) like bank account and social security information that might be used to identify a specific person. When this information was made public on the Dark Web, it put customers (as well as the investment company) at risk.

Market	Total Listing	Drug Listings	Market URL	User Guide	Reg	Multisig?	Commission	Vendor Bond	2FA	Forced Vendor PGP	Created	Screenshot
⬇ Berlusconi Market Down / Offline	6475	3812	http://berluscoqu3nj4qz.onion/	/	Open	✗	2%	0-250$	✓	✗	07.7.2017	👁
⬆ CGMC Up / Online	949	453	http://cgmcoopwhempo6a5.onion/	/	Ref	✓	2-3%	0$	✓	✓	06.7.2016	👁
⬇ The Hub ☑ Down / Offline	Forum	Forum	http://thehub7xbw4dc5r2.onion/	Click ↗	Open	/	/	/	/	/	/	👁
⬇ The Majestic Garden ☑ Down / Offline	/	/	http://talismanrestz7mr.onion/	Click ↗	Ref	✗	Donnation Based	Ref (Invited Vendors)	✗	✗	01.4.2014	👁
⬆ DNM Avengers ☑ Up / Online	Forum	Forum	http://avengersdutyk3xf.onion/	Click ↗	Open	✗	/	/	✗	✗	01.11.2015	👁
⬆ Dream Market ☑ Up / Online	62834	59108	http://6khhxwj7viwe5xjm.onion/	Click ↗	Open	✗	4%	0.1 BTC 400$	✓	✗	11-15-2013	👁
⬆ WallStreet Market ☑ Up / Online	7048	3569	http://wallstytlzjhkrvmj.onion/	Click ↗	Open	✓	2.5-5%	80$ Free For Trusted	✓	✓	10-19-2016	👁

FIGURE 4.6 Comparison between the two sites.

Credentials for administrative and remote terminals in numerous countries were accidentally disclosed on the Dark Web by a Middle Eastern website (it is not known how or who did it). Although the problem was discovered in time, it still poses a threat.

Due to a problem with the requisite login credentials for the system that houses the information, a prominent US healthcare firm was discovered to have sensitive human resources and internal network information exposed on the Dark Web by a threat intelligence business. No recurrence was found once the problem was fixed.

ACCESS

Most people utilize Tor, a technology developed by the US Army Science Lab, to access the Deep Web. Consider Tor as an alternate to well-known web browsers such as Chrome and Firefox, both free to use. Instead of taking the shortest link between your laptop and the farthest reaches of the internet, the Tor browser takes a random routing of encrypted servers, commonly known as nodes. As a result, when individuals connect to the Deep Internet, their browsing history and actions aren't traced. Anyone running on the Deep can't be tracked down owing to Tor's privacy-preserving features.

People now use Tor to access both the surface and deep web simultaneously using a single browser. For others, there is no choice but to use Tor customers and virtual private networks in countries with strict access and use regulations, which prevent them from accessing even public websites unless they use government entities or perhaps Internet Providers to understand what they see online. Of course, anonymity has a sinister side, as thieves and malevolent hackers prefer to work in the shadows to protect their identities. President critics and other loud advocates fearing retaliation if their true identities are uncovered feel the same way.

USE AND MISUSE

Some Deep Internet users may bypass regional restrictions and use TV or movie services that aren't available in their own countries. Those who want illegally obtained music or movies will take tremendous measures to get their hands on them. It gets scary, frightening, and downright strange toward the conclusion of the net's darkness. *"The Guardian"* reported that Mastercard information can be acquired on the Dark Web for a few dollars per record. At the same time, ZDNet claims that everything from bogus citizenship certificates to passports and even the services of professional hitmen are available if you know where to look. Interested parties can also obtain personal information by threatening or extorting frequent internet users. See how Ashley Madison was recently hacked, which revealed an abundance of sensitive information such as real names, addresses, and phone numbers. It doesn't matter if you use the dark web or not; if the sites you often visit are infected, you're open to blackmail (or worse).

Illegal narcotics are a significant draw on the Dark Web. According to Motherboard, the Silk Road drug market sells anything to anyone who wants it at any price. You'll find strange things in the Deep, including a DIY ablation kit and virtual treasure hunts that led to a "hunter" ringing up a New York City payphone at 3 a.m.

THE TRUTH ABOUT THE RISKS

Law enforcement is virtually nonexistent in the shadows because of both users' and websites' widespread encryption and anonymization techniques. As a result, anything that violates decency and taste standards can be discovered online. This includes obscene, illegal "adult" material that will leave a lasting impression on the viewer.

SOME GENERAL DANGERS

The sale and purchase of illegal substances, firearms, and even human trafficking are possible on the Dark Web. It's harder to know who you're buying from on marketplaces because of the anonymity. Is it safe to rely on them? Will they make off with our cash? Thieves and fraudsters can purchase personal information like card numbers and bank accounts on the Dark Web for use against us. This can result in your documents being falsified. Here's another reason to avoid disclosing sensitive personal data on the Dark Web.

Anonymity is essential to black-hat hackers because they aren't afraid to share their exploits with the world on the Dark Web. Yet another aspect of hackers' dark web presence is that they hone their skills by tricking unsuspecting users into doing something that gives them a vulnerability or attack vector to exploit.

Always exercise caution while deciding which links to click on. Never click on executables or anything else that seems shady when downloading. The Dark Web is littered with malware. Several types of malware were discovered there in 2017, including:

* 2017 – Karmen Ransomware RaaS.
* 2017 – MACSPY – The Dark Web offers a Remote Access Trojan as a service.

- 2017 – First-ever RaaS-based Mac ransomware, called MacRansom.
- 2017 – RAS called Shifr RaAS enables ransomware creation by assembling three fields of a form.

Botnets, particularly Tor-based botnets, are another threat on the Dark Web. They'll be able to demonstrate.

- Authenticated hidden service accessibility.
- Private Tor network access is possible.
- The potential for flooding of the exit nodes.

Security researchers use traffic analysis to look for botnets and the C&C servers that control them. Intrusion Detection Systems and network analyzers are used. The following steps can be followed to get rid of a botnet:

- The C&C servers and infected hosts are being cleaned.
- Domain name revocation.
- Obscuring the C&C server's supplied IP addresses.

Because botnet traffic is sent through the Tor network, it is encrypted and difficult to decrypt. Legal traffic generated by Tor can be used to disguise botnets. Most intrusion detection systems cannot detect botnets based on Tor. In addition, it isn't easy to locate the C&C servers in question. Reusing the botnet's secret service's generated private key allows the botnet's operator to hop between the botnet's C&C servers effortlessly.

Terrorists communicate, recruit, and organize via the Dark Web (themselves and their attacks). The Dark Web is the preferred distribution method to avoid detection and monitoring. When it comes to gambling, people addicted to it adore the Dark Web because it allows them to indulge without worrying about breaking local regulations.

Another risk is being accused of misbehavior or illegal activities. As previously indicated, law enforcement agencies establish Dark Web websites to entice and arrest those who commit crimes. Unfortunately, this leads to the arrest of innocent people who have accessed or used content that was not intended to be illegal and did not intend to break any laws.

Additionally, internet service providers and governments are developing new ways to keep tabs on what's going on in the Dark Web. As a result, distinguishing thieves from legal users is becoming increasingly challenging. The following Figure 4.7 shows how NASA, for example, has been working on a search engine to track down illegal activities, as shown in the figure.

Every new technology has some drawbacks. In addition to anarchists and weapon traffickers, the Dark Web is also home to perverts and drug dealers. Here, the threat is more psychological than physical, and people can be harmed by seeing or hearing gruesome photos or videos or being exposed to any other kind of content.

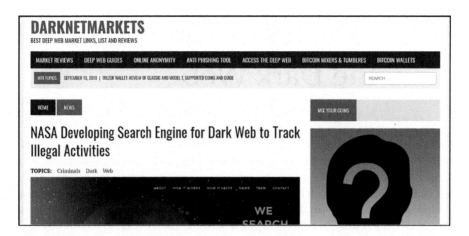

FIGURE 4.7   Illegal activities.

SUMMARY

These dangers on the Dark Web were addressed in this chapter, and we also spoke about the best ways to protect oneself and how to implement best practices. The most important thing I've learned from this chapter is that there's risk everywhere, even on the Dark Web. There's no reason you can't benefit from the variety of knowledge and topics available on the Dark Web if you take the required safeguards and are cautious.

Only when you use the Dark Web responsibly, privately, and ethically, will you help those who value privacy and don't want their personal information released realize their dreams of using it.

5 Cybercrime on the Dark Web

The dark web is a haven for criminal activity, including cybercrime. Because of this, many cybercriminals have found fertile ground here, and the results are starting to show. Data and money stolen by cybercriminals are disappearing at an accelerating rate, making it more difficult for police to track them down. This is due to the way the shadow economy is organized on the darknet. Attack actors have many varieties, and they've all been honing and improving their skills. Exploit writers and virus distributors have improved their skills. Anyone involved in money laundering, such as drug traffickers, has improved their ability to conceal the revenues of their attacks. An advanced cyberattack is challenging to stop and equally complex to examine when the efforts of the several players who make up a cyberattack today are combined. As cybercrime categories, darknet activities, and new value chains have bolstered cyber attackers' capabilities in recent years, this chapter's primary objective is to familiarize you with them. Specific issues will be discussed in depth, including:

- Categories of cybercrime.
- Cyberterrorism.
- Using DW for cybercrime warfare and cyber extortion.
- Money laundering and malware-as-a-service.

CATEGORIES OF CYBERCRIME

According to this definition, cybercrime is any crime that uses a computer or network illicitly. Fraud, identity theft, and infringement of a third party's copyright are only a few examples. Surface-net cybercrime has been around for a while now. However, as the darknet has grown in popularity, fraudsters now have a safer location from which to operate. Trails of illicit activity that lead back to a cybercriminal are the most challenging things for them to avoid. They will likely be caught, charged with a crime, and sentenced to significant time in prison if they are located. The dark web provides cybercriminals with a nearly perfect operational environment. The following is a list of the different types of cybercrimes.

COMPUTER FRAUD

To get someone to do or not do anything, the facts must be distorted, which results in a loss. As a result, it's a common form of cybercrime to which many individuals and businesses have fallen victim. Computer fraud entails falsifying data by entering false information or unauthorized instructions into a computer system. Online transactions may be tampered with, destroyed, suppressed, or stolen. Finally, it may

DOI: 10.1201/9781003404330-5

entail modifying or erasing previously saved data. As a result of the rise in unlawful activity, businesses are losing millions of dollars each year. People and organizations have reported the following computer fraud occurrences the most.

BUSINESS EMAIL COMPROMISE

This is a well-known fraud that preys on companies. The scam is excellent when a company has overseas partners to whom monies are routinely delivered electronically. The scam begins with the theft of a high-level employee's company email account. Attackers who have gained access to an executive employee's email will see what form of communication that person uses. It is common for them to contact the accounts or finance department through email and request that future payments be made through new foreign bank accounts on behalf of particular businesses they work with. They can make a killing by instructing their employees to spend significant sums of money as monthly payments to their overseas suppliers or business partners, with the money going to the hackers instead (Figure 5.1).

Ubiquiti Networks was the target of one such attack. Hackers constructed a fake email account for a high-ranking member of the company's personnel and told the accountants to make payments to suppliers using fictitious accounts in foreign countries. The corporation had already lost over $44 million by the time the scheme was discovered. Hackers are currently using this elaborate hoax, and it is effective.

DATA INFRINGE

This is yet another common form of computer fraud. If data from a seemingly secure storage system is accidentally released or spilled, this is the moment at which it was compromised. Hackers get their hands on private information, which they either reveal to the public or use as a ransom to extort money from their victims. One of the most significant data breaches at a well-known corporation is Yahoo, the email service provider. According to reports, hackers have accessed millions of Yahoo users' personal information. The company hasn't been hacked once, indicating that the hackers are either collaborating with an insider or have been on Yahoo's networks for a long time. One other significant instance was the theft of voter data from the Republican National Committee (RNC) in the United States. Private information on over 200 million Americans was taken from the RNC, resulting from the Amazon S3 bucket storing data insecurely. A data breach occurred at Uber, although the situation was handled haphazardly by the company's administrators.

| Cybercriminal compromises employee email | Compromised account is used to send notifications to customers | Payments are transferred to cybercriminal'saccount | Cybercriminal receives money |

FIGURE 5.1   An illustration of a business email compromise intrusion.

According to reports, a hacker gained access to the company's network and stole the personal information of 57 million customers. Some high-ranking officials gave the hacker a hefty sum of money to keep the hacker quiet. This attempt to conceal the intruder instead of dealing with him ended in the dismissal of some executives. Because of its involvement in computer fraud, Kaspersky Lab has already been forbidden by the US White House from using its wares on federal computers. According to reports, the NSA contractor's laptop running Kaspersky antivirus was attacked by Russian hackers. Data was stolen from the computer, which was running the antivirus and was owned by the contractor.

In this deliberate attack, the hackers are believed to have taken advantage of the program's ability to obtain any file on a hard disk. When a data breach was made possible by an antivirus application, the attacker demonstrated just how low security had sunk. WikiLeaks also reported on a data breach in which an unusual criminal was implicated. Exposed claims that the US CIA possessed a database of exploits to track Windows users.

DENIAL-OF-SERVICE

Because they are done to suppress or prevent regular operations, denial-of-service (DoS) attacks are included in the definition of computer fraud. DoS attacks disrupt lawful access to systems or networks by flooding them with unauthorized requests. Organizations fear this kind of attack because it occurs without warning and is difficult to halt once it has begun. Most of the attack is the work of botnets, which have enlisted thousands of devices and bombarded servers with requests. Dyn, a domain name resolving service, fell prey to a distributed denial-of-service (DDoS) attack in 2016. One hundred thousand botnet devices were used to launch the attack, which delivered queries to the company at a rate estimated at 1 Tbps. Because the firm responsible for converting domain names into IP addresses was targeted, the attack was particularly audacious (Figure 5.2).

FIGURE 5.2 Depiction of a DoS attack.

Since Dyn was attacked, many websites' names could not be resolved, preventing them from being accessible. As a result of the attack, the rest of the business world took notice and began to take the capabilities of determined attackers more seriously. Another DDoS attacker successfully took down investigative journalist Brian Krebs' website after a massive attack with a throughput of up to 620 Gbps. In this attack, the degree of force utilized against the investigative journalist was significant. The Mirai botnet was blamed for the attack, which infected thousands of machines linked to the web with software and forced them to participate in DDoS attacks. Finally, a wave of DDoS attacks on Russian banks was alleged to have been perpetrated by a botnet of around 24,000 computers in 2016. Five banks were the targets of attacks, which lasted more than 2 days. However, according to reports, the invading botnet failed to take down the websites. DDoS attacks increased by 915% last year, according to data. As Internet of Things (IoT) devices have become more widely used, this has happened. Because of their lack of security, IoT devices have become prime targets for hackers looking to enroll many devices in their botnets. Organizations were targeted to disrupt operations or divert attention from a data breach.

MALWARE

Malware can be used to open a door for an attacker, mainly if it contains exploits. Malware has become a critical component in nearly all criminal operations. Unsecured devices can readily be infected with malware, which can subsequently be used to perpetrate further crimes, including identity theft and data theft. Malware can be programmed to download itself to a user's computer or mobile device when they visit a specific website. Without an antivirus program, the user can't identify if their device has been infected. Malware can steal data and keep a direct line of communication open between the hacker and the target computer. Before launching their attacks, hackers can keep tabs on everything a person does for an extended period of time. When hackers targeted businesses and financial institutions, they followed a unique value chain that compromised PCs and kept tracking infected devices for extended periods. To complete the attack, they would have to become familiar with the systems used by their targets first. This is where they exploit the infected devices' systems to authorize or generate transactions to transfer money to their accounts, depending on which they choose. Types of malwares are shown in Figure 5.3 below.

EMAIL ACCOUNT COMPROMISE

In many ways, this resembles the previously discussed compromise of business email. However, corporations are not the only targets of this kind of attack. Targeting a broad population and even those who aren't expecting it can be done with great success. Hackers utilize compromised email accounts belonging to professionals to trick others into delivering money or sensitive information to their attackers. Attackers are most likely to target those who work in financial organizations, real estate, or law companies to steal their email accounts. The intruders will pose as professionals and engage with clients, demanding money or favors for their services. Password guessing or social engineering tactics are used to access the accounts. When hackers gain

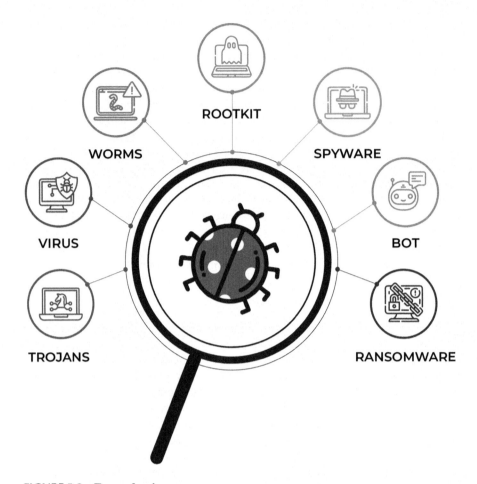

FIGURE 5.3 Types of malware.

access to a company's email, they can use that information to target clients, acquaintances, and relatives, or even carry out transactions in their name. Email account compromise is shown in Figure 5.4.

PHISHING

This type of computer fraud occurs when users are tricked into giving money or personal information to cybercriminals through emails. Phishing attempts generally do not target a single person because they send multiple recipients the same phishing email. Senders who claim to be from a respectable company will ask the receiver for information or credentials to launch an attack. Another type of phishing assault involves fooling the receivers into believing they've won a lottery or other competition and then demanding personal information or money to collect their prize.

Phishing has evolved to include elements of technology. The email is specifically personalized to the recipient's needs using spear phishing, making it more sophisticated than

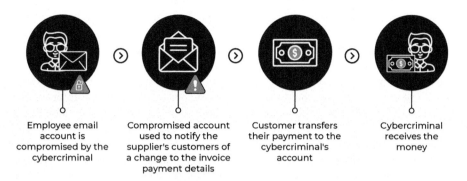

Employee email account is compromised by the cybercriminal

Compromised account used to notify the supplier's customers of a change to the invoice payment details

Customer transfers their payment to the cybercriminal's account

Cybercriminal receives the money

FIGURE 5.4 Email account compromise.

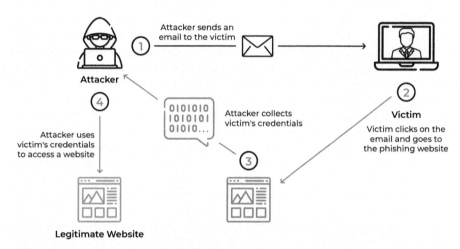

FIGURE 5.5 Depiction of phishing.

standard phishing. The assailant will know something about the victim, so they'll know exactly where to aim their attack. Using a fake HR email, the attacker might trick the victim into disclosing their tax information or other sensitive information by making the email look like it came from the HR department of the target organization. Requesting personal data from the target will not be perceived as inappropriate by HR; hence, it will be provided. For years, phishing emails used to be riddled with spelling and grammar faults and blatant forgeries. Recently, a new breed of attackers has emerged.

These intruders send out professional-looking emails. Cloning tools exist; all it takes is changing the domain name to run a false website for the attacker. Phishing emails inform the victim that their account has been compromised and they must log in by clicking on a provided link to rectify the problem. This is how an attacker uses phishing. You will redirect your intended victim to an impersonation of the authentic website, where they will be asked to check in using a similar interface after clicking the link. Whenever the victim signs into the account, the attackers receive their credentials, and the victim is put on a never-ending round of authentication requests (Figure 5.5).

With the different ways, attackers are adopting. Phishing has become an extremely practical attack in recent times. Fraudsters will tell customers that their PayPal accounts are having problems and that they must immediately log in using the link provided to fix the problem. The link would take the recipients to a cloned site that looked exactly like PayPal's login page, prompting them to input their login credentials. The cloned website would then ask the user for further personal information in several steps after they'd done that and submitted the information. As a result of giving away so much information during the attack, the victim is now completely defenseless against the assailants.

Affected PayPal users received emails with recommendations on how to prevent being a target in the future. PayPal was informed of the situation. During the 2017 US tax season, phishing assaults were once again successful. Hackers took advantage of people's haste to finish their tax returns to scam them. Their emails would generate fake IRS requests, claiming to be from the agency itself, and ask the recipients to comply by sending information or money. Later, the phishing network was tracked to India, where the ringleader was apprehended. In the wake of millions of dollars in American losses, they agreed. If the attackers employed the same methods and technologies somewhere else, it would be possible to carry out the attack.

Hackers have taken notice of phishing's efficacy. Because of this, they are using this method to reach a large number of individuals while spending very little money. Many additional attacks have been as successful as the two just mentioned. In just the first three months of 2017, one in every 25 Qataris was the victim of a phishing scam. A phony postal service campaign took place in the Czech Republic. The hoax campaign invited consumers to use their postal services via an app they might download. That malware program stole their banking information, so they had to uninstall it immediately.

Companies tricked out an energy solutions pdf file in more than 50 countries in the same year. Any device opened with the malware-infected PDF file became affected. After hackers sent phishing emails suggesting that Amazon offered discounts on certain items, the e-commerce site suffered the same fate as PayPal. After clicking through to a clone site and entering their login credentials, users were sent to the original site, where they were informed that the discounted products were out of stock and could not be purchased. However, the hackers could utilize the data they'd previously provided to them to continue their attacks in the future.

Many more phishing efforts were made to infiltrate the company via email. It was projected that in 2017, 75% of all firms received phishing emails as part of a security survey conducted among a representative sample of organizations throughout the world. According to this estimation, phishing has made a strong comeback and is growing more prosperous. According to the study, phishing can result in malware infections, compromised accounts, and data loss.

RANSOMWARE

A new sort of malware has emerged that uses cryptography for nefarious ends. Once a computer has been infected with malware, its files will be encrypted, rendering it useless. Any encrypted file or software cannot be opened. Because of this, the infected machine is unavailable for any task. Phishing emails are a typical way

for ransomware to spread. Whenever an end-user opens an email with a malicious attachment, their PCs become infected. Some ransomware variants spread to other machines in the infected network. Because they can quickly encrypt files, consumers have a slight possibility of stopping an assault once it has begun. Once the machine has been encrypted, malware will display a warning that it has been encrypted and that the user must pay to get the decryption key. This allows the victim to decode the machine locally. In some instances, attackers may provide a decryption program to the victim. Due to the difficulty of tracking payments made with traditional methods, most payments are now made with Bitcoin.

These ransomware assaults in 2017 hit people all around the world, showing how many still don't understand the new cybercrime realities. It's becoming more widespread and successful at the same time as becoming more indiscriminate. In 2017, the biggest ransomware outbreak was WannaCry, which has been tied to North Korea since its start. Over 150 countries were affected by ransomware, which was widely publicized. The hackers seek a $300 Bitcoin ransom for each encrypted machine. According to reports, there were 150,000 instances recorded throughout the world within a few days. The effectiveness of the ransomware was proved by the fact that it targeted a Microsoft exploit known as EternalBlue. Even though the vulnerability had been patched two months prior, many users still had not done so. According to reports, the National Security Agency had EternalBlue, and as a result, the agency was slammed following the attack. A vulnerability in WannaCry's code was discovered only through static analysis, leading to the entire attack's termination. However, it was too late for the tens of thousands of machines that had already been encrypted. Computers in hospitals infected with ransomware were being utilized to provide life-saving services when they were infected. Several people lost their lives due to the cessation of these computers' services as a result of this. Figure 5.6 shows how ransomware works.

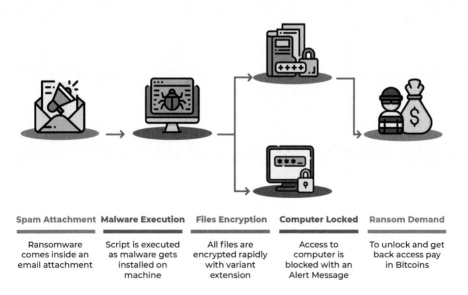

Spam Attachment	Malware Execution	Files Encryption	Computer Locked	Ransom Demand
Ransomware comes inside an email attachment	Script is executed as malware gets installed on machine	All files are encrypted rapidly with variant extension	Access to computer is blocked with an Alert Message	To unlock and get back access pay in Bitcoins

FIGURE 5.6   How ransomware works.

BADRABBIT

Hundreds of Russian and Ukrainian organizations fell victim to less-effective ransomware. The victims were Russia's media outlets, Kyiv's metro system, and an airport. In South Korea, the United States, and Poland, there are few reports of malware. Unlike WannaCry and Petya, the BadRabbit ransomware does not exploit the Microsoft Windows operating system flaws. When the ransomware had finished encrypting the PCs, it wanted 0.5 Bitcoin as ransom, as shown in Figure 5.7.

LOCKY

This malware was first identified in February 2016. However, it has been disappearing and reappearing since then. It's been determined that it spreads via spam emails sent by botnets. It's been linked a lot to Necurs, specifically. It was sent out via 23 million emails in August of last year in a single day. Pictures and downloadable attachments were included in the emails' bodies, making them interesting to read. VBScript was included in the zip file of attachments. Once opened, this script would start the ransomware.

NOTPETYA

Nearly a month had passed since WannaCry was discovered when it was discovered. The problem first hit power firms in the Netherlands and Ukraine. Later, the United Kingdom and Spain reported similar ransomware outbreaks. NotPetya had infected over a hundred people in over a dozen nations in just a few days. Compared to WannaCry, this ransomware encrypted the Master Boot Record. However, the ransomware continued to take advantage of WannaCry's EternalBlue exploit. NotPetya

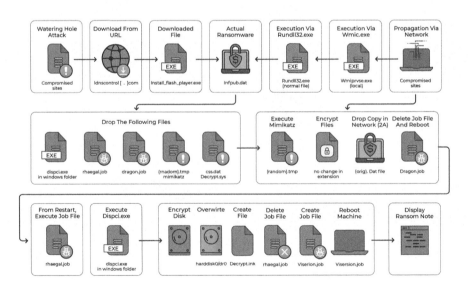

FIGURE 5.7   BadRabit ransomware.

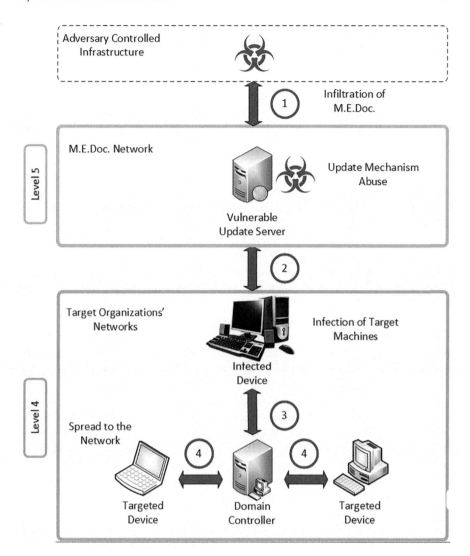

FIGURE 5.8 Ransomware's impact.

was given this name to distinguish it from the considerably less widespread ransomware known as Petya. Companies took the brunt of the ransomware's impact, with some reporting losses of $300 million, as shown in Figure 5.8.

CYBERTERRORISM

Governments worldwide must deal with a new form of terrorism known as cyberterrorism. Online terrorism is rising on the public internet and the dark web. This has law enforcement agencies like the Federal Bureau of Investigation (FBI) concerned. An attack group known as cyberterrorists uses computer attacks to frighten

or coerce governments and other organizations into supporting terrorist propaganda. Terrorism is directed at computers and perpetrated via computers or networks; that's what it becomes. There is a slew of things that fall under the category of cyberterrorism. If a blogger publishes an article and then shares it on social media claiming that bombs have been planted and will go off on a specified date, that might be termed cyberterrorism. Cyberterrorism includes terrorist propaganda disseminated via social media with the intent of causing harm to the people of a certain country. To commit cyberterrorism, one must hack into a government website to spread panic or demonstrate one's dominance and subversion of a country.

Some countries' systems have become progressively digitalized. Smart grids supply some countries' electricity, and basic services are much more heavily digital in other nations or large cities. Even industries like nuclear power generation rely on information systems to function. Critical infrastructure can be targeted by terrorists who use computer systems to control it. US and Israeli officials said they deployed a virus known as Stuxnet to shut down Iran's nuclear reactor. The malicious software compromised the control systems for the nuclear reaction process, so the nuclear power station spontaneously combusted. After the incident, investigators concluded that it was state-sponsored.

Armed with a large enough team of competent hackers, terrorists could bring entire communities to their knees by disrupting essential services like electricity and water. Fortunately, none of the well-known terrorist organizations have people who possess such abilities, and most of them would rather engage in actual conflict than one based in cyberspace. Since Stuxnet, only a few isolated incidents have shown concerted attempts at cyberterrorism. Attacks against Ukraine's energy provider networks, for example, resulted in power outages. Once, a researcher exploited a vulnerability in the system that controls traffic lights to take control of traffic systems throughout the United States. Other attacks in many countries can be classified as cyberterrorism.

Estonia was one of the nations hit hard by a massive cyberattack that rendered all online services unusable. The internet was brought down in 2007 after a DDoS attack was launched against Estonia. With no internet connectivity, the country regressed to its preinternet days with no online banking, phone carrier networks, or government services. Since Russia and Estonia had been at odds over removing a Soviet statue from Tallinn, the country was the perpetrator. The attack on Estonia served as a sobering reminder of how reliant modern states have become on technology and how vulnerable they are. The cyberterrorism conceptual framework is shown in Figure 5.9.

The number of cyberterrorism assaults is still modest, as seen by the few high-profile occurrences. Even so, this might not be the case in a few years. Terrorism will soon be fought on the online battlefield. The IoT is being more widely used across a wide range of sectors and infrastructure. Many people rely on them for practical reasons.

On the other hand, these gadgets are fragile targets for criminals. Many market items are vulnerable to cyberattacks because they lack proper security protections. Cyberterrorists may start attacking interconnected sectors and infrastructure via

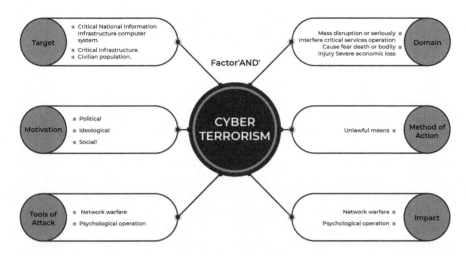

FIGURE 5.9 Cyber terrorism conceptual framework.

the IoT. The absence of members with hacking expertise no longer ensures terrorist organizations' inability to carry out cyberattacks. Experienced individuals can now be recruited on the black market for malware and directed to cause political disruptions in computers and network systems in a particular country. They could be hired. Terrorists are already showing signs of moving on that path in the future, as evidenced by recent events.

There are currently plans in place worldwide to deal with such a danger. Institutions have already been set up to assist in the fight against cyberterrorism. The US military has previously established joint task teams tasked with preventing and responding to acts of cyberterrorism. When cyberterrorism attacks occur in member countries of NATO, a cyber defense force is set up to deal with them. As a result of its high level of connectivity, South Korea is particularly vulnerable to cyberattacks. Several terrorist attacks on the country have already proven this. The country has increased efforts to secure important institutions like the National Intelligence Agency (NIA). China's contentious defense force, the Blue Army, was developed expressly to deal with cyberterrorism. The Blue Army is a hotly debated topic due to allegations that it has infiltrated other countries' networks and threatened other governments. More countries recognize the threat of cyberterrorism and are taking steps to protect themselves against attacks of this nature.

CYBERWARFARE

A cyberwar is a conflict fueled by political motives between groups, states, or countries. To disrupt business operations, engage in industrial espionage, and obtain data that can be utilized for military strategy, states hack each other's computer systems and networks. There are various types of cyberwarfare. Malware could compromise the infrastructure or organizations of a country's government agencies. The malware aims to disrupt both traditional corporate activity and vital public infrastructure, such

as power grids. Iran's nuclear reactor was attacked with malware known as Stuxnet, which is considered cyber warfare and is used by the United States and Israel.

Another type of cyberwarfare is a DoS attack on government computing systems or important industries in a certain country. DoS attacks have the potential to impair online transactions and processing. It's possible for DoS attacks to completely disable internet connectivity in a country, as in Estonia. Hacking and data theft from significant government organizations and companies in a country are examples of cyberwarfare. Many countries have accused Russia, China, and North Korea of infiltrating international systems and stealing critical information by utilizing hacking units within their governments or hacking and data theft activities. Even though many of these allegations have yet to be confirmed, tensions are rising, and a cyberwar may break out shortly. Countries have also been stockpiling weapons in preparation for such an assault. Finally, ransomware can be employed in cyberwarfare by sending spam-carrying malware to important government entities. The ransomware can potentially encrypt machines crucial to the operation of the country's infrastructure, rendering them inaccessible.

Cyberwarfare has various goals, but they all attempt to attack a country's crucial infrastructure and its most important sectors and organizations. Even if a country's networks are safe, adversary governments can engage expert hackers to find and exploit any vulnerabilities. The most frequently targeted assets are critical pieces of infrastructure. It's not hard to envision massive blackouts in the event of an attack on a country's power distribution network. For example, electricity-dependent sensitive services would come to a screeching halt. Nuclear reactors are used in some countries, whereas hydroelectric power facilities are used in others. The country's electrical generation could be harmed if these plants are targeted. Hydroelectric power facilities' control systems are vulnerable to attack, and floods could result from manipulating the controls.

Government agencies and institutions' computer systems are likewise vulnerable to assault. These systems' data could be hacked and misused by adversaries for their political ends. Secret agents' and spies' identities, as well as government secrets, could be made public. On the other hand, ransomware can render systems inoperable. It is possible to hack into government communication networks to silence the flow of information. Sensitive information can be gleaned from messages sent via public communication channels. Information on a country's residents could be made public if critical institutions are breached. Finally, adversary states might attack military databases to find where the troops are stationed, their equipment, and what weaponry they employ. Enemy states may get a backdoor into military communications by infiltrating the channels used to give commands.

CYBER EXTORTION

There's a new form of threat in town, in which organizations are threatened with DoS attacks until they pay hackers. The hackers promise not to assault the systems, provided the requested sum is paid. Alternatively, hackers may repeatedly launch DoS attacks against the servers to demonstrate their prowess before asking the business to pay a ransom to end the attack. As a result of this form of cyberattack, companies

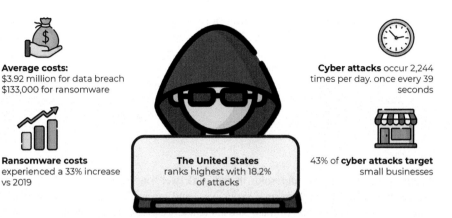

Average costs:
$3.92 million for data breach
$133,000 for ransomware

Ransomware costs
experienced a 33% increase
vs 2019

The United States
ranks highest with 18.2%
of attacks

Cyber attacks occur 2,244
times per day. once every 39
seconds

43% of **cyber attacks target**
small businesses

FIGURE 5.10   US cyber extortion.

have typically agreed to pay the attackers rather than sit back and watch their systems and networks crumble under their feet. Approximately 20 occurrences are reported to the FBI every month; however, many more go unreported, especially by companies trying to protect their good name while not disclosing their security weaknesses. Statistics are shown in Figure 5.10.

USING THE DARK WEB FOR CYBERCRIME

This section will discuss only a few of these activities in detail.

DRUGS

There are numerous underground drug markets where drugs are sold. Some of the darknet markets are where the dealers list their goods. Buyers pay using Bitcoin and receive their medication by mail. Customers rely on suppliers with a history of reliability because few rules exist. Buyers can update their trust score on some platforms based on their interactions with various sellers. On the other hand, legal firms have taken down the majority of marketplaces. If past trends are any indication, new markets will emerge to meet the needs of vendors and buyers who previously bought and sold on defunct markets.

HUMAN TRAFFICKING, SEX TRADE, AND PORNOGRAPHY

According to researchers, one-fifth of the darknet's adult websites were once found on Tor. Pornographic material was available along with human trafficking and the sex trade. The darknet and surface web trafficked 2.5 million people in 2014, despite popular belief that these crimes are now confined to the past. As a result, the black market for human trafficking may still be active. A Defense Advanced Research Projects Agency (DARPA) program dubbed Memex was created in response, searching the dark web for possible human trafficking activities and keeping tabs on them.

When it came to the dark web, child pornography was a troubling problem that revealed human depravity. The FBI had taken down nearly every darknet site that featured child pornography, and they had also tracked down and arrested the sites' creators. In addition, many darknet marketplaces forbid the sale of child pornography. For example, child porn was one of the things that had to go from Silk Road 2.0. It's a good thing there aren't many sites remaining that host this kind of offensive material.

WEAPONS

Weapons can be bought and sold on the dark web on Amazon and AliExpress. Among the weapons are firearms, explosives, and ammo for each type of weapon. Security is jeopardized due to these sites because weapons are offered to those with malign intentions. Terrorists have bought weapons on the dark web and then carried them out in assaults. In terrorist acts like the one in Paris, weapons purchased on the dark web were used. The massacre at Charlie Hebdo left 130 people dead and 350 injured. Armed ISIS militants with military-grade weaponry, nonetheless. On Tor's underground markets, weapons abound and are not prohibitively expensive. Terrorists' desire for more lethal weaponry has grown significantly. Those who want military equipment that performs better than their standard armament are willing to pay a premium. These markets also make it easy for radicalized individuals to obtain weapons (Figure 5.11).

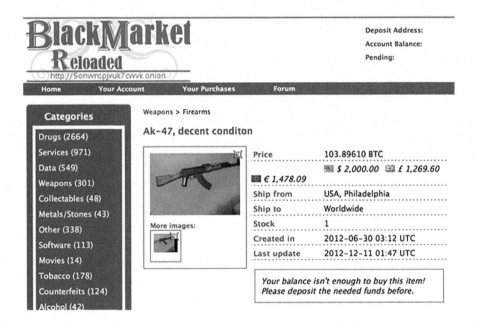

FIGURE 5.11   On the dark web, a weapon is for sale.

FAKE DOCUMENTS

Fake citizenship is available for a few hundred dollars, and fake passports are used to accomplish this. Forgeries of passports and driver's licenses are commonly found in the same places. Those who want to enter or leave the country anonymously, such as terrorists and illegal immigrants, can get fraudulent passports to cover their tracks. For example, some of the given documents are of such excellent quality that a nonspecialist would have difficulty telling the difference between them and a genuine one. There is a great distribution system for these documents, so people can use them to enter foreign countries right from their home countries (Figure 5.12).

ATM PIN Pad Skimmers and ATM Malware

Automated teller machine (ATM) fraud has been reported, with victims reporting that their funds were stolen immediately after using the machines. Using ATM PIN pad skimmers, thieves can take money from victims' ATM accounts. These can be installed on ATMs to allow hackers to capture keystroke data from ATM users. Even if banks do catch up with the criminals, the money they stole will be gone. Cash machine PIN pad skimmers are available for purchase on the black market.

ATM malware is a class of malicious software designed to steal money from ATMs. Third parties can install malware on ATMs. The intruders will then use the ATMs to withdraw money from their cassettes using instructions sent to the machines. Once the money is gone, it will be in the hands of the assailants.

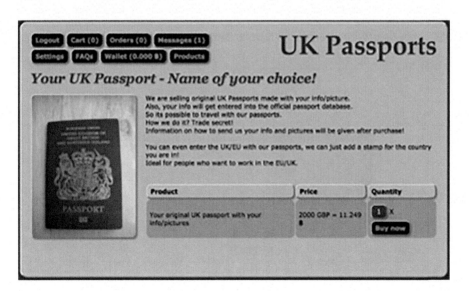

FIGURE 5.12   Passports of the United Kingdom are available for purchase on the dark web.

COUNTERFEIT CURRENCY

People can find high-quality counterfeit cash on the dark net's markets. Stores, restaurants, and other businesses can accept this currency for normal transactions without realizing they are paying with counterfeit money. Small firms, which lack the resources to verify the currency's legitimacy, stand to lose a great deal if they use the phony currency. Some dealers in fake currency claim that their currency will pass a simple UV test. Counterfeit Currency website is accessible on the Tor browser, as shown in Figure 5.13.

DATA DUMPS

Data dumps with stolen information can be purchased on the dark web. As far as you should know, the data may include personal information like your name and age, physical address, phone number or email address, and login credentials for some websites. It's the buyer's responsibility to figure out how to decode any encrypted data they might uncover in a dump. Data dumps are priced based on the monetary value and volume of data they include.

FAKE WEBSITES

Today, many elements can be used to fool even the most vigilant users into falling for phishing scams. Modern-day phishing attacks make great efforts to appear legitimate. When it came to traditional phishing emails, the content was needed to get people to do what they wanted. Nevertheless, today's phishing emails rely on more than simply content; they also rely on recipients' faith in the sender. They attempt to

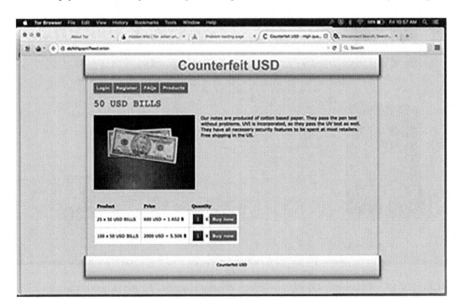

FIGURE 5.13 Counterfeit currency website.

deceive their victims into believing reputable organizations have sent them. Targets are given login information for the fictitious companies the emails claim to have come from. The links will take you to a copy of the legitimate site. The website will look authentic, so the target will have no reason to suspect its veracity. This is because hackers may buy cloned versions of popular websites on the darknet. Some of their work includes cloning online banking sites, government entities' web portals, and a variety of other high-quality replicas of legitimate websites.

EXPLOIT KITS

For cybercriminals, the dark web offers exploit kit distribution services. The dark web has supplied exploit kits for quite some time now. As a result, their services are in high demand, as few cybercriminals are proficient programmers who can create their attacks. Explicit authors' job is to research different systems, look for flaws, and then design exploits for those systems.

DATA EXFILTRATION

Data theft is a common goal of today's cyberattacks, instead of the theft of actual money. Data can be more valuable than money in some situations, and it's also less dangerous to take. Money trails may be left behind when someone steals money, making it possible to track the perpetrator. Data, on the other hand, is much easier to manage. Data exfiltration refers to transferring data from one storage medium to another. As a word used in cybercrime, taking data from compromised systems and saving it on the hackers' own devices is known as data exfiltration. To steal data, hackers must first access networks and storage systems within those networks. This has happened to several businesses. When hackers stole the personal information of almost 2 billion individuals, Yahoo was one of the companies affected. A review of data exfiltration is schematically shown in Figure 5.14.

Most data exfiltration attempts result in the data being sold on darknet markets. There are markets where data dumps can be listed for sale, and interested parties can purchase them. Advertising businesses will use the data to create user profiles

Exfiltration Diagram

Released to Public Domain 2014 by File Transfer Consulting, LLC

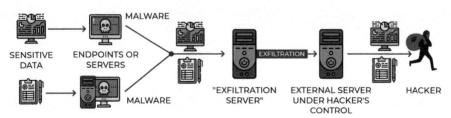

FIGURE 5.14   Data exfiltration.

and target advertisements across all communication mediums. An advertising company or another hacker will most likely pay for your personal information. In the future, fraudsters will use stolen data to target anyone whose personal information is included. They may, for example, employ it to send phishing emails to the recipients of such emails. A better understanding of their targets can help them write more persuasive emails to entice them.

In rare cases, hackers obtain encrypted data after making data exfiltrations. When this occurs, you have a choice between two paths. The hackers' first choice is to resell the stolen information on the black market for a small profit, and Decrypting the data is the second option. Decryption attempts can be successful on rare occasions, especially with less-than-stellar encryption schemes. Hackers allegedly stole encrypted versions of user data from Yahoo in the beginning. However, MD5, one of the weakest encryption techniques, was employed as the encryption algorithm. Over 2 billion user accounts' data were compromised when hackers finally decrypted it after multiple failed attempts. Data exfiltration may result in encrypted data, but attackers may attempt to decrypt it even if it is useless.

A new security measure allows companies to hire experts to scour the darknet and the surface web for stolen data. This type of action occurs only after an organization confirms a hack and the theft of personal information. Using these, you can track down stolen data and investigate who put it online in the first place and for what purpose. Organizations can now keep tabs on data leaks thanks to new services. PwnedList. com is one of them. Searching and indexing fresh data on the dark web is a continuous process for the service. PwnedList can determine if an organization's data has been compromised by performing a sample search. If any results come up, the organization will know that its data has been listed on the dark web. It can then pursue the matter further with the appropriate authorities to identify the individuals responsible. Using this database, a business can find out if any stolen data has been made public on the dark web. However, these services have a problem in that stolen data is often sold on the dark web. In addition, hackers will not reveal all of their information. They can only define what kind of data it is and what it does if they sell it.

Cybercrime Profitability

In the beginning, the major motivation for hacking was not money. In other words, it was just a way to show off one's skills. Most attacks also used scripts copied and pasted from the internet or free software found on various forums. They were simply in it to make trouble and get notoriety, not for financial gain. However, hackers' skills improved over time, and they sought financial rewards for using them. There was no known technique to turn them into cybercrime elites at the time. Because of this, they began developing a market for monetizable hacking services and tools.

The first dark web exploit kits appeared on the Russian market in 2006 and quickly spread throughout the country. They ushered in the age of cybercrime's commercialization. There were even more kits for sale on the black market. For example, some came with an attack launcher with a graphical user interface. These kits were purchased by individuals who then resold them to organized crime organizations, which would use them to attack unsuspecting victims. Back then, the same exploit kit would be applied to various targets. Thus, the hacker only had to purchase the

equipment once. However, today's cybersecurity tools make it impractical to exploit the same flaw repeatedly. Once a threat signature is identified, the same threat cannot target protected systems again.

More hacking tactics have been developed by cybercriminals, though. The following is a list of them.

EXTORTION

Making money through extortion is an option. Extortion has become a standard money-making method with the advent of ransomware, which encrypts computer equipment and then demands a payment to release the information. In the past, such an attack would have been carried out only for entertainment purposes, with the threat actors making no demands of the victims. Ransomware assaults now affect the entire continent, with criminals demanding large sums of money as ransom. When the WannaCry ransomware was active, it requested $300 in Bitcoin to decrypt the files within a week. The price would rise to $600 if the money were not paid in time. The computer would be permanently encrypted if the victim failed to deliver. Other malware has imposed similarly hefty fees, with some requesting as much as 0.5 Bitcoin. As if their threats weren't bad enough, some ransomware sends out warning messages that seem to be from the FBI. The most common explanation is that your computer has been locked because you were browsing or downloading unlawful content. Those who don't want to pay the ransom will be threatened with having their laptops permanently locked up or possibly being arrested if they don't.

PHISHING

Phishing is another way that cybercriminals make money. Due to sophisticated new phishing techniques, millions of dollars have been stolen from unsuspecting victims. Due to their lack of technological sophistication, traditional phishing attacks were relatively easy to detect. The Nigerian Prince's phishing email was widely distributed. Ultimately, any help the recipient provides to a Nigerian Prince to get their hands on an enormous windfall will be amply remunerated. Once a person decides to help, they will be advised that they will have to pay a small fee to help with the money transfer process. After spending a certain amount, another request would come in for additional money, making the costs appear to never end.

Phishing is another means of making money via cybercrime. Victims have lost millions of dollars due to sophisticated new phishing tactics deployed by hackers. Since previous phishing attacks did not use technology extensively, they were relatively easy to detect. The Nigerian Prince was the target of a widely disseminated phishing email. The sender promised to pay the recipient a substantial amount of money if he helped a Nigerian Prince get his ancestral inheritance. When someone chooses to help, they will be required to pay a fee to facilitate the money transfer. Even if you paid a certain amount, there would be no end to the charges because you would be asked to pay again.

Phishing sites look and feel much like PayPal's, and login credentials and personal information are harvested from the site. Emails sent by PayPal phishers look and feel just like those sent by PayPal. Afterward, they explain why a user's account has been restricted. When PayPal restricts an account, no money may be withdrawn

or deposited into it until the restriction is lifted. Because of this, it is reasonable to assume that a user would try to find a quick solution.

ADVERTS

Ads are another method of monetizing cybercrime. Criminals who profit by displaying advertising to unsuspecting victims are known as cybercriminals. The hackers rely on payments from advertising companies, which are derived from the number of impressions or clicks an ad receives. A large number of PCs were infected with adware due to this attack. The adware will show popup advertising on your computer's screen. This isn't necessarily bad, but it's annoying for consumers to have ads interrupt their online activity constantly. Popup ads are shown in Figure 5.15.

IDENTITY THEFT BY USING LOGIN INFORMATION

Cybercriminals can sell stolen login information on the black market for profit. Banks, institutions, social media sites, personal emails, and even conventional websites may use login credentials. Malware can be used to steal passwords on purpose. Because so many people save their login credentials in their browsers, the virus instantly downloads and installs itself when they visit particular websites. Infected computers will be infected with malware that steals and sends the attackers' login credentials. To extort money or steal it directly, the logins could be exploited.

PREMIUM-RATE SMS

Unfortunately, researchers have identified malicious apps sending messages to high-cost numbers to offer specific features. This problem appeared in the app stores for Android and iOS. It had the impact of causing a lot of money to be lost by phone

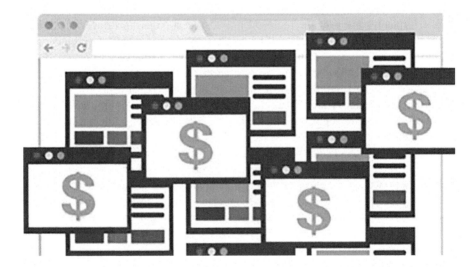

FIGURE 5.15   Ad pop-ups are depicted here.

users who didn't realize it was their apps. As a result, Android and iOS both saw significant gains. Android tightened its grip on the permissions that installed apps might request. Both platforms have also strictly controlled the apps available in their app stores. However, premium-rate SMS attacks continue to occur. Surveys are being used to gather this data. Survey participants are prompted to provide their phone numbers and text a code they get to a predetermined number. Sending the code back costs them more, and they're charged accordingly.

BANKING MALWARE

It wasn't long ago that people were worried about key loggers stealing their username/password combos when they logged in to websites. Login information entered into unprotected websites is at risk of being sniffed from packets. It's possible to get Trojans that capture incoming messages and screen activity, and these can collect a large amount of data that hackers can use to access a user's account.

MONEY LAUNDERING AND MALWARE-AS-A-SERVICE

Malware-as-a-service is one of the new value chains that attackers use in their underground economy. When cybercriminals buy malware from the cloud, they can infect various devices. Assailants need not create malware in this scenario, and Malware can be rented or purchased on the dark web from other experts. Following is a list of some malware delivery experts (Figure 5.16).

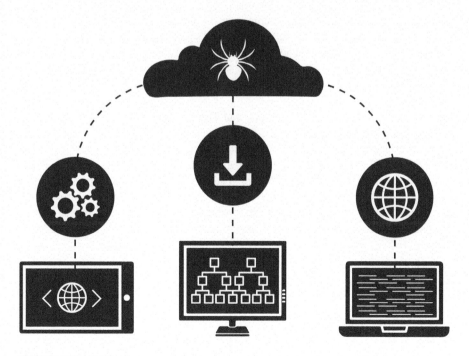

FIGURE 5.16 Malware-as-a-service.

EXPLOIT WRITERS

These hackers are always discovering new vulnerabilities in systems, and exploits are constantly being created. One or more vulnerabilities in a system will be exploited. For instance, EternalBlue was an exploit for a Windows flaw. Many ransomware attacks, including those caused by WannaCry and NotPetya, have used this vulnerability. Cybercriminals who lack coding expertise can buy exploits created by exploit authors and use them. By nature, exploit writers are rarely involved in an actual attack. They make their living by renting or selling their exploits to others. The intricacy and efficacy of an exploit are factors in its price.

A zero-day exploit is one of the most expensive types of exploits. Attackers use exploits to take advantage of security flaws their victims haven't noticed yet. As a result, they're effective. Many zero-day exploits are believed to have been employed by Stuxnet. which fueled the narrative that the government orchestrated the attack. Common cybercriminals cannot afford to waste multiple zero-day exploits in a single attempt with no financial benefit. In the underground market, other low-quality exploits sell for less money but can be just as harmful to those who use them.

BOT HERDERS

As DDoS attackers increase, they get better and better at their attacks. When an attacker sends so many unauthorized queries to a company's servers, the server goes down for a while. These assaults can be carried out by purchasing attack infrastructure on the dark web. Botnet recruitment is a specialty of some hackers. A malicious client version of zombies enables the attackers' complete control over the functionality and behaviors of an infected computer. Figure 5.17 shows an example of the harmful communications delivered by a bot herd's program, which instructs all zombie computers in that area to send spam to a list of specified addresses.

MALWARE WRITERS

Malware writers create viruses, worms, and Trojan horses. These writers can compromise operating systems, browsers, file systems, and networks. To avoid detection, malware authors can include a variety of behaviors in their programs. As well as being polymorphic, they're capable of exhibiting a wide range of behaviors, which makes it difficult to find them. Antivirus software vendors are in a perpetual state of conflict with malware developers. Until antivirus systems have indexed the malware signatures, malicious software authors must constantly release new iterations to remain relevant. Darknet markets are places where malware can be purchased and resold.

MONEY LAUNDERING

When cybercriminals earn money, they go to great lengths to obscure their activities. Law enforcement utilizes the money transfer trail to apprehend cybercriminals. To avoid this, experts on the dark web provide money-mulling services. The importance of money mules in the cybercrime supply chain cannot be overstated. The money stolen from a victim by a cybercriminal cannot be withdrawn from a bank. His task

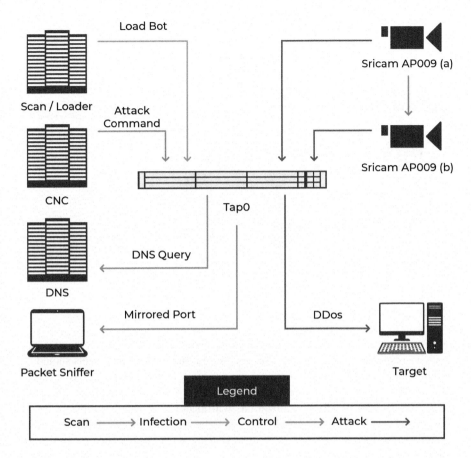

FIGURE 5.17 A botnet setup.

is to make it easy for hackers and clearing platforms to shift money from their bank accounts back to the banks where the money originated. Money trails are either fully deleted or rendered nearly impossible to follow by those who perform cleaning services. Money mules frequently transmit stolen funds between cryptocurrencies as a medium of exchange. Often, cybercriminals get compensated in cash, which is then resold to money mules for a profit. As a result, recovering money that cybercriminals have stolen is nearly impossible. The money mules wait for the cybercriminals to give them the go-ahead to clean up the funds as soon as they arrive in bank accounts or Bitcoin addresses. Figure 5.18 depicts this.

SUMMARY

The darknet has been the subject of much discussion in this chapter. It was the first time that cybercrime had been classified. Computer fraud is the first type of cybercrime. Data breaches, DoS attacks, compromised business email accounts, phishing, and ransomware fall into this category. This chapter also examined a second type of terrorism: cyberterrorism. Terrorists are increasingly threatening critical services

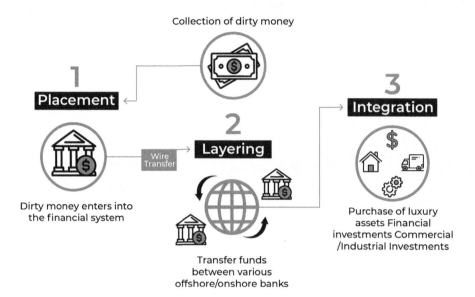

FIGURE 5.18 Money laundering.

and infrastructure with hacking. A rationale has been offered for how various countries have responded to this threat. This chapter outlines why governments should be on the lookout for potential cyberterrorism attacks, even though there haven't been many incidences thus far. Cyberextortion is the next type of cybercrime. The study shows that hackers threaten organizations with hacking or DDoS attacks to extort money from them. Finally, the study examined the topic of cyberwarfare. According to the findings, there have been numerous cyberspace clashes between nations, indicating that cyberwarfare is not far off.

China, Russia, and North Korea have all been implicated in small-scale conflicts that can escalate into full-scale cyberwarfare. Industrial espionage and election tampering have occurred due to shutting down other countries' internet. The darknet's role in aiding cybercrime was also addressed in this chapter. Data exfiltration was discussed, and what occurs when large amounts of data are taken from corporations was explained. Hackers could decrypt Yahoo data despite it being encrypted because of a flaw in the encryption algorithm. Cybercrime monetization has been a topic of discussion in this chapter.

The monetization of cybercrime's beginnings has been briefly described. After that, this chapter examined the most recent methods for generating revenue from cybercrime. Exploit kits, extortion, advertisements, login credentials theft, premium-rate SMSs, and banking malware have all been discussed. Last but not least, malware-as-a-service and money laundering have been examined in this chapter. Many hackers do not have the coding skills to create their viruses, so they hire professionals to do it for them. It's also been brought up that money mules provide laundering services. A focus has been placed on the methods employed by money mules to cover their tracks and hide the illegal proceeds of cybercrime.

6 Red Room Deep Web

Internet users answer in red rooms are frequently asked about on sites like Reddit and 4chan. So many people have shared their stories and given guidance to spectators in the past that it is hard to keep it all straight. The red room became popular in Japan after a pop-up commercial asking "Do you like the red room?" appeared on people's screens. Close it, and a full-sized window containing the names of people would pop up. According to legend, the names on the wall belonged to those who had previously entered the red room but had been discovered dead. Anyone who saw the pop-up ad suffered the same fate. A "myth," an "urban legend," is exactly what everyone who hasn't been on the deep web will tell you about red rooms.

In general, red rooms can be thought of as video gateways. They are also hidden pages where the visitor can see a person being tortured live (streaming) and even contribute to the torture by making suggestions or requests for the person being tortured. You can participate to varying degrees based on your financial commitment. Payments are made with cryptocurrency (such as Bitcoin) to ensure privacy and eliminate hassles.

Using search engines, are you trying to find information about the "Red Room" or the "Deep Web Red Room"? The spot you're looking for is right here. However, unlike widespread belief, they do exist! We have also supplied a link and a step-by-step explanation of how to join! Aside from the tiny and bing points, the Red Room on the deep web has everything you need.

For those just starting with Red Room, I ask you to read all the following points first. They will give you a good understanding of what to expect in Red Room, how to stay safe in Red Room, etc. As shown in Figure 6.1.

This chapter will cover the following topics:

- What is the Red Room Deep Web?
- What is Available on the Red Room Deep Web?
- How to Join the Red Room Deep Web?
- Red Room Deep Web Pricing Plans and Payment Methods.
- Is Accessing Red Room Deep Web Illegal?
- Why is the Red Room considered Non-Existent?
- Our Take on the Red Room: Disclaimer.
- Deep Web Links to Access the Red Room.

RECOMMENDATION: NEVER EXPLORE GIVEN RED TEXT WITHOUT VPN SERVICE
SYNTEX LINKS: http://(Red Text Put Here).onion
For Example: http://xxxxxxx.onion

WARNING

FIGURE 6.1   Accessing red rooms format.

DOI: 10.1201/9781003404330-6

WHAT IS THE RED ROOM DEEP WEB?

Let me try to be as concise as possible. It's a site that broadcasts live violent, sexual, and other 'bad' videos for the amusement of others over the Tor hidden network (deep web). Although this software is not free, it is incredibly expensive and allows users to give the protagonist a list of orders or suggestions they want to perform. The clearnet is where people locate things they can't find on the internet, such as violent or painful living streams. Generally, red rooms welcome you with a note, as shown in Figure 6.2.

The word "Redrum" is thought to be a punishment for the word "Murder," which is spelled backward when you say Red Room!

Streaming live shows is possible on websites like Red Room (primarily on the dark web). These live performances have terrible content, such as rape, murder, and torture, among other things. The owner(s) of the website get to profit from the sale of access to these programs in exchange for Bitcoin. They're usually quite pricey. As you'll see in the following sections, a variety of "plans" give you varying degrees of influence over the video's events. When I tried to gain access, numerous plans seemed expensive (purely for educational and myth-busting purposes). The lowest I could go was 0.5 bitcoins ($25,000) in terms of price.

FIGURE 6.2 Welcome note.

WHAT IS AVAILABLE ON THE RED ROOM DEEP WEB?

The Red Room can be described as a "Video gateway." You might think of it as a deep web market for criminally motivating videos that is "more advanced" and "real-time." As a result, anything and everything related to inflicting pain on others will be available online.

CHILD PORNOGRAPHY

Child pornographic content is prohibited from most deep web markets because most normal-minded individuals would not go for it. The following types of child pornography are included in the category of child pornography:

- Torture: Inflicting physical injury on the youngster while reveling in their suffering.
- Rape: Inflicting sexual harm on a youngster, regardless of their sex.
- Nonactivity: In this type of pornography, nothing is done to or to the youngster; the victim is tied to a bed or chair and, in most cases, dressed in undies, while a camera broadcasts the scene to the public.

MURDER

One option is to watch a random person kill another random person, or you can pay the administrators a certain amount to kill (or torture) a specific person. You are believed to be in on the killer's plans by watching the Red Room stream of the act. It's also possible to select from "categories" like "slow death," "neck-slicing," and all other unimaginable ways to kill someone.

RAPE

Further aggravating the situation, on the Red Room Deep Web, "Rape" appears to be available for purchase as a "commodity" and is "in-demand." Anyone, male or female, can be the victim of rape in the Red Room and have their suffering chronicled for the public's benefit. Again, there are various types of rape, and as you can guess, there are numerous methods to cause sexual anguish to another person. Almost anything you can think of is claimed to be possible in the red chamber.

GENERAL TORTURE

Not only do the Red Room tapes show "classified" crimes, but they also show general torture. A few examples of "very painful" procedures include slicing the tongue or taking the eyes out.

CHAT

There may be a "talk" option in some Red Rooms. Instead of watching the movies, utilize the chat feature to communicate with other "like-minded" individuals without revealing any personal information about yourself. People who fall into various "sadistic categories" can use it as a social network because locating other "like-minded" people in the actual world is incredibly difficult. As a result, different pricing plans differentiate between "video-watchers" and "chat-users," and so on.

HOW TO JOIN THE RED ROOM DEEP WEB?

You can't access the Red Room over your regular internet connection, and only the TOR browser can access the "Deep Web," where it's only available. TOR is a secure and anonymous web browser that protects your online privacy.

NordVPN is required for improved security or anonymity (Onion over VPN server). Most of the time, it's utilized to access the deep web, where you'll find the mysterious red chamber. TOR, by default, hides your IP address from prying eyes, but you should still use a virtual private network (VPN) when utilizing it to access the Red Room's dark web.

Third parties have audited NordVPN's no-log policy and found it to be accurate. NordVPN has servers in over 60 locations, with over 3,600 different active IPs. All your internet traffic is migrated from TOR nodes to specialized onion servers, which further enhances the security of your internet connections.

Below is an example of what you may see on a Red Room Deep Web home page. While the "join" button may not be present in every Red room, I'll click on it to move you along for the time being. I'm then offered multiple "plans," such as the "spectator" plan, which lets me merely "watch," or the more expensive "Commander" plan, which allows me to order the person in the video to carry out a specific activity. Red Rooms plans are shown in Figure 6.3.

As a result of selecting "Spectator" just to write this post, I am redirected to the "Payments" page. A Bitcoin address is provided to me, along with the exact amount of Bitcoin I'm supposed to transfer. The payment mode is shown in Figure 6.4.

The Red Room Deep Web will enable us to continue our investigation if we pay the required fee. Every Red Room platform has a Bitcoin address on the home page, sends money to that account, and then sits tight for instructions to arrive via email or text message.

RED ROOM DEEP WEB PRICING PLANS
AND PAYMENT METHODS

To use Red Rooms, you must have a Bitcoin wallet on hand. Bitcoins are the most widely used cryptocurrency and can't be tracked. As a result, you have no reason to fear for the safety of your personal information while making payments, and the administrators of the Red Room can make money without fear of repercussions from law authorities. Some Red Rooms may accept other cryptocurrencies like Monero (XMR), and some Red Rooms may accept Ethereum. Unlike some platforms, which

FIGURE 6.3 Red rooms plans.

offer a single set of packages to all users, others have packages with varying access levels. This was illustrated in the preceding sections, and platforms have different packages.

IS ACCESSING RED ROOM DEEP WEB ILLEGAL?

Totally! Yes. A witness fee is "criminal," as the saying goes. As a result, it can only be found on the "deep web," and using a VPN in addition to the TOR browser is highly advised for increased security. Taking security measures isn't required, but if you do and are found out, you'll be charged as an "accessory to the crime" because you didn't just fail to report the crime, and you actively encouraged it to continue.

WHY IS THE RED ROOM CONSIDERED NON-EXISTENT?

Because most internet users do not believe in the reality of Red Rooms, I went into great detail in the preceding section to clear up any misunderstandings. They're considered "nonexistent" for the reasons listed below.

- Since most internet users aren't familiar with the "Deep Web," it's difficult to find this information anywhere else. Some people are terrified to explore the "deeper" parts of the deep web, such as the Red Room.

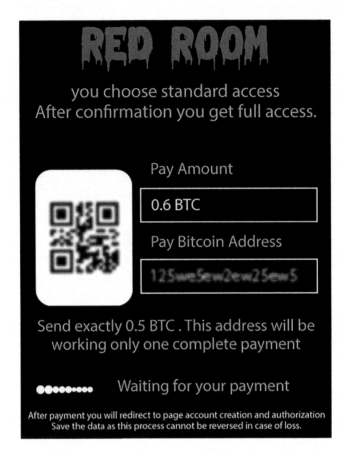

FIGURE 6.4 Payment .method.

- Red Rooms are out of reach for many people.
- It's important to note that those who can buy the Red Room Deep Web aren't just any kids who would publish screenshots online; they're responsible adults who are often well-educated and know how to keep it a secret.
- Because it's a crime to do so, no one would put evidence of it online and therefore implicate themselves.
- Most users are unlikely to have a social profile or even an "ordinary existence," as we understand it, in the Red Room because only a small group of people are allowed to "enjoy" torturing others and to "pay" to watch or control this behavior. Those who "enjoy" it in the Red room aren't mentally healthy.

There are also many fakes and scams in the Deep Red rooms. As a result of serious customers paying and being cheated, the general perception of red rooms is that they are all fraudulent. This means they have no recourse and no way to tell others about the loss of their money if they don't tell the authorities and post openly about it. Since

7 Terrorist Acts on the Surface and Dark Web

INTRODUCTION

Terrorists have relied on social media to disseminate their messages and post images, videos, and other media related to their attacks. While using social media sites like Twitter and YouTube has led law enforcement to collaborate with organizations like Europol and Interpol to identify extremists from their online activities and wipe and disable their websites to stop them from being used.

Terrorists continue to use the most well-known social media platforms to spread their propaganda, radicalize, and recruit people, even though they've recently discovered a new way to communicate with other members of the terrorist group or other terrorist groups or their supporters, and potential recruits. In this group are young people who have experienced injustice, exclusion, or humiliation due to their social status, possibly because of the Dark Web.

There is a "hidden" area of the internet known as the Dark Web, which is used by many internet users who wish to remain anonymous and unnoticed. Meaning that modern-day terrorists usually communicate and disseminate bomb-making instructions, attack planes, and other useful information with their supporters or recruits on the dark web. Using encrypted platforms and applications by terrorists to avoid being identified by law enforcement, their physical position, and eavesdropping on their communications is another example of end-to-end encryption. There is a great deal of "freedom" provided by these apps for terrorists, and they are not concerned about how to keep their talks and transactions secure while remaining undetectable.

The dark web is also used by terrorists to safeguard the long-term viability of their group. The terrorists need an ever-increasing supply of cash to buy the weapons and commit their crimes. Because it is fully anonymous, the Dark Web is the best place to achieve this. The Dark Web gives terrorists the ability to gather funds from their followers, sell oil and weapons, and purchase anything they need to carry out their operations.

TERRORISTS' ONLINE ACTIVITIES

According to Europol, the internet is a critical component of terrorist plots in Europe. The number of terrorist websites has grown significantly, indicating how important the internet is to terrorists. These sites have multiplied by orders of magnitude in several years, now numbering in the thousands. Because all major terrorist organizations have their roots in non-EU countries, they were forced to conduct their operations over the internet. A key weapon in terrorists' hands is now the internet. They utilize it for everything from recruiting new members to communicating propaganda, sharing

DOI: 10.1201/9781003404330-7

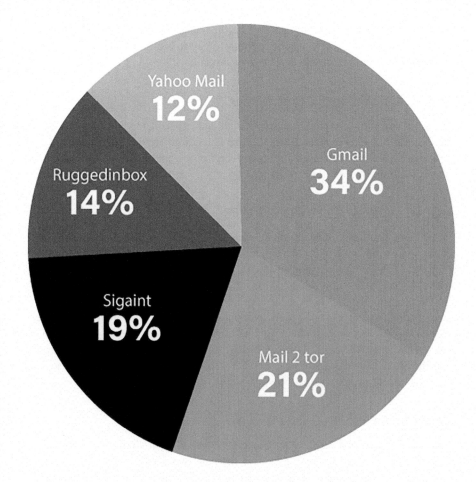

FIGURE 7.1   Technologies used by terrorist organizations.

important information and knowledge, coordinating attack plans, and generating money. Following are the technologies terrorist organizations use for all propaganda, as shown in Figure 7.1.

They've turned to the Dark Web for anonymity and to avoid being tracked by government enforcement agencies. Although the Surface Web may have a larger audience, the Dark Web appears to be better for recruiting, financing, planning, and training. The Dark Web is also more secure.

PROPAGANDA

Traditional media outlets such as television, radio, and newspapers publicize terrorist causes and activities, but their multistage editorial selection processes make it impossible for terrorists to disseminate propaganda. To get around these restrictions, terrorists created their own websites. The fact that terrorists have complete control over the content means that their messages may be readily targeted at specific

demographics. Terrorists outside the EU use the internet to spread propaganda to EU member states. Terrorists intend to use this strategy to recruit people in the EU who may be particularly vulnerable to their armed conflict.

PROPAGANDA AND SOCIAL MEDIA

It's been a while since terrorists have worked and experimented with social media, and the results have persuaded them to use it for their terrorist actions. Terrorists abuse over 150 social media sites to spread their propaganda, according to Europol's European Union Internet Referral Unit.

PROPAGANDA AND THE DARK WEB

On the Dark Web, militants communicate with one another and disseminate propaganda in films, images, and public declarations (announcements). Smartphone programs like Orbot, which can only be downloaded through the Dark Web, communicate.

There were also translations of several Daesh-issued statements in Turkish, Russian, and English on the website. For its Tor-based privacy and anonymity, this website nonetheless relied on freely available public domain content like YouTube videos to host its propaganda materials. URLs can only access video content on the Dark Web to get to the surface of websites. Furthermore, all of this media is removed from the hosts' websites. The new website also led readers to the terrorist group's encrypted Telegram messaging network, which they used to communicate.

CONTENT OF PROPAGANDA

There is no doubt that terrorist propaganda is growing in strength. Terrorist propaganda has improved its strategies over the past two decades to impact its target audience positively. Terrorists' ability to gain notoriety has risen dramatically due to the internet. Terrorist internet messaging is now attempting to include lifestyle and online gaming parts to appeal to a younger demographic. Investigators must have a firm grasp of propaganda topics and their underlying reasons to be successful.

It's a common misconception that terrorist websites exist solely to publicize their heinous deeds. Instead, one of the project's primary goals is to persuade a large online audience about two issues: the limitations placed on free speech and the plight of political prisoners. While one point may elicit sympathy with Western viewers that support free speech, the other may serve to silence those in government who disagree with their views. To still instill fear and embarrassment in their adversaries, they drew attention to the antidemocratic measures against them. The internet represents free, limitless, and uncensored communication for its users, making terrorists, as mentioned above, well-suited to the medium.

RHETORICAL STRUCTURES OF TERRORIST WEBSITES

Terrorist websites have utilized three rhetorical structures to support their commitment to violence in the past. The first is that terrorists have no choice but to resort

to violence because they are typically seen as the weaker members of society. As a result, violence is their sole option for dealing with an oppressive foe. On the other hand, terrorist websites are reluctant to admit to their heinous deeds, while government operations against them are referred to as "slaughter," "murder," and "genocide." A strong state uses a method that makes terrorist organizations appear to be persecuted, with their leaders appearing to be assassination targets.

The legality of using violence is the second rhetorical tactic. In this discourse, you may have noticed that the terrorist blames the adversary for the carnage. The movement's members must fight a relentless foe to defend the rights of their people.

To combat the terrorist violent image, the third and final rhetorical structure is to deploy the language of nonviolence on a big scale. These organizations use international pressure on a repressive regime to achieve their primary goal of a diplomatic settlement.

CRIME AS A SERVICE

Another activity of terrorists on the Dark Web is the hunt for "hiring" criminals who are prepared to sell their criminal abilities for money. For example, on June 14, 2016, an advertisement for the Dark Web website of Albanian assassins and hackers was shared via the terrorists' Telegram channel. To access the webpage, someone utilized Tor, as shown in Figure 7.2.

COMMUNICATIONS

As technology has advanced over the past two decades, terrorists have taken advantage of the change in tactics to become more high-tech and clever. There has also been a global network consisting of hundreds of websites whose goal is to invite

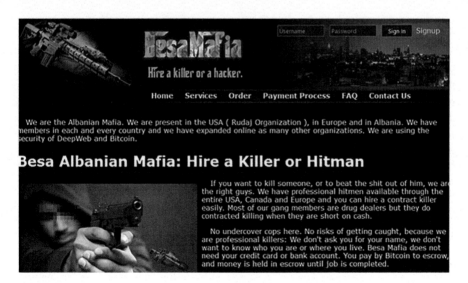

FIGURE 7.2   A secretive website where you can find and hire criminals.

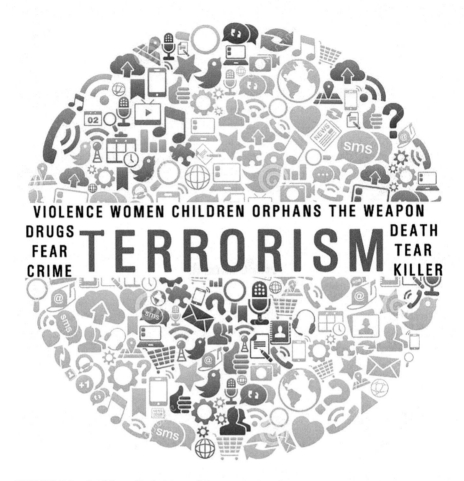

FIGURE 7.3   Social media that terrorists use.

young people to join the fight against Western nations, train them, educate them, and then recruit them. Terrorists used secret and open conversations to do this. With the popularity of social media sites like Facebook, YouTube, and Twitter, which hundreds of millions of people use daily, online recruiting has blossomed in recent years for public relations. While terrorists use the Dark Web and encrypted communication to hide their activities from law enforcement authorities, the reverse is true. This has led to the need for encrypted communication being recognized by major terrorist organizations like ISIS, RAW, and others, and they've "embraced the DarkWeb more than ever before" (Figure 7.3).

DARK WEB AND ENCRYPTED COMMUNICATION

Terrorists use a wide range of encryption methods and technology to keep their communications hidden from law enforcement and intelligence organizations, leaving them with only the metadata with which to operate. Terrorists utilize the Dark Web

and social networking sites, public and private websites, and other technologies to conceal and protect their communications. The best options to communicate anonymously and secretly are email, webchats, personal messaging housed on Tor (The Onion Router), or particular tools that provide users with anonymous and secured communications. To put it another way:

- Typically, email service providers ask for a username and password when signing up new customers. Providing additional identifying information or verification data, such as a phone number, is usually wholly voluntary on the user's part. Because email messaging and storage are encrypted, the privacy of the conversation is protected. Terrorists frequently employ cryptic email services like Hushmail and ProtonMail instead of standard email providers.
- Utilize Tor-based web chat applications such as "Chat.onion," an anonymous and secure way to communicate with friends and family over the internet. Every message passed through a network of proxies is hidden using onion routing (Tor), used by "Chat.onion." In addition, 16 character checksums are used to identify people whose public keys are used. You can connect with other users by sending your ID, showing your QR code, or scanning theirs using your camera (Figure 7.4).

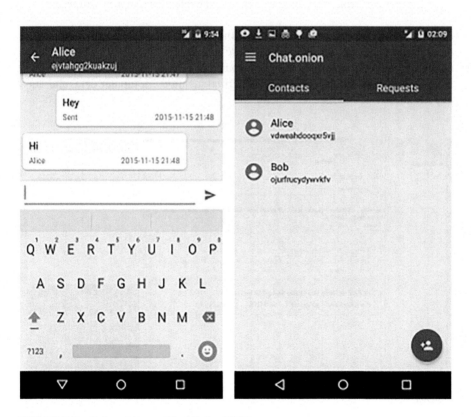

FIGURE 7.4 Onion chat app (Chat Onion 2016).

- For example, Tor Messenger can be used for private communications, and all of its traffic is routed through Tor, making it secure by default. It works across platforms. Additionally, it supports many transport networks, such as IRC, Twitter, and XMPP. Additionally, it permits off-the-record messaging and automatic security updates (Figure 7.5).
- Bitmessage is a peer-to-peer (P2P) messaging protocol for sending encrypted messages to multiple recipients. No one can be trusted because it's decentralized and trustless. Because it employs high levels of security to prevent the sender and recipient of communications from being imperson-ated, Using warrantless wiretapping programs to listen in on "noncontent" data, such as the transmitter and recipient of messages, will no longer be possible (Figure 7.6).
- Ricochet uses the Tor network to communicate with contacts instead of mes-saging servers. When you use this service, your IP address and location are hidden. Ricochet addresses provide an added value to the user by giving them an exclusive address (letters and numbers). If you want to contact another Ricochet user, you can use this address. To swiftly send messages to online contacts, the user can use the new features and files. Network activity moni-toring services and networks do not have access to contact lists. By encrypting the message from beginning to end, only the intended recipient will read it.

Finally, Tor has over 50 chat rooms, while the Dark Web hosts many private messag-ing services. These programs and tools are already used by many ISIS, Al-Bardar (India), Akhil Bharat Nepali (India), Tripura Tiger Force (India), and Communist Party of India members to protect their virtual identities, computer data, and, most importantly, contact with each other.

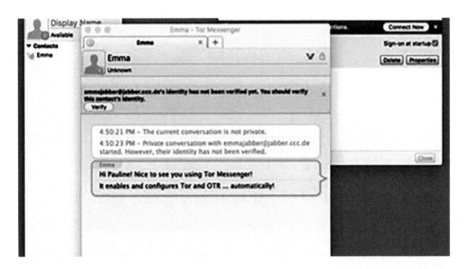

FIGURE 7.5   Tor messenger (Wired 2015).

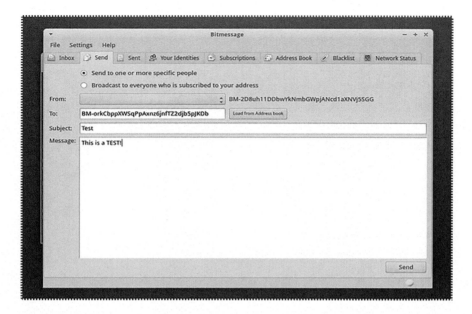

FIGURE 7.6 Bitmessage (BBARCESAJ 2013).

MAIL2TOR

Using Mail2Tor, anyone can send messages to anyone anonymously. Users can access it using a standard email service like Gmail, AOL, or Yahoo Mail for a more private experience. The Tor Project provides this service, and to use it, one must first install the Tor browser extension. In this way, users' privacy, relationships, and other sensitive data are not jeopardized due to network spying. The interface is shown in Figure 7.7.

SIGNAL

Android and iOS users can communicate securely using the Signal app. One-to-one and group messages can be sent over the internet with it. Images and videos can be sent, and files and one-to-one voice and video calls can be made. End-to-end encryption is used by Signal to protect all communications with other Signal users, and regular cellular telephone numbers are used as IDs in that communication.

TELEGRAM

Other encrypted social media services, such as Telegram, were heavily used by terrorist groups to prevent being shut down. It has the advantage of not being indexed by search engines, which is a huge plus. It's a text and multimedia messaging program for Android, iOS, and Windows phones and tablets. The Telegram company is so confident in its encryption security that it offered a $300,000 reward twice as many times to the first person to break it. Telegram can be used on any

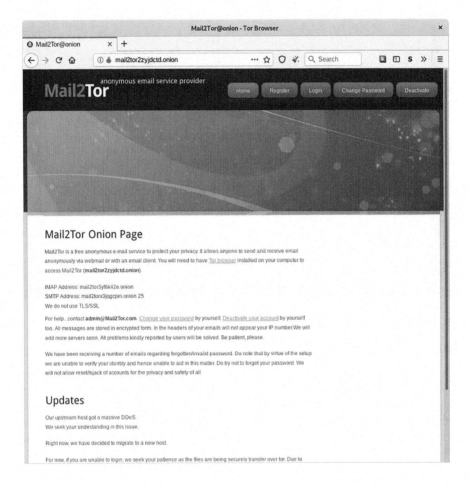

FIGURE 7.7   Mail2Tor interface.

internet-connected device, such as a desktop computer, a laptop computer, an Android phone, or an iPhone. Communications can be encrypted, shared indefinitely, and deleted after a specified period with Telegram, among other capabilities. Telegram also allows you to coordinate up to 5,000 individuals, encrypt messages, and exchange unlimited media files. There is no doubt that its user base has risen significantly since 2013.

SURESPOT

ISIS and Al-Qaeda both use the Surespot encrypted communications technology. Because it's not tied to phone numbers or email addresses, users can have several identities on a single device. Users can even send voice messages using this service. You can download Kik from the Play Store or the iPhone App Store on any Android-powered or iPhone-powered smart device and use it to communicate securely. Kik protects the privacy of its users by not requiring them to provide a phone number

when they sign up. Then, after creating a user name, you can use your smartphone's data or Wi-Fi connection to send and receive things like text messages and photographs. You may also use it to create doodles and access mobile websites. ISIS and Al-Qaeda both make extensive use of it.

WICKR

Also utilized by ISIS is Wickr, an app that encrypts messages before they are sent. Wickr protects users' messages and identities through multi-layered P2P encryption technology. Other Wickr users can receive encrypted files that expire after some time, similar to how Telegram works. Wickr is a photo, video, and file-attachment-sharing app for iOS, Android, Mac, Windows, and Linux, available on all of these platforms. ISIS and Al-Qaeda both prefer it. The application interface is shown in Figure 7.8.

ZELLO

Zello is a push-to-talk app for mobile and PC. It's a Russian-developed encrypted chat software with a Texas base of operations. ISIS terrorists often use it for online communication. According to reports, terrorists in last year's Stockholm attack communicated using Zello. For chatting with others and listening in on conversations, Users of Zello can create private or public channels. It costs money to operate the

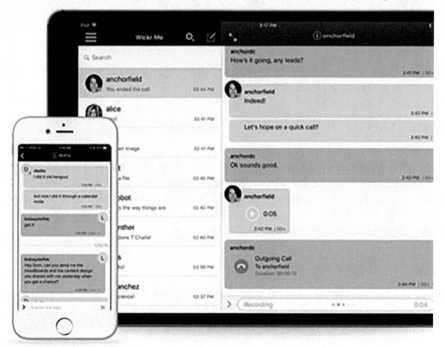

FIGURE 7.8   Wiker application interface.

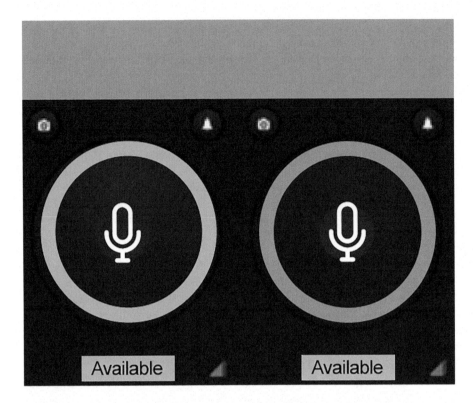

FIGURE 7.9   Application interface.

Zello@Work app, although the ordinary Zello app is free to use. The application interface is shown in Figure 7.9.

WHATSAPP

In mobile texting, WhatsApp Messenger is one of the most popular options. End-to-end encryption is used, and it's free for everyone who has an Android, iPhone, or BlackBerry. Various terrorist organizations have been observed using the communication platform to carry out operations and communicate with their supporters, including ISIS, Al-Qaeda, and others. WhatsApp can also be used to disseminate false information via the internet.

KIK

Any Android-powered smart device may download and use Kik, an encrypted instant messaging program, via the Google Play Store or App Store. For security reasons, Kik does not request a phone number from new users. Users can send and receive messages, pictures, videos, doodles, and mobile web pages after creating an account with a username using a smartphone's data or Wi-Fi connection. Both ISIS and Al-Qaeda heavily rely on it.

STEGANOGRAPHY, INTERNET MEMES, AND WATERMARKING

For clandestine communication, terrorist organizations like ISIS and others turn to high-tech techniques like steganography and watermarking. Steganography is a cryptography technique that incorporates memes. In another way, it's a tool that lets you hide a message inside another message on the internet. With the right subject title, JPEGs or GIF-encoded digital images can theoretically be utilized to transmit additional data. Dual-Tone Multi-Frequency (DTMF) audio files, Morse codes, and barcodes or QR Codes are also used to convey sensitive codes, maps, and auto messages using GPS coordinates or location. Generally, barcodes track things like serial numbers, pricing, and inventory. Quick response codes or barcodes can also communicate. Using this technology, terrorist organizations that want to communicate covertly can do so securely.

TERRORISTCRYPT

This steganography and encryption tool, known as TerroristCrypt, was first launched in January 2018 and cloaked messages within images. Since TerroristCrypt is so widely used and the actual encryption and steganography algorithms used in TerroristCrypt are still unknown, it's practically impossible for law enforcement agencies to check every image on social media platforms like Facebook, Twitter, and Telegram (Figure 7.10).

VIDEO GAMES

Online video game communication (such as WoW) is becoming increasingly common for online "gamers" to conceal messages in seemingly innocent exchanges. Comparing PlayStation 4 to WhatsApp, it's nearly impossible to keep up with everything, which makes matters worse. There are numerous ways to communicate privately on the PlayStation 4, and it allows gamers to make and receive audio calls and text messages via online chat. Terrorists could also exchange secret messages within specialized video games without speaking or writing words. Terrorists, for example, may use

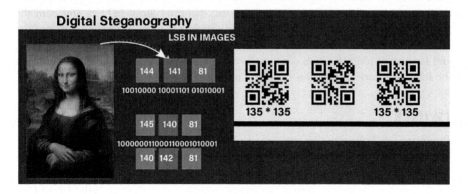

FIGURE 7.10 Altered images with hidden content.

Super Mario Maker coins to scribble down an attack strategy and send it to a pal, or two Call of Duty gamers could use a shower of bullets to scribble notes on a wall.

EMAIL DEAD DROPPING

Terrorists might "dead drop" discussions over the internet using a simple email account. It's a well-known technique for drafting emails without sending them, allowing several users with the same email account to read them without fear of being intercepted.

CYBERSECURITY IN VOICE COMMUNICATION

Linphone, Silent Circle, and RedPhone guarantee caller identity while encrypting audio communications.

TERRORIST MEDIA

Terrorists communicate over various platforms and switch between them frequently to muddle an investigation by law enforcement authorities. On the other hand, the media played an essential role in every aspect. It is based on religion; if it even happened, it was labeled terrorism and related to Muslims most of the time, as shown in Figure 7.11. All terrorists have developed their weapons systems. For terrorists and criminals, smartphone applications and other software are becoming increasingly important tools for communicating securely without building or maintaining their infrastructure. It's possible that people's reliance on these devices is waning, but it's important to let law enforcement know about them anyway since terrorists can use them to communicate.

SOCIAL MEDIA AND SURFACE WEB

Because of its accessibility, terrorists continue to use the public internet, the dark web, and encrypted communication. Social media sites like Twitter and Facebook are used to get their message out to a wide audience. However, they don't simply use them to spread misinformation; they also use them to recruit fighters and gain the support of their followers by justifying their violent behavior. At the beginning of the terrorist campaign, social media can help recruit new members, gather intelligence, and keep the group in touch with each other. Terrorists primarily communicate on the following surface websites on social media.

TWITTER

Terrorists use Twitter to disseminate propaganda. Twitter hashtags, which are popular among anti-ISIS activists in the Middle East and Europe, assist terrorists in disseminating their message in areas of interest, including Europe and other Western nations. Terrorists use these hashtags to help spread their propaganda throughout the world.

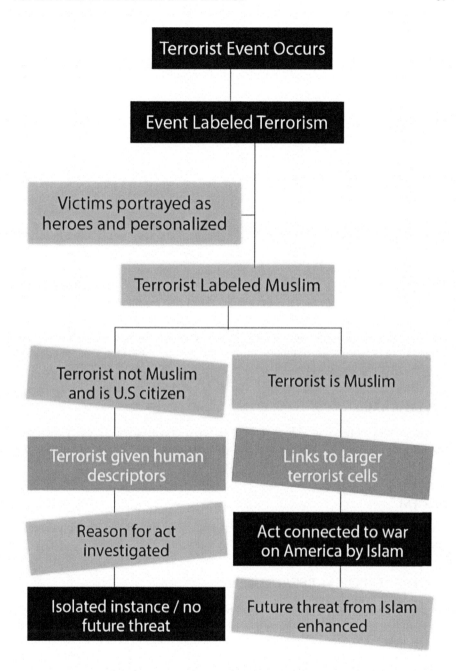

FIGURE 7.11 Media coverage module.

YOUTUBE

Terrorists use YouTube to post videos depicting the atrocities committed by terrorist groups like ISIS, Al-Qaeda, and other terrorist organizations.

FACEBOOK

It is common for terrorists to use fictitious social media personas to propagate their message and recruit new members or followers.

PINTEREST

Both communists and terrorists utilize Pinterest to spread their ideas, articles, photos, and videos.

TUMBLR

Half microblogging, part social networking, this online media platform has a little of everything. More than 3 billion blogs have been created with 100 billion entries since 2007. There is no need to sign up unless you want to comment on or follow other people's blogs when using Tumblr. Immediately, communication can be achieved simply by typing the "correct" blog.

INSTAGRAM

#hashtags on pictures and videos refer to terrorist organizations or other sites with recruitment materials or propaganda. Instagram is also used to project images of terrorist attacks and brutality by posting videos and photos.

ASK.FM

Daesh has communicated with its members and sympathizers via this social media platform.

ONLINE TERRORIST RECRUITMENT

On top of all that, they utilize the internet to build relationships with people who are receptive to their propaganda and recruit new soldiers and followers. Terrorists use the internet to accomplish more than just communicate. People under 30 make up the bulk of internet users, making it very easy to recruit them. Terrorists, on the other hand, actively seek out and cultivate relationships with potential victims rather than simply waiting for them to show up. To spread their propaganda and recruit new members, terrorist organizations like ISIS make extensive use of social media. There is growing concern about the radicalization of youngsters on social media, with ISIS reportedly owning 90,000 Twitter accounts dedicated to recruiting and enlisting schoolchildren and other marginalized youth. Now that these operations

are under scrutiny, terrorist organizations are scrambling to find a new, less risky online communication method. It's been stated that the Dark Web is the best solution because it's completely anonymous.

SURFACE WEB

Terrorists use the World Wide Web to disseminate propaganda and find recruits who share their ideas. Social media networks like Twitter and Facebook can help you achieve your goals faster and more effectively.

SOCIAL MEDIA

Terrorists have recently used social media to target thousands of youngsters and young adults. According to studies, to reach their intended audiences (often lonely young people), terrorist organizations such as ISIS and Boko Haram use social media sites such as Facebook, YouTube, and Twitter.

WEBSITES AND CHAT ROOMS ON THE INTERNET

There are a variety of other online publications used by terrorist groups and social media. Because more people are using the internet, terrorist-run websites have risen astronomically. Terrorist websites were active 20 years ago, when there were just six, and this number has now surpassed 7,000 in modern times. Terrorists and their supporters also maintain several social media identities to disseminate propaganda, publicize group activities, and recruit new members.

Combining internet and technology trends, recruiting is now easier and faster than ever before. Terrorists don't sit around and wait for potential recruits to approach them. They instantly come to them if they believe a person has the appropriate profile for the group's aims or can carry out any group's activities. They look for information about the people who visit their websites. In addition, a large number of these websites are concerned with "training" recruits. Anyone with access to these prohibited sites, including potential recruits, has the opportunity to learn how to make explosives, carry out particular terrorist attacks, receive firearms, and become a member of a terrorist organization from terrorists. Potential terrorist recruits are inundated with religious messages, propaganda, and how-to manuals.

VIDEO GAMES

Many terrorist organizations recruit new members using online video games, popular music videos, and computer games like home-built websites. These video games portray violence against Western countries and political leaders in multiple languages to appeal to a broad audience. This is especially true for youth and young adults, who may make up the largest users. Most of this is done by the European Union and the United States, which created video games to destroy sacred Muslim sites. Examples include the Special Forces and Special Force 2 video games, which show Hezbollah fighters waging war against the Israeli military. The Global Extremist

Media Front and Al-Qaeda put the Quest for Bush video game on the internet. The game's main objective is to assassinate the US president. The European Union also created the "Pubg" Game Map, which requires players to attack the Muslim holy site of Khanna Kaaba. Recruiting such young people who adore harming Muslims hurts their feelings.

COVERT RECRUITMENT AND TRAINING

Terrorists first used the Surface Web to spread their message and recruit new members to assist them in achieving their aims and objectives by broadcasting propaganda. This means, as previously mentioned, that a lot happens publicly on the Web, via social media, online journals, chat rooms, and so on. It's easy to see why this might be the case. They become more active as soon as they realize they must connect with potential recruits. As the conversations become more heated, terrorists use encryption software to ensure their communications remain private and are not leaked to the public.

CYBERTERRORISM

Terrorists' limited financial resources make crimes like cyberattacks more appealing because they require a smaller number of individuals and unquestionably lower sums of money to be carried out. Because cyberattacks may be carried out from virtually anywhere, cyberterrorists have a significant edge over traditional terrorists. These cyber terrorists know how to hide their "traces" when carrying out cyberattacks to stay anonymous, unrecognized globally, and technologically undetectable. When cyberterrorism is coupled with physical terrorism, experts see the most devastating results. Cyberterrorists could target government systems and financial networks to create havoc for the general public. Data can be erased, websites damaged, or virus inserts can damage a security system if terrorists access crucial information and resources, like classified information. Through cyberattacks, terrorists can raise money and disseminate propaganda.

Crimes such as cyberattacks are becoming increasingly popular because they require a considerably fewer number of assailants and certainly less money to carry out than traditional terrorist acts. Terrorists use cyberattacks to raise money and disseminate their propaganda. Terrorists who are well-versed in computers can also mask their "traces" when launching cyberattacks, allowing them to go unnoticed and unrecognized on a geographical and technological scale. The major advantage of cyberattacks is that they can be carried out from anywhere by cyberterrorists while maintaining their privacy at the same time. Cyberterrorism is most effective when used in conjunction with physical terrorism. Cyberterrorists could target financial and government networks to create havoc in the general populace. Data theft, data erasure, website devastation, and virus injection are just a few ways terrorists might compromise a security system.

CONCLUDING REMARKS

Terrorists' extensive use of the Dark Web puts our time and peace on the line. This is because terrorists have discovered new methods of hiding from law enforcement agencies, making it easier for them to carry out their plots. Because of this, terrorists have a significant edge over law enforcement because they cannot be tracked or identified through online behavior. Many more people are becoming radicalized and influenced by terrorists. Governments and law enforcement agencies often cannot spring on terrorists after learning of their communications and whereabouts because of the encrypted messaging provided by the Dark Web and other end-to-end encrypted apps like Telegram or WhatsApp. This is a major issue because we won't know what terrorists will do next.

The Dark Web makes it easier for terrorists and their backers to fund their operations as far as attack preparations go. Terrorists don't give a damn if their financial transactions go through; they gain greater influence by getting donations from people who buy guns and ammunition.

8 Dark Web Markets

INTRODUCTION

As new terminology has been developed in recent years, online criminal marketplaces built and operated in the Dark Web environment are known as Dark Web markets, darknet markets, dark markets, or crypto markets. New online marketplaces like Amazon, eBay, and others on the Surface Web are very similar to these relatively new online marketplaces in that they provide their customers with illegal goods, trading services, and transaction facilities while using advanced encryption to protect the anonymity of their users; as a result, they make the entire market anonymous.

The underground economy is known as the new and growing trend in dark market transactions. When it comes to the darknet market on the world's evolving internet, mobile technologies and digital currencies are known as cryptocurrencies, and criminals may conduct their unlawful trading activities more efficiently by making payments between vendors and purchasers. Due to money laundering and terrorism financing concerns, it also risks the financial system. Money should be changed to cryptocurrencies before any transactions can be started.

DARK NET BLACK MARKETS

An estimated $100 million is generated annually by criminal operations on the deep web. The majority of this money is stored as bitcoin (BTC), and this revenue may even be higher now that BTC prices have swung so dramatically. Vendors have utilized dark net black markets to list a wide range of illegal items and services in the past and continue to do so today. Several deep web crackdowns have shown that unlawful deep web activities earn far more than expected. In 2015, the Federal Bureau of Investigation (FBI) seized $34.5 million after raiding a well-known deep web bazaar for drugs. During a crackdown on online marketplaces for guns and drugs in May of the same year, police seized $80,000 in BTC. Only if additional successful crackdowns are conducted in the future will these figures be higher than they are today.

CHARACTERISTICS AND FEATURES

Cryptocurrencies such as BTC, Monero, and others are used for secure trade and payment transactions. When the legality of a substance or product is questioned, sales tend to transfer from the open web to the dark web. Using a virtual private network (VPN), only a few security options are available on these sites, including a Tor or I2P browser and pretty good privacy (PGP) encryption/decryption and authentication. The market developers also place a high value on the aesthetics of the display and the user-friendliness of the market's interface.

DOI: 10.1201/9781003404330-8

For the most part, dark marketplaces demand that buyers and sellers sign up by providing their personal information on registration forms. If keeping your identity anonymous is a top priority, avoid providing personal information such as phone numbers and email addresses.

Another important factor in the industry's overall trust is vendors' confidence. Several variables influence vendor confidence, but one of the most important is how engaged the vendor is in your marketplace. On many marketplaces, customers can rate merchants by giving them stars or using other reputation-based methods. Vendor ratings from other darknet marketplaces are shown for markets that focus on the reputation of vendors or are relatively new. When customers submit neutral or negative feedback about vendors, it decreases buyer confidence in that market.

As a result, darknet market participants have noticed the sudden absence or migration of certain marketplaces. Once a considerable amount of BTC money has been moved to these marketplaces, it is common to shut down the site to prohibit outgoing transfers and take the money you've locked into it. For example, the Sheep Marketplace and The Real Deal Market both went dark in 2016 after their administrators and owners vanished with millions of dollars worth of marketplace funds. The Nucleus Market, which suddenly vanished on April 13, 2016, was a suspect in this type of exit fraud.

Whenever a well-known darknet market is closed, all of its customers transfer to other well-known darknet markets instead, boosting their membership and activities significantly in a short period of time. Agora and Evolution marketplaces had a 20% surge in membership after Silk Road 2.0 was shut down in 2015. Many of AlphaBay's users switched to the Hansa market once it shut down. The Dutch police have identified a number of these users who have temporarily taken control of the Hansa market.

GOODS AND SERVICES

In other Dark Web categories, the goods and services offered on the Dark Web sites themselves could be categorized as follows:

Arms – revolves around the unlawful sale of weapons, including guns, to individuals, organized crime groups, and terrorists by gun traffickers.

- **Drugs:** Nonpharmaceuticals and pharmaceuticals (including illegal prescription medicines) are produced or trafficked in large quantities. The spectrum of drugs on offer includes anything from methamphetamines, cocaine, marijuana, heroin, and other acids to markets like those that traffic anabolic steroids and Viagra-made medications.
- **Jewelry and Gold:** Mostly goods made of silver and gold.
- **Fraud and Counterfeits:** Online trafficking of fraudulent, forged, stolen, and counterfeited documents and cards such as fake passports or identification cards and credit cards or accounts that have been cloned and stolen is a new and fast-increasing market for all types of criminal activities, including terrorism. On the Dark Web, there are a variety of niche markets.
- **Guides and Tutorials:** A wide range of security and anonymity-related issues for darknet market consumers.

- **Services and Goods, e.g.:** Software, malware, game keys, hosting, VPNs, and security services; currency exchanges and financial services, botnets; and so on.

Dark markets descend from those in which limited or prohibited commodities are listed, so buyers and sellers know that particular products cannot be transferred there. If these limitations are breached, a permanent ban can be applied.

According to the Serious and Organized Crime Threat Assessment, only 1% of the most effective vendors account for 51.5% of dark market transactions. Preliminary research has also suggested that drugs account for 80% of trade, with the other 20% covering fraud and counterfeiting, other digital items, and services like online gambling. One study found that 57% of currently active sites are involved in criminal activity.

MULTISIGNATURE OR TRUSTED MARKETS

When transactions require more than one signatory, a market is classified as a multisignature market. You're probably used to single-signature transactions, where payments only require one signature using a cryptocurrency network. However, multisignature transactions (also known as "multi-sig") demand multiple signatures before funds can be transferred and thus require multiple keys to authorize. All three keys must be created to release the payment in a multi-sig market. Vendors, buyers, and the market each hold the key to unlocking the third. If only two keys are generated, the payment is not released. Darknet marketplaces that use multi-sig transactions are referred to as trusted markets since they often have a strong reputation, with no security concerns, fraud, or other technical issues.

ESCROW MARKETS

However, other marketplaces use traditional escrow, which entails having an escrow account where funds are held in trust until a purchase order is issued. The Dream Market, the Berlusconi Market, and the Majestic Garden Market are all active escrow markets.

'FINISH EARLY' MARKETS

Using this approach, money is paid straight to the vendors' bank accounts. This technique is employed with well-known vendors or with whom you've had previous success transaction. Purchases made for the first time are riskier because the vendor has no prior payment history, and payments cannot be refunded if products purchased are never received.

INVITE/REFERRAL MARKETS

Affiliate programs are common in these markets, and they reward users who bring in new customers by referring them to the site using their referral links. For example,

different vendors in a marketplace may use various payment methods. Or, payments may be made directly between buyers and sellers when they first meet, without the market being involved. Active marketplaces include the Wall Street Market and the Dream Market.

CHARGES, TRANSACTIONS, AND PAYMENTS

The market comprises three major characteristics: the mediator and service provider, who link buyers and sellers in a single location while providing anonymity, security, and trust to their users. The sellers, purchasers, and dark market are all represented here.

CRYPTOCURRENCIES

This digital or virtual peer-to-peer currency uses cryptographic principles to be sent from one person to another. There is no financial organization controlling fiat currency; thus, it can be used just like the US dollar or the country's currency where a person lives. Cryptocurrencies are presently accepted as payment by more than 100,000 sellers and companies, and that figure is only expected to rise in value (Figure 8.1).

Cryptocurrencies are bringing new types of economic crime organizations that are difficult to uncover using conventional police and financial/tax investigation techniques due to the main concern that they might be utilized to enable illicit transactions and services. Various methodologies and technologies have been developed to help law enforcement detect transaction flows and track the illicit use of cryptocurrencies. Instead of a single centralized authority, each successful transaction is added to the blockchain as a list of data called a block. The entire community and other cryptocurrency users can verify and relay the transaction. It was created primarily as a BTC accounting system and is one of the technologies used to keep track of and verify digital currency transactions in a digitized, decentralized public ledger.

COMPARING CRYPTOCURRENCIES AND FIAT CURRENCIES

As shown in Table 8.1, the main distinctions exist between cryptocurrencies and regular fiat currencies (Figure 8.2).

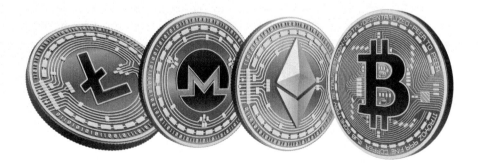

FIGURE 8.1 Cryptocurrencies.

TABLE 8.1

Fiat Currency vs. Cryptocurrency: The Pros and Cons

Fiat Currencies	Cryptocurrencies
Government-issued	Computer-generated
There is an endless supply, and the government can manufacture more if necessary.	There is a limited supply and a maximum price.
The actual, hands-on method of exchanging currency types.	A computerized method of exchanging money Code, both private and public, is used to present.
Centralized and regulated by the government and financial institutions.	Dispersed and independent of any particular government or organization.
The market and government regulations decide its worth.	There is supply and demand for it, which determines its price.
Individual countries have their own currencies and utilize them.	Borderless monetary units.

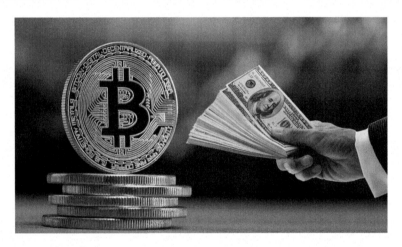

FIGURE 8.2   Fiat currency vs. cryptocurrency.

CRYPTOCURRENCIES AND DIGITAL CURRENCIES DIFFERENCES

Many BTCs, a digital currency, represent any fiat money used to move between banks. Some differences between digital currencies and cryptocurrencies are summarized in Table 8.2.

HOW TO OBTAIN CRYPTOCURRENCIES

Mining and trading/exchanging are the two primary methods of obtaining cryptocurrencies.

MINING

BTC and other cryptocurrencies are issued by individuals who are not part of the government or financial institutions, such as banks. The term "mining" refers

TABLE 8.2
Comparison of Crypto-currency and Digital Currencies

Digital Currencies	Cryptocurrencies
Identifiable only by a unique ID number.	Encrypted and anonymous.
Regulated by a country's government and central bank.	As previously stated, these are non-centralized currencies.
Inconsistency in the exchange of ideas.	The supply and demand for currencies immediately determine exchange rates.
Limits on the amount that can be transferred.	There are no restrictions on the amount you can transfer.
Banks levy exorbitant fees for money transfers.	Reduced transfer fees.
The long wait period for money to be transferred.	More rapid distribution of funds.
There is complete power in the hands of the banks.	Amounts are sent to each person's digital wallet, where they are stored. They are in charge of the bank and have complete authority over the money.
Digital currencies can be created and circulated with no restrictions.	There will only be a finite number of cryptocurrencies created; hence, their value is expected to rise for the foreseeable future.
It's incredibly commonplace in society.	The low level of acceptance by society is related to gray and dark transactions by the public. Not accessible by anybody; specialized knowledge is required.

to producing new cryptocurrencies as a way to reward the people who put in the time and effort to verify and secure them. To solve the cryptologic problem, the miners compete with one another, and the cryptocurrency will then be created once this process is complete. The proof-of-work technique of mining refers to this race to solve a mathematical challenge, with the winner receiving the prize for doing so first.

The more BTC miners there are, the more transactions are verified, and as a result, the network is more secure. If you want to work in the mining business, you'll need specialized computer hardware and software. Because of the growing use of cryptocurrency as a store of value, the network has seen a surge in people trying to solve arithmetic problems. To get around this, miners have devised a system for working in groups to identify solutions more quickly than they could individually. Individual pool miners receive cryptocurrency according to the amount of effort they contribute to the mining pool.

TRADING/EXCHANGING

Hundreds of exchanges enable trading with cryptocurrencies and fiat money, so this is the quickest way to get your hands on some. Person-to-person purchases of cryptocurrencies are also possible. And, however, these transactions are almost always conducted via exchange platforms. If you're going to buy cryptocurrency, be sure you know everything there is to know about the market and the risks involved.

To store the purchased coins, a digital wallet must first be selected. Instead of sending and receiving email messages, an e-wallet lets you transfer and receive digital money. Digital wallets can be found on computers, smartphones, other mobile devices, cloud servers, and other remote storage facilities. These digital wallets will track all of the cryptocurrencies, making it possible to conduct, monitor, and keep track of previous transactions.

POPULAR CRYPTOCURRENCIES

No matter how frequently and dynamically the top 20 cryptocurrency lists change. The following paragraphs will focus on the top five most popular cryptocurrencies used on the darknet markets for the past several years that are still included in the lists below.

BITCOIN

BTC is an open-source, peer-to-peer platform that allows anybody to participate without a specified owner or central control. It was the first and largest cryptocurrency globally. BTC was created by a man going by Satoshi Nakamoto's pseudonym and is often referred to as "digital gold" by industry insiders.

The current market capitalization of BTC is approximately $92.5 billion. BTC's price quickly became unreasonably costly after increasing from $746 to over $11,000 in value over a year beginning on December 1, 2016. To confirm transactions and release new BTC blocks, over 16 million have already been mined. This means that the total number of BTCs in circulation will be 21 million.

The SHA-256 algorithm used by BTC is often regarded as one of the most difficult, even though it allows for increased parallelism. As a result, BTC miners have developed ever more complex ways to mine digital currency. BTC mining with application-specific integrated circuits (ASICs) has become the most popular technique in recent years. In contrast to previous generations of CPUs and GPUs, these new systems may be specifically configured for BTC mining. As a result of this innovation, BTC mining has become more out of reach for the common person.

Compared to other cryptocurrency networks, BTC has a far stronger network effect and is quite popular among new users. As the original and longest-running cryptocurrency, Bitcoin boasts the largest community. Most darknet markets and dark web vendor businesses accept BTC, which should be noted.

ETHEREUM

The digital token Ether was established by the Ethereum blockchain corporation, whose name is Ethereum (ETH). It's common to hear the terms ethereum and ether used in the same sentence while discussing cryptocurrency. Ethereum, created by Vitalik Buterin and released in June 2015, is a relatively young cryptocurrency that is still developing but shows great promise. The currency is issued at 18 million ETH per year via mining, and many people see it as a possible BTC successor. The Ethereum blockchain is oriented toward businesses rather than consumers, like the

BTC blockchain. This platform allows complex physical and financial supply chain procedures to be automated using smart contract technologies and compliance processes involving numerous parties, giving businesses the tools to create their services and products. Blockchain technology is being used by Fortune 500 companies like Microsoft, Intel, BP, JPMorgan, and Cisco as part of the Enterprise Ethereum Alliance (EEA), created in February 2017. The EEA's membership has greatly increased since then.

While BTC users are ideologically driven, Ethereum users are less so. They are more interested in the technology's potential economic and financial applications than fighting against central banks and major governments.

Ethereum had a market capitalization of approximately $79 billion as of December 20, 2017, when its value soared from $100 to $823. The rise of Litecoin (LTC) has made it the second-largest digital currency globally, after BTC.

LITECOIN

A former Google developer, Charlie Lee, published LTC on GitHub on October 7, 2011. It has since gained a lot of popularity. According to its founder's concept, it was meant to operate as a complement rather than a competitor to BTC, serving as the silver to the gold. LTC is regarded as the younger sibling of BTC, even though there are 84 million available LTCs compared to 21 million available BTCs. A surge of 72.91% has been recorded between LTC and BTC in 2017 since the start of the year. Investors becoming more daring may be a factor in the rise of BTC's value. They may be looking for other investment options using lower-cost cryptocurrencies and newer entrants to the market.

For merchants who need to handle a high number of minor transactions quickly, LTC is a good option. The LTC network is faster than BTC's 10-minute transaction processing time, making it more desirable. The long-term average confirmation time of a transaction is 2.5 minutes. In other words, the time it takes for a seller to get payment in BTC is four times as long as it takes in LTC. The differing encryption algorithms used by BTC and LTC represent another technological distinction between the two cryptocurrencies. LTC uses the scrypt algorithm, which is relatively recent compared to BTC's usage of the longstanding SHA-256 algorithm.

However, because many exchanges only allow trading in BTC and not USD or EUR, buying LTCs requires first purchasing BTC, which must then be exchanged for LTCs. On the other hand, some exchanges allow you to purchase LTCs right away.

MONERO

Monero (XMR) is a relatively new and emerging cryptocurrency based on the CryptoNight PoW hash algorithm from the CryptoNote protocol, which is opensource; anonymity and decentralization are all essential considerations. Monero has a mining method that favors ASICs rather than relying on a small number of farms and mining pools. Anyone with a CPU or GPU can participate in the mining process. When it comes to Monero, the privacy features are always on, which sets it apart

from other cryptocurrencies. Monero transactions cannot be traced back because encryption protects the sender and receiver wallet addresses, keeping them secret. As a result, when you receive Monero, you cannot know who sent it to whom. Like most digital currencies, Monero uses a special mechanism called "ring signatures" to swap the public keys of its users, making it impossible to track down a single one of them. This makes it untraceable. Monero is a fungible currency because of its secrecy. As a result of their past involvement in transactions, suppliers and exchanges cannot place Monero units on a blocklist. It is practically impossible for outsiders to do a blockchain analysis of Monero since the cryptocurrency generates so many one-time public addresses that only a single message receiver can collect and analyze them.

DASH/DARKCOIN

Dash stands for Digital Cash and was created in January 2014 by Evan Duffield under the name "Darkcoin." It changed its name to "Dash" in March of that year. A new InstantSend function has been added to Dash, which freezes funds immediately after they are sent, even if the transaction has not yet been validated. The funds spent on the first purchase are still available in most cryptocurrencies when a buyer makes two transactions simultaneously. Therefore, a buyer can spend more than he has available in his wallet. You'll never have to worry about accidentally overspending by using this option. According to CoinMarketCap.com, Dash's price has increased by over 80% since January 2017. It's worth noting that Dash differs from BTC and other cryptocurrencies. It contains a layer of "master nodes" that decide which projects are funded and enable private transactions on the blockchain. Some detractors claim that the network isn't genuinely decentralized because of the master node structure, which concentrates power in the hands of a few users.

ACTIVE MARKETS

Vendor shops, the dark market's suppliers, have their own websites and stores, either separate or embedded within marketplaces. The Dark Web marketplaces are divided into two major groups. In addition to offering trading services, most marketplaces serve as forum spaces for the communities of people who use them.

Based on the information in Darknet Markets (2019), a resource that provides a comprehensive list of underground marketplaces as well as user ratings, we can conclude that 15 marketplaces and 14 vendor shops were online as of the beginning of May 2019, while about 175 others remained dormant, as shown in Figure 8.3.

Considering that most darknet markets sell more than one commodity or service, Figure 8.4 illustrates the percentages of active darknet marketplaces by the types of goods and services currently sold in active darknet markets.

Thirteen of the 15 active marketplaces make up 87% of the drug market; five of the 15 active marketplaces produce 33% of the fraud and forgery market; and the same for guides and lessons. These most popular and long-lasting active markets each get a short description below.

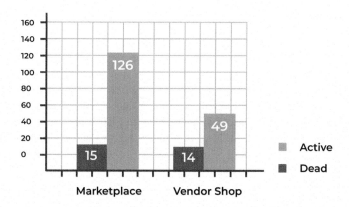

FIGURE 8.3   Active and dead marketplaces and vendors shops.

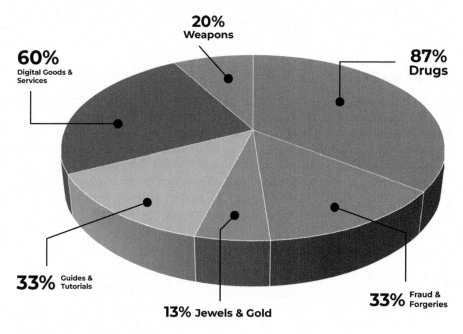

FIGURE 8.4   The 16 active darknet markets have a mixture of products and services.

WALL STREET MARKET

One of the most inventive and up-to-date markets for physical and digital commodities, with only a few merchants, is selling drugs, fraud, and guidance as to most of their product and service listings. To become a vendor or seller, you must create a seller account, although no charge is indicated on the site.

DREAM MARKET

It has been one of the world's largest and longest-running darknet markets since November/December of last year, known for its security and dependability as well as its user-friendly design. Recreational drugs, drug paraphernalia, digital items outlawed by the government, hacking and falsification services, counterfeit goods, and weapons are included in the company's product and service lists. Electrum is an open-source wallet that acts as an escrow service for BTC transactions. As a marketplace focused on buyers, Dream Market places a high value on vendor evaluations by including ratings from other big marketplaces and its own. There's also a Dream Market forum for official discussions.

NIGHTMARE MARKET

Even though Nightmare Market is a newcomer to the multi-signature darknet marketplace scene, it offers innovative features, active support, and enhanced buyer/seller security, including direct deposit support. It is possible to pay with many cryptocurrencies, such as BTC and BTC Cash.

EMPIRE MARKET

In early January 2018, Empire Market established a multi-signature market modeled after the recently shut-down AlphaBay Market. According to the website, the new market was created as a tribute to AlphaBay Market. Digital products, guidelines, tutorials, software, and viruses are only a few of what's accessible on the market, including drugs, scams, counterfeits, and digital products. Drugs are the most common product type on this marketplace, and it includes a forum where anybody can participate. There is a place for each post type, so there is always somewhere to put your thoughts. LTC, Monero, and BTC are all accepted cryptocurrencies.

POINT/T•CHKA FREE MARKET

Since January 2015, the Russian marketplace T•chka, now called Point Marketplace, has been dominated by drug listings. Although it isn't as large as some other prominent Dark Web marketplaces, it is well structured and attractive. Prescription drugs, digital goods, services, and how-to guides and tutorials are all available. A buyer or vendor account can be opened using a simple and quick registration process available to everyone. For 0.2 BTC, users can upgrade their accounts to premium status, granting them more rights. T•chka receives a 5% referral fee, which is reduced to a 2% charge for premium members if a customer purchases something through the website. Using traditional escrow, T•chka holds on to the transaction payment for up to 10 days before disbursing it to the vendor upon receipt of the goods.

SILK ROAD 3.1

Silk Road 2.0 was the successor to Silk Road, although it was doomed to failure after a year. At Ross William Ulbricht's introduction in 2011, Silk Road was one of

the first and most well-known darknet markets. Due to the founder's imprisonment in 2013, the market has been shuttered. Additionally, authorities arrested the man behind Silk Road 2.0. Users who had money taken during the seizure were quite disappointed. Silk Road 3.0 was thought to be a fraudulent extension of Silk Road 2.0. It wasn't long until the crew behind the original Silk Road 3.0 emerged with a Crypto Market fork. It was an exact clone of the original Silk Road but with much-increased security. After Silk Road 3.0's administrators shut it down in 2017, a new darknet bazaar called Silk Road 3.1 emerged. Most items on the shopping list have something to do with narcotics.

CANNABIS GROWERS AND MERCHANTS COOPERATIVE (CGMC)

Since June 2016, it's been a restricted-access cannabis market for guests. A bewildering array of brands and graphics fill one of the most intricate screens. Most of the listings on CGMC are for concentrates and flowers, so there aren't many sellers or listings there. Vendors have been properly vetted before being approved to work with us. This market's currency is BTC, and funds in your BTC account are required to pay for transactions. Payments on CGMC can be escrowed using multi-signature payments or a direct-type payment technique.

BERLUSCONI MARKET

It features a design that feels reminiscent of Hansa market and has an easy-to-use interface. It only takes a few minutes to sign up, and BTC and LTC payments are made directly from the user's wallet to the seller's wallet rather than via the account's wallet. In addition to pharmaceuticals and chemicals, there are many categories and a significant number of listings in each one, such as frauds, counterfeits, manuals, tutorials, jewels, and gold. The vendor pages offer a wealth of information to help consumers narrow down their options. Data on their profile pages includes, for example, feedback ratings, the number of transactions made, the date of the first sign-up, and the most recent active status. Making a purchase is accomplished by placing an order online.

THE MAJESTIC GARDEN

No categories or listing pages are provided because it is a platform for presenting and exchanging psychedelic-related knowledge rather than a native marketplace. Despite this, several threads contain vendor information and reviews, making it easier for people to trade psychedelics over P2P networks. Vendor accounts created with this method do not require wallets, deposits, or other costs. There are simply three fields to fill out when making an account: username, password, and a different email address from the one you use often.

HYDRA

Hydra is a company that deals primarily in narcotics and recreational drugs. Although it facilitates trade between buyers and sellers on the Russian darknet, it stays out of

trading. Instead, it aids in the resolution of disputes. It has a brief registration form that is quick to complete. Vendors must construct a store in the marketplace to sell their products. Customers must place their orders and wait for the seller to contact them to confirm them before the purchase can be initiated. Only BTC and QIWI are mentioned as payment methods on Hydra's help pages.

WAYAWAY

A darknet market known as WayAway has been operating since 2009 and is located in the regular web's history. Like the RuTor market, it's a Russian forum-based market for popular recreational drugs and research compounds. Rather than targeting the foreign market, it focuses on the Russian one. Products are not classified; the focus is on merchants or dealers. The procedure for creating an account is simple and quick. The sale terms have no market involvement because they are all defined and agreed upon by the vendors. WayAway only accepts BTC as a form of payment.

RUTOR

In addition to being a darknet forum for Russian-speaking users, Darknet marketplace functionality is also included, selling various goods and services in Russian. Seller profiles have a cost attached to them. There are only a few posts and vendors on RuTor. Therefore, most things fall into one of these three categories: drugs, weapons, and services. Instead of employing an escrow system, it accepts deposits in BTCs using a BTC wallet address that the administrator issues once a buyer requests it, not an automated system.

CANNAZON

It's a Cannabis-specific multi-signature marketplace, and BTC and Monero are both accepted as forms of payment.

ACTIVE VENDOR SHOPS

Not markets, but sites managed by individual merchants who offer their products on the dark web in different locations. According to statistics collected as of early May 2019, the following are the Dark Web's top 14 vendor shops.

CHARLIEUK

To put it another way, CharlieUK is a UK-based cocaine dealer who has been active in the online markets since 2013.

DUTCHDRUGZ21

DutchDrugz is a veteran drug dealer who still trades in psychedelics and other illegal substances.

RECHARDSPORT

Located in Shanghai, China, RechardSport is a well-known sportswear supplier.

ELHERBOLARIO

A Middle-Eastern drug dealer named ElHerbolario sells marijuana. Darknet markets and drug-related themes are among the many possible discussion topics open to users.

GAMMAGOBLIN-PUSHING TABOO

Gammagoblin, a distributor of hallucinogenic chemicals since SR1, has created a personal storefront on the Dark Web. The LSD Avengers community has given it a rating out of five stars.

THE CHURCH-JESUS OF RAVE (JOR)

JOR, an old-time vendor who has been selling since 2013, is the only place to get LSD or MDMA.

TOYOUTEAM

Since 2012, ToYouTeam has been a merchant, offering a wide range of goods.

THE FRENCH CONNECTION

Mr. Nice Guy or Nucleus can get H, XTC, meth, and other narcotics through The French Connection.

EU COCAINE

It only sells cocaine, as the name implies. They send everywhere globally and use personal delivery technologies based on the order amount. They exclusively accept BTCs as payment.

GLASSWERKZ

The owner of GlassWerkz, an Agora seller who launched his shop, came up with the idea for the store. For reasons that remain a mystery, the store was closed.

COCAINE MARKET

Only cocaine is for sale in this vendor's store, and only BTCs can be used to purchase the item.

CHEMSPAIN

Only BTC can be used to pay for their services, including domestic and worldwide shipping from Spain. GBL, RC, Benzos, GHB, and Bulk are the main products sold by this vendor shop.

MAGHREBHASHISH

The Maghreb, a vendor of hashish and cannabis on Crypto Market and AlphaBay, launched MaghrebHashish as a side project.

VENDORS AND MARKETS THAT ARE FULL OF DEAD OR SCAMMED PEOPLE

A total of 126 marketplaces and 49 vendor businesses had been identified as inactive or fraudulent by 2019. While some of these marketplaces are still up and running, their value fluctuates greatly, earning them the temporary moniker "scam/dead." The most common are briefly explained here.

ALPHABAY

AlphaBay was one of the world's largest darknet markets before it was shut down, with more than 200,000 members and 40,000 vendors. In addition to counterfeit goods, digital goods, and guns, there were also listings for carded gadgets and appliances among the more than 250,000 items included in the database. Other categories included carded clothing, jewelry, gold, and other precious metals. There were also guides and tutorials on using the various services and solutions. Cryptocurrency exchange AlphaBay supports BTC and Monero (XMR).

AGORA

Exit scams have caused Evolution, the world's largest darknet drug market, to close its doors since March 2015. Agora, which replaced Evolution, has been quite trustworthy; it started in 2013 and ended in 2015.

EVOLUTION

Multi-signature escrow services were in demand when Evolution started in January 2014, and it was the second or third largest market based on trade volume. It was known for its excellent uptime and high level of security. The site's operators stole around $12 million worth of BTCs before it was shut down in March 2015.

HANSA MARKET

However, it didn't have the same user traffic level as other major Dark Web marketplaces. No matter how many times you tried, you couldn't get past the first page since there were many categories.

OUTLAW MARKET

When Silk Road 1 was still operational, it was one of the first darknet markets to be established. It was built with security in mind and away from open-source platforms to reduce hackers' exploitation risk. Weapons, drugs, and data dumps were all available at the Outlaw Market. On the May 16, 2017, it was taken offline. According to a notice on the homepage, site hackers took down the site. The wallet of the platform has also been stolen, according to the report. It's possible that because Outlaw Market concentrates on greater security features, there are fewer opportunities for hackers to gain access, leading many users to believe that the site's administrators were behind the exit scam.

AERO MARKET

Additionally, a highly skilled team developed this darknet black market platform using cutting-edge server security technology. The Aero Marketplace and Forums were included in that. Buyers and sellers will appreciate the user-friendly interface that streamlines the transaction process. The process of signing up was quite simple. Buyers and sellers can share the same account. To open their store and begin selling, vendors had to pay a one-time cost based on their selected plan. Medicines accounted for more than 60% of all goods sold in one market. Digital items and services were also listed: scams and counterfeits, how-to guides, diamonds, and gold. Escrow and 'finalize early' transaction types were available, as was multi-signature functionality with BTC and Monero as options. The market had plummeted due to scam alerts by the end of November.

LIBERTAS MARKET

This Monero-only darknet store features a clean UI and a simple design. The distinguishing color green serves as the website's motif. The lengthy registration form that must be filled out makes the registration process time-consuming. Drugs, forgeries, jewelry, and lab supplies are just a few of the numerous entries.

THEREALDEAL MARKET

In November of 2016, TheRealDeal was shut down. Code and zero-day software exploits were for sale on this darknet market, associated with the cyber arms trade. Because of all the scammy Dark Web sites out there, the marketplace was built by its designers, who told DeepDotWeb in an interview that it was a response to them. Experiments and fraud accounted for more than 40% of the listings on the site. However, pharmaceuticals accounted for well over half of the commercials.

MERCADO NEGRO

Brazilians and the Netherlands have launched a Black Market initiative, which means "black market" in Portuguese. It aims to liberate consumer products. Developed on one of the world's most secure platforms, it aims to provide security, ease of use, and facilitation. It accepts Monero as a payment method.

VALHALLA (SILKKITIE)

Silkkitie was the initial name, and it targeted the Finnish market when it was first released in October of that year. After two years of operation, it rebranded and began serving the Dark Web globally. Valhalla used an invite-only registration technique to keep a lid on the market's growth while incentivizing its customers to refer their friends. Escrow/multisig/FE, Escrow/multisig, and multisig alone were the three payment options available for most listings.

APPLE MARKET

Authorities have already taken down some dark web marketplaces, including Apple Market. Customers appreciated Apple Market's escrow services, which made them feel secure and at ease when making purchases. Even though it had fewer listings than more well-known black marketplaces like AlphaBay, purchasers praised the interface's aesthetics and usability. Drugs, accounts, cards, hacking tools, software, and keygens are still available in the Apple Market. You can also purchase eBooks. Vendors that listed their goods on the site were responsible for creating the listings. Another unique element of this darknet market was the inclusion of a search tool. It made it easier for customers to locate the products they wanted on the site. The site's user interface was cutting-edge, with features often found on well-known e-commerce sites like Amazon. The website offered a feature allowing users to store cryptocurrencies in a wallet created by the website. The wallet would be debited or credited according to the user's preference. Instead of transmitting them directly from an exchange, the customer recommended that a BTC mixer be used to promote anonymity. Because of this, sending money directly from an exchanger to a BTC address would be deemed security risky. As previously stated, this is because most items available on the black market are illegal.

YOUR DRUG

According to the latest available data, darknet markets were up and running as of November 2017. These hidden internet markets are now home to a darknet store with years of experience in the drug-selling industry. The shop boasts that it offers high-quality pharmaceuticals at competitive costs and fulfills its consumers' needs. Its target market is resellers and final customers, to whom it promises to comply with its shipment timelines, package standards, and privacy expectations. The store declares that security is its top priority, which suggests that it does pay attention to it.

STONED 100

This is a well-known vendor on the dark web, having previously appeared on the Dream Market and AlphaBay. Due to AlphaBay's recent crackdowns and Dream Market's current uncertainty, this merchant has kept its darknet externally present. Speed, ecstasy, hash, sildenafil, and marijuana are just a few of the illicit substances sold by the dealer.

QUALITYKING

This dealer set up their presence on the darknet to avoid overdependence on the large black markets such as AlphaBay, Dream Market, and others. To judge by how quickly law enforcement has shut down the major markets, this strategy appears to be working. This vendor solely sells opioids, and that's about it for products. There was no sign of the seller's darknet activity as of November 2017.

FIGHT CLUB

The darknet seller Fight Club, whose snappy moniker was also used as the title of a popular Hollywood film, has shifted from one black market to another. This vendor solely offers unlawful documents for sale. He is a dealer in international driving licenses and identification cards. Before, vendors like this were active on sites like Dream, Abraxas, AlphaBay, and Nucleus. This merchant has been operational on the dark web as of November 2017.

L33TER

This dealer has been around for a long time yet is still active on the underground market. Since the beginning, the vendor claims to have played a significant role in the darknet markets. A well-organized dispatch and delivery system is used to sell digital and physical products. The vendor uses a customer ticket system to ensure customers get their orders on time. A consumer's digital products are automatically sent to them after payment is made to the vendor. According to our records, as of November 2017, this supplier was still operating.

AGORA MARKET AND FORUM

In addition to Silk Road 2, government authorities also shut down the darknet marketplace Agora Market. Like Silk Road 2, it was a well-known market, although inconveniently frequent outages plagued it. Typical suspects, like narcotics and fake money, are permitted to use weapons on the site. Owners reaped profits by charging a 4% fee on any products listed for sale on the market for the public to see. To access it, you needed a referral link from another website. However, despite all of these precautions, legal authorities were able to remove them. The Agora Forum was a place where dealers and purchasers could converse. When the police showed up, this forum was doomed to the same fate as the market.

ATLANTIS

When the dark web started, this was a popular area to buy and sell drugs. At the end of 2013, when law enforcement agencies stepped up their efforts to shut down darknet markets, they were still operational. According to reports, the owner of this marketplace shut it down due to security concerns rather than law enforcement.

A marketplace was shut down in 2014. It was a respectable size based on the number of merchants and customers registered on it. There was a 5%–10% vendor commission on the products listed on the platform, which was charged by the marketplace. On the other hand, the market had forbidden the sale of guns to keep the media off of it.

CARAVAN MARKETPLACE

After the FBI took down Silk Road 2, this was the first place consumers could go for refuge. In addition to hard drugs, it listed stolen credit cards, stolen identification cards, and compromised PayPal accounts. There was a sophisticated messaging system in the marketplace to facilitate user participation. In addition, administrators were always on hand to help users with any problems they encountered. In 2014, it was temporarily taken down, and a new site was launched in its stead. On the other hand, the new site lasted just until the beginning of 2015, when law enforcement authorities pulled it down.

DARKNET HEROES LEAGUE

As a result, it was designed to be a trustworthy marketplace for darknet suppliers. As a result, it would be more trustworthy than existing darknet markets because customers would feel more confident dealing with long-time sellers. The site sent out invitations to all vendors it thought suited the description. When Hansa and AlphaBay went under in 2017, they were taken down. In just a few short months after they were removed, it met the same demise at the hands of law enforcement authorities.

THE REALDEAL MARKET

It served as a marketplace for hackers searching for exploits to employ in their hacking endeavors. There was a market for exploits, hacking services, and source codes. Other than electronic things, the market also featured pharmaceuticals and other everyday commodities, like counterfeits marketed on other markets. Its demise occurred on October 31, 2017, when the site went down. In the same way that they had done with a slew of other darknet sites.

SHEEP MARKETPLACE

This was a pharmaceutical market that went out of business in a hurry. However, because thieves have no respect for honor, this marketplace's proprietor patiently waited until it was well-stocked with BTC from customers before departing with the money. For many sites, a customer would deposit money with the site and then use that money to make a purchase. Instead of using the clients' BTC, the owner came up with other creative ways to make fast money, and when the opportunity presented itself, they jumped at it. Exit scams come in many forms, and this was a textbook example. It was shut down in December of last year.

RUSSIAN ANONYMOUS MARKETPLACE

Darknet market takedowns like this one were common in 2017. After Hansa and AlphaBay were shut down, Russian authorities targeted the Russian Anonymous Marketplace (RAMP). There have been sporadic distributed denial-of-service (DDoS) assaults since the marketplace began in 2012. As users and administrators of RAMP, we were shocked to find out that Russia shut the site down. We had hoped to avoid the problems that other marketplaces face under FBI and Dutch police control. In an interview with Russian media, one of the site's administrators claimed that Russian law enforcement was unconcerned about hidden online services and did not perceive them as a threat. According to reports, the Russian government appears to be lenient when it comes to cybercrime. The law enforcement agencies took it down faster than AlphaBay when they struck.

UK GUNS AND AMMO

This is a darknet store specializing in selling firearms and ammunition, as implied by the name. The store only sells goods made in the United Kingdom. They prefer using BTC as a transaction medium.

USA/EU FAKE DOCUMENT STORE

Passports to various nations are for sale on the website, and consumers are promised free delivery. The shop claims to have British, American, Japanese, and Australian passports.

THE DARK WEB IS A MARKET FOR ILLEGAL GOODS AND SERVICES

As seen by the darknet mentioned above, existing criminal threats are emerging. The following are the most common criminal threats, although many more are undeniable.

DRUGS

Narcotics appear to be in high demand at all times. For this reason, drug users prefer to buy their drugs online when the opportunity arises rather than through street vendors, which can be extremely unsafe. Drug addicts have gone to online chat forums to express their dissatisfaction with the closure of certain black markets, on which they relied for their supplies. Pharmaceuticals were the most popular product for sale on all of those marketplaces.

WEAPONS

The sale of guns through the dark web is one of the most hazardous crimes. Pistols, rifles, and explosives are all available on the underground market. The sale of these weapons is completely unregulated, so anyone may get their hands on them. Because

black markets have strong peer ratings, customers can easily screen fraudulent merchants from the marketplaces. The only remaining suppliers are the tried-and-true ones who consistently deliver. As a result, the weapons offered for sale on these websites will reach their intended recipients. Terrorists, the mentally ill, and vengeful individuals are all possible purchasers.

COMMUNICATION CHANNELS FOR TERRORISTS

Many communication platforms are under surveillance due to the international hunt for terrorist groups. According to Edward Snowden, in 2015, certain people were forced to be observed. An NSA whistleblower resigned from his position and released a slew of documents detailing the agency's eavesdropping on phone calls and text messaging across many carriers. He also claimed that the NSA was spying on people's communications across different platforms. Due to this, terrorists resort to using the dark web as a communication channel. The dark web is ideal for terrorists to communicate because of the easy access to chat rooms and the little chance of being caught by law enforcement authorities. Terrorists can use the darknet as a haven to plot and coordinate attacks without worrying about being discovered.

HACKING

On the dark web, experienced black-hat hackers can be hired on a contract basis. According to a hacker's description on the dark web, this is what it looks like: A modest work is claimed to cost less than €250 by the hacker. The hacker claims to be proficient in zero-day vulnerabilities, bespoke Trojans, bots, and DDoS attacks when it comes to hacking. In addition, the hacker claims to have some knowledge of social media. As well as inflicting technical problems on websites and disrupting networks, they're also capable of economic sabotage. One tactic is to portray them as child porn customers to get their attention.

Antivirus software is commonly used to find and get rid of infections on a computer. There is malware for sale on the dark web in various locations for those who don't want to hire a hacker. Zero-day security flaws are also sold on the dark web, and Zero-day exploits use vulnerabilities that haven't been fixed yet.

ASSASSINATIONS

Among other things, Silk Road founder Ross Ulbricht was accused of hiring an assassin to kill some of his clashes. They were allegedly hired on the dark web by him. Even if concealed, assassination marketplaces exist where people can pay assassins to kill specific targets. The assassins claim a high success rate, and they charge accordingly depending on the difficulty of the task at hand. Even though the darknet may be full of swindlers, there are assassins for hire who are honest and will kill for pay. Because of the dark net's anonymity, people believe they are safe. Assassination agreements on the dark web go down in horrific detail. These service providers prefer not to draw the attention of law enforcement by routinely turning down requests for verification of previous work or feedback from satisfied clients. Before ordering

an assassination, customers must provide documentation proving they have the funds necessary to complete the task, and that money is then held in trust by the assassination company. An assassin's evidence of completion is required after the killing, so the money is released.

For example, mercenaries and ex-soldiers operate on the dark web under C'thulhu. They assert that they have solutions to common problems and the ability to carry out operations wherever they are on the globe. They go into detail on their dark web page on why they're the ideal company to work for. According to them, other hitman hired physically pose a concern since they may assist the authorities if apprehended and threatened with jail time. They claim, they say. If they accept a plea deal, they can help authorities find the person who paid them while simultaneously receiving favorable punishments for their crimes. The darknet assassins claim that offering their services on the darknet is in the interests of both parties. As long as the payment is made anonymously, neither they nor the person paying for the service can be taken to prison. According to the pricing listed on their website, their services are rather pricey. The most affordable is the $3,000 thrashing of a predetermined target. The most costly service is the accidental death of a high-ranking politician. They also provide rape, bombing, and crippling a target as additional services.

According to some deep web specialists, the hitman services marketed on the dark web are scams. However, many advertisements for assassinations and hitman services appear to be scams. For example, the FBI first accused Ross Ulbricht of Silk Road of hiring a hitman to kill six people. Contrary to what happened with the FBI, his name was later cleared. The hitman they were alluding to turned out to be scams, and they had no intention of using them on Ulbricht. The fact that the hitman guarantee they can kill any target anywhere in the world raises suspicions.

Fraud

There are many opportunities to make quick cash on the dark web. The majority of them are obtained through deception. Fake currency is available in a few places. They promise that standard UV light scans will not pick up the fake currency, despite this being true. Some shops sell goods worth around $6,000 for around $600. Other businesses offer ATM cards for sale. The prices on these cards are set according to the available balance on the associated ATM card. They promise to provide the cards along with a working PIN for the buyer to withdraw the money.

The sale of hijacked PayPal accounts is another popular scam on the dark web. Vending companies claim to transfer money to their bank accounts by providing the buyer with compromised login credentials. The prices of these accounts are likewise determined by the sums they have. There are two types of accounts for sale: standard and premium. The accounts in the first group have been hacked, and the buyers balances have been verified.

On the other hand, unverified accounts have not reviewed their balances, but there's a good chance that some money will be in them.

While surfing the dark web, I came across an advertisement offering 100 PayPal accounts for $100 in one of the businesses. Because the buyer cannot know how

much money will be in these accounts, they're selling them for $1 each. In comparison to unverified accounts, verified ones command a higher fee.

It's crucial to keep in mind that no one can be certain that the rapid money they're promised will be made or that they won't get scammed. The payment is made using BTC, and you will not receive a refund if you buy the wrong one. Even yet, there is a powerful peer-review network on the darknet that can guide buyers to reputable providers in the dirty sector.

Fake IDs/Driving Licenses

It is true that some immigrants enter First World countries via backdoors, but this is far from universally true. One challenge they face once they're inside is obtaining identification cards and driving licenses that will allow them to travel freely around the rest of the world. These extremely potent documents may help them land jobs or stay out of trouble if they contact law enforcement. People in some countries may have a criminal record and want to change their names to something more honorable. Some people only want a false identity to open bank accounts, get loans, buy lands, etc., without compromising their true identities. Fake identification cards and driving licenses are available on the dark web from vendors specializing in their creation. They ask for a photo and perhaps a desired name from the buyer to be put on the fictitious documents. The price varies by country for identity cards and driving permits. For €900 on the dark web, you could buy a bogus US passport, ID card, and driver's license. Documents from Switzerland cost €850 as opposed to €900 in other countries. At the time of writing, the lowest price was €650 for a German ID, passport, and driver's license.

Illegal Wildlife Trade

Poachers sold rhinoceros spikes, bone, and tiger skins on the darknet, among other endangered species products, according to an INTERPOL investigation published in June 2017. Also, because the transactions were made using BTC, it was more difficult to identify the individuals responsible for them. Advertisements appeared over five months, most of which promised rhino horns and ivory. This is a frightening discovery when you consider the efforts to reduce poaching by prohibiting the sale of these products. Security agencies are stepping up their efforts to shut down unlawful marketplaces, and poachers are responding. There are fewer barriers to entry for poachers now that they can operate anonymously and safely on the dark web.

Child Porn

After the FBI shut them down, a few well-known dark websites that published or sold child pornography remained online. Brutal content is published and sometimes sold to darknet users on these sites. Most of the dark websites selling this stuff were shut down due to coordinated takedowns. However, darknet users can still pay to acquire this content from some lingering websites if they hunt hard enough. Fortunately, several of the dark net's major black markets disapproved of the sale of such content

and hence forbade vendors from disclosing their intentions to do so online. When it came to child pornography, Silk Road was very clear about not selling any of it. This type of criminality is seen as being on a higher level in the mainstream black market, where decency prevails.

MALWARE FOR SALE

Many security firms were alarmed about the spread of ATM malware toward the end of 2017. Despite ATMs' apparent high level of security, it appears that hackers have discovered ways to exploit ATM hardware and software. Early this year, manuals on how to hack ATMs and cause them to dispense cash were for sale on the dark web. The dark web had these instructions listed for sale for $5,000. When the FBI took AlphaBay offline, they found ATM malware sales transactions and how-to guides. Important details about the April 2017 transaction to purchase ATM malware have been published on the site, including the following:

When the salesman promoted the ATM malware, he said it would let users withdraw all the money stored in the machine. The merchant was supplying a choice of three software programs. The first one was for checking the ATM's balance. Second, all the money in the ATM was supposed to be cashed out using the software. The third and last piece of software served as a bridge between the first and second pieces. Aside from providing training videos and answering any buyer's concerns, the seller also stated that he would support the software. Vendors also asserted that their malicious software was compatible with any ATM worldwide. This would be undetectable by ATM antivirus software. According to the suppliers' instructions files, a USB port on an ATM might be exposed and used to insert malware into the machine.

There is malware out there, which means crooks have figured out how to develop ATM-dispensing programs. These applications can be purchased for up to $5,000 on the dark web. Since third parties can't run their programs on ATM computers, banks must move quickly. Even though this malware wasn't designed to target ATM customers, it will impact their financial institutions. In addition, banks may have to make sure that ATMs are adequately secured on a physical level. Thus, thieves will be unable to break into ATM booths and drill their way into the machines' USB ports.

Additionally, the USB port security on ATM computers must be improved. Until banks are ready to do their updates, the USB ports on the network should be deactivated. Because of this, criminals will be unable to utilize their own devices, like thumb drives, to run malicious programs and steal information from the PCs if the ports are disabled. Banks can ensure that their ATMs are safe from fraudulent software by using antivirus software. For example, Kaspersky Labs has a solid track record of dealing with this type of attack, and Kaspersky was one of the first security firms to warn about an attack against ATMs.

BOTNETS

A computer network infected with a DDoS attack can be launched by sending unauthorized requests to a target. DDoS assaults are a major concern for enterprises due

to the potential financial and reputational damage they can cause. DynDNS, a large DNS provider, was a high-profile target of a DDoS attack last year. Those behind DDoS assaults are hacker botnets, which they deploy to flood targets' networks with unauthorized traffic. As a result, legitimate traffic is halted. Botnet networks posted for sale on the darknet are readily available to anyone who wants to launch a DDoS attack on a target. A huge botnet of 100,000 computers was posted for sale on the dark web. Police shut down a large black market called AlphaBay after discovering the listing. This botnet cost $7,500 to purchase. The merchant might be used for DDoS attacks, spam, and ransomware.

According to the merchant, the botnet could generate significant traffic, namely 1 TB/s. The DynDNS DDoS attack generated 1.2 TB/s of traffic, the same as the botnet's total output. Later, the corporation determined that around 100,000 zombie machines were delivering the erroneous queries. It's safe to suppose that DynDNS, as a large networking firm, had a variety of protection procedures in place to deal with a DDoS attack up to a point. As a result, if the botnet mentioned on AlphaBay generated 1 TB of bandwidth and directed it to the networks of several businesses, it might wipe them out. Many companies will be unable to cope with the traffic volume they are subject to because they lack adequate security measures. Other botnets, it's safe to suppose, are available on the dark web for purchase by anyone with evil intent.

Other companies provide botnets with fewer participants and lower-priced options. Buying 1,000 US-based botnets costs $200, whereas buying 1,000 EU-based botnets costs about $120. On the other hand, small purchases keep devices off the blocklist. The EU-based bots, for example, cost $12,000 to buy in pieces, whereas the total cost is roughly $7,500 to buy all at once.

Botnets are popular on the dark web due to their effectiveness. Takedown attempts are most likely to succeed if the motivation is revenge, harassment, or unethical competition. If a competitor's website is taken down for a few days by an e-commerce store, customers will most likely migrate to that store's website. As the Internet of Things (IoT) grows, so will botnets and DDoS attacks. This is due to the sheer number and small size of IoT devices. As soon as IoT-based botnets debut on the dark web, expect them. Future zombie botnet armies will rely on IoT malware to take over infected devices and attract new members. This malware has previously been discovered and is under investigation.

BTC LAUNDRY

Although BTC is a decentralized digital currency, it does not provide complete payment anonymity. This is because all of the transactional information is available to the public. To execute transactions more quickly, BTC uses a technology called Blockchain. An open ledger is used by Blockchain technology to keep track of transactions. This system is powered by peer computers all around the world, rather than centralized servers. Everything is made available to the public to facilitate the collaboration required by peers to complete transactions. BTC transactions can therefore be traced, but with considerable difficulty. To engage in unethical activities, one must first ensure that their misdeeds cannot be traced. For example, a person using the darknet to hire an assassin will not want a trail left behind that may be traced back to them.

BTC laundry makes it considerably more difficult to trace a user's transactions. Darknet shops provide the service of combining one's BTC with those of others. They achieve this by transferring BTC in a series of microtransactions, and then they return a similar amount of BTC to the user's wallet after subtracting a few fees. As a result, transactions pile up and become difficult to track. Finally, some BTC owners want their digital cash converted into traditional fiat money. When BTC is converted to money and placed into a bank account, some darknet shops offer anonymity to prevent the deposit from being tracked. Services exist that convert BTC into fiat currency and anonymously deposit the funds into a user's bank account of choice.

INFORMATION ABOUT GOVERNMENT AND CELEBRITY OFFICIALS' SECRETS IS BEING LEAKED

There's evidence that a few people did awful things. WikiLeaks is a well-known publication in the field of disclosures. As part of WikiLeaks, there is a dark web page where anonymous information about other people or organizations can be submitted. Many additional sites on the dark web provide personal information about high-ranking politicians, law enforcement agencies, FBI agents, and celebrities that may be found there. Obama's personal information, including his Yahoo and AOL email addresses, was listed on one of these sites when he was president of the United States. The list also included IP addresses that Obama allegedly used to access his email.

Some sensitive information about well-known people can be found on Cloud Nine, a dark website. You'll find a list of people who are either FBI agents or snitches for them. Kim Kardashian and Kimberly Brown are just a couple of the well-known faces featured on the website.

BTC AND CRYPTOCURRENCY FRAUD

It's not uncommon to find dark net shops whose sole purpose is to commit BTC fraud by defrauding unwitting clients. First, stay away from places that promise to double your BTC. It's impossible to double one's BTC with software or a system, and more BTCs may only be obtained by purchasing or receiving them as payment from others. In exchange for goods or services, one must send BTCs from their wallet to a certain address, where they will be doubled and given back to the scam businesses on the dark web. However, scammers don't show up once you send BTC to their provided address. It is illegal to pursue scammers on the darknet, and knowing where to seek tracks that could lead to them lawfully is impossible. These dishonest con artists have opened shop in their neighborhoods, where they target unsuspecting customers hoping to profit from the BTC-doubling schemes.

Exit scams are another form of darknet BTC and cryptocurrency fraud. This occurs when a store or vendor disappears with BTC or other cryptocurrencies supplied as payment by a customer. The seller disappears with the money after failing to deliver on their promise to provide the product or service the client ordered. This form of fraud has been seen in both new and shut-down darknet shops. Since the darknet is so anonymous, new shops have little to lose if their customers' cryptocurrency

disappears. As a result of this form of fraud, some well-known criminal enterprises have promised their customers that exit scams would be guarded against. These shops include Dream Market, which boasts that no vendor or even the site itself can steal a customer's BTC deposits. The shop's proprietor defrauded customers who made deposits to Sheep Marketplace's BTC wallet and operated under Sheep Marketplace.

TERRORISM

Terrorism has been one of the dark net's most troubling overuses. Once upon a time, terrorists were active on various platforms, but they have decided that the open internet is too dangerous because it is easy to monitor and trace them. This decreased their dark web usage, as they preferred to communicate using open networks such as email and social media instead. Terrorism is on the rise, thanks to the anonymity provided by the dark web. Although extremists chat in chat rooms on the open internet, they prefer to hang out in the shadows. These secret chat rooms allow them to talk freely without worrying about being tracked down and apprehended by law enforcement. Many countries watch the internet for inflammatory words that could be seen as encouragement for terrorism, and they take action when they find anything. However, they cannot get the same results on the black market. People may visit the darknet site to learn more about the organization, promoting the group's ideas. The Telegram network has links to private messaging portals and propaganda archive content. When the terrorists began inviting others to join them on the darknet site, it became increasingly difficult for authorities to track them down and shut them down.

When terrorists use the dark web, they're using tactics they've previously used on the surface web. Terrorists use the dark web to gather intelligence, recruit new members, radicalize individuals, and generate funds. They may even use it to plot terrorist strikes. As evidenced by recent terrorist incidents, attacks are coordinated on the dark web. American intelligence agencies were successful in 2013 when they intercepted communication between two top Al-Qaeda officials. They learned that the two had been plotting attacks on each other through the darknet. To communicate while on the move, terrorists have started turning to the Telegram messaging app. The creators have previously offered large cash awards to anyone who can crack the system to discourage hackers. Terrorists are increasingly using Telegram, according to a study done in 2015. Terrorists use it to reach many people at once with their messaging. Many Al-Qaeda and ISIS affiliates have started using Telegram covertly to reach a larger audience.

Terrorist organizations have used the dark web to raise money. People were encouraged to join the European resistance on the dark web, but the page quickly disappeared. People might make BTC donations to an address provided on the page. The darknet has been used to conceal famous individuals' and governments' support for terrorist organizations. According to rumors, major nations may have funded and equipped ISIS for political purposes. Terrorists utilize the darknet to obtain weapons from within nations to carry out attacks. According to investigators, DW Guns, a darknet shop selling German-made weapons, was thought to be the source of the Paris attack. Terrorists may potentially be selling human organs on the dark web. According to reports, these organs were snipped from human slaves. Human organs

are highly sought-after on the black market because of the great demand. A terrorist organization may utilize the dark web to market its seized antiques. Several historic cities and villages, including Syria, have been attacked and looted for artifacts.

POLICING THE DARK MARKETS

Black market policing utilizes three investigation processes: strategic investigation, identification, and prosecution of suspects. To be successful in the initial strategic phase of Dark Web policing, law enforcement must engage within a wider ecosystem that includes technological and environmental factors as well as organizational and governance factors. After suspect identification has been completed, the next stage is to watch those suspected of involvement in the crime to learn more about their identities and what role they played in it. Any time a law enforcement investigation uncovers black market services offered in a specific location. A local operation is usually set up to address the issue at hand.

EXPECTATIONS OVER THE NEXT FIVE YEARS

The sophistication of the Internet and mobile technology has expanded in the past decade, making it easier to establish dark web services and darknet markets for trading illegal products and delivering illicit services. As a result, the underground economy has grown by using new digital currencies known as cryptocurrencies to conduct transactions between buyers and sellers.

Roughly 130 black markets emerged this decade, although only about 12% are still operating now, e.g., around 15 markets, with a tendency to disappear further. Vendor stores are no different in this respect. It's easy to understand why there are so few active marketspaces.

1. Those entering the market aren't familiar with the rapidly emerging security and vulnerability issues that need to be addressed. Thus, they're doomed to failure quickly.
2. When their markets flourish, darknet market owners and administrators take the money amassed there and vanish in a flurry of exit frauds.
3. More and more darknet markets are being shut down due to effective coordination and actions by LEAs.

For the time being, there are just a few cryptocurrencies in use on the darknet markets that can be considered more reputable because of their rapid value and price gains in a relatively short period, such as BTC, Monero, and others. Because cryptocurrency prices are rapidly rising, the cryptocurrency market resembles a stock exchange. Users are investing in new currencies in anticipation of large profits from purchasing and selling their existing currencies without exchanging anything.

While multifunctional, decentralized, and less vulnerable systems are becoming increasingly popular in the darknet market, the blockchain technology that underpins cryptocurrencies is increasingly being extended into other business applications and platforms, bringing corporations together in production and commercial alliances.

9 We Are Anonymous
We Do Not Forget We Do Not Forgive

Before I go any further, let me say how much I admire Anonymous, the ephemeral hacktivist collective. Anonymous, a prank squad with no morals, got its start on the troll forum 4chan. Since then, it has evolved into a vigilante justice movement that is changing the world for the better because of its desire to act outside of conventional society's bounds (Figure 9.1).

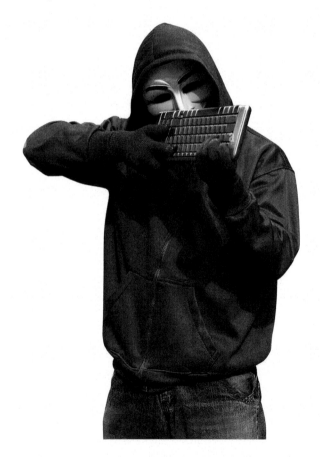

FIGURE 9.1 Cyber hacking collective Anonymous announced it is going after ISIS after the terrorist militants killed over 130 individuals in Paris on November 13, 2015.

                                    DOI: 10.1201/9781003404330-9

The website 4chan, which launched in 2003 and quickly became infamous for its "anything goes" random section known as the board, is where Anonymous started. A web forum with no author names, archives, and entries about anything was discussed on the board.

There's a culture known as "anonymity" that exists. It does not have a leader, membership lists, or committees. Anyone who wants to exploit the brand to advance their cause can be included in this nebulous group. If you declare yourself Anonymous, you are doing so voluntarily. Anyone with an idea can engage other people in further discussion. Other Anons may or may not come to your aid based on what you've said.

Anonymous has had numerous important "raids" since the turning point, including cyberattacks against governments, significant organizations, financial institutions, and religious institutions. The organization launched a coordinated attack on targets for perceived offenses.

Distributed denial-of-service (DDoS) assaults – overloading websites with false traffic to cause them to fail – and doxing – exposing targets' sensitive information – are the most common methods.

However, Anonymous never seemed to have a clear goal in mind. Raids may be deadly or hilarious, but you can look at them either way. They happened swiftly, like a tornado on the internet. When Anonymous first emerged, it was never considered a member of anyone's army, and it rarely stuck to a single theme.

PROJECT CHANOLOGY

It was Tom Cruise, in a shockingly manic Scientologist film revealed in January 2008, who changed everything and gave Anonymous a political conscience. To make matters worse, Anons decided to demolish the Scientology church due to the organization's aggressive legal tactics to get the video taken down (Figure 9.2).

While working on Project Chanology, the Anons became more politically aware. They also developed new tactics for organizing large-scale protests. According to Anons, people were harmed, money was stolen, and lies were told as caregivers and teachers by the Church of Scientology. Project Chanology served as an excellent springboard for the anti-Scientology movement to join the Anonymous collective.

After seeing this video, Anonymous was inspired to take action against censorship, support-free speech, and stand up to the government's oppression, all of which are reflected in the manifesto. This video has the potential to go down in history, and YouTube has received an Anonymous video submission.

OPERATION PAYBACK

Anons had a new aim in mind in September of that year. It was reported at the beginning of September that an Indian company called AiPlex claimed to have been contracted by the Motion Picture Association of America (MPAA) to send takedown requests to piracy sites and controversially DDoS those that did not respond, such as the infamous anti-copyright BitTorrent site "The Pirate Bay," which took pride in rejecting takedown requests (Figure 9.3).

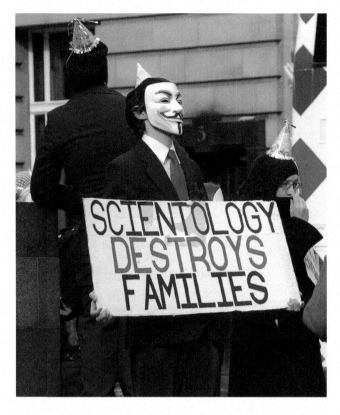

FIGURE 9.2   Screenshot from the video "Project Chanology: The Rise of Anonymous."

After Bradley Manning disclosed hundreds of thousands of diplomatic papers to WikiLeaks in 2010, the US government began an aggressive legal attack. Senator Joe Lieberman called Amazon and successfully pressured them to block WikiLeaks materials from being hosted. To put it another way: due to political demands from the US government and other financial institutions, several companies have stopped dealing with WikiLeaks or frozen their clients' donations; Assange himself has had his Swiss bank account frozen. The reactivation of Operation Payback was announced (Figure 9.4).

The Swedish Prosecution Authority and PostFinance targets Operation Payback's DDoS strikes. On December 8, 2010, Operation Payback launched a DDoS attack against MasterCard and Visa's websites. After a persistent DDoS attack on PayPal's website caused a modest interruption in its operation, PayPal said on its blog on December 9 that it would refund the frozen monies in the Wau Holland Foundation account that raised money for WikiLeaks but would not reactivate it. Amazon could repel a DDoS attack, and Anonymous' attempts were hampered. According to CNN, Amazon's enormous website "is virtually impossible to crash" (Figure 9.5).

The focus of Operation Payback was primarily on the show. Many media outlets overlooked the fact that none of the attacks impacted the targeted organizations'

Dear College or University,

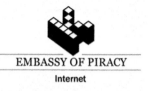

Stop playing cops for the RIAA and MPAA! Schools are under **no legal obligation** to do the bidding of these oppressive and downright abusive trade groups without a court order. Harvard stands strong and encourages other schools to resist as well.

Sharing, **duplicating**, and creating a *copy* of content, **information**, ideas, is **NOT** the same or even on par with **STEALING** property. Television, VHS, cassette tapes, radio, and even the printing press were all strongly opposed by those who owned and controlled the information of the age. The *internet* is our final battle and will be our final victory.

Illegally downloaded songs **do not** translate into lost purchases or stolen profits. *Quite the contrary.* The decline in music sales correlates much more with other factors like the increase of video game sales[1], not to mention as record label profits go **DOWN**, artist incomes have steadily **RISEN**[2]. Those who download illegally spend *more* money on music than those who don't[3], but figures continue to be downright **fabricated** to feed the media[4].

Copy restrictions are **not** about due credit nor the interests of artists but merely the market control and exploitation of creative work for financial gain by a few corporate giants. Copyright is the weapon wielded by the goliaths of a *dying* industry, a weapon **rejected** by the artists of this new generation.

Criminalizing everyone with ill-conceived laws to protect an industry which refuses to adapt is harmful to society. File sharing cannot be stopped. We will always find new and innovative ways to share with one another. We have embraced this name **"PIRATE"** provided by perjurious propaganda so prepare to be **pillaged** and **plundered**!

To all students:

DOWNLOAD

AS A CIVIL

DISOBEDIENCE

1. http://www.guardian.co.uk/news/datablog/2009/jun/09/games-dvd-music-downloads-piracy
2. http://labs.timesonline.co.uk/blog/2009/11/12/do-music-artists-do-better-in-a-world-with-illegal-file-sharing/
3. http://www.independent.co.uk/news/uk/crime/illegal-downloaders-spend-the-most-on-music-says-poll-1812776.html
4. http://www.guardian.co.uk/commentisfree/2009/jun/05/ben-goldacre-bad-science-music-downloads

FIGURE 9.3   Flier aims to convince students not to abide by the warnings of antipirate groups, urging readers to download as civil disobedience.

operations for long, instead of leading the public to believe that they would be unable to use their Visa or MasterCard to pay for gas or groceries as a result of Anonymous' actions. However, Anonymous took advantage of the publicity and issued sweeping proclamations of victory, becoming famous.

FIGURE 9.4 The Anonymous collective was encouraged to send faxes of random WikiLeaks cables, letters from Anonymous, Guy Fawkes, and the WikiLeaks logo to the target fax numbers all day long.

OPERATION TUNISIA

A poor Tunisian fruit trader named Mohamed Bouazizi from the rural town of Sidi Bouzid then set himself on fire on December 17, 2010, to protest the crushing corruption he could no longer live with. He'd done it out of desperation, and it showed. Bouazizi's self-immolation would have far-reaching effects on American society, the Middle East, and the internet. Anonymous would be altered forever if such a non-anonymous act of protest were to occur.

A street vendor in Tunisia named Mohamed Bouazizi supported his widowed mother and six siblings, but he lacked the proper permits. Bouazizi resisted handing over his wooden cart to the authorities in December 2010. After that, he was harassed by police, and his business was shut down. Bouazizi took to the streets and burned himself on fire in front of a government building with no other option. People in his hometown of Sidi Bouzid were moved by his desperate act right

Target	Site	Attack time
PostFinance	*postfinance.ch*	2010-12-06
Swedish Prosecution Authority	*aklagare.se*	2010-12-07
EveryDNS	*everydns.com*	2010-12-07
Joseph Lieberman	*lieberman.senate.gov*	2010-12-08
MasterCard	*mastercard.com*	2010-12-08
Borgstrom and Bodström	*advbyra.se*	2010-12-08
Visa	*visa.com*	2010-12-08
Sarah Palin	*sarahpac.com*	2010-12-08
PayPal	*thepaypalblog.com*	2010-12-09
Amazon	*amazon.com*	2010-12-09 (Aborted)
PayPal	*api.paypal.com:443*	2010-12-10
MoneyBookers	*moneybookers.com*	2010-12-10
Conservatives4Palin	*conservatives4palin.com*	2010-12-10

FIGURE 9.5   Target and attack time.

away. This was the first day of protests. The demonstrations' pictures and videos were posted to social media sites worldwide, including Facebook, Twitter, and YouTube.

Uprisings sparked by the events in Tunisia spread across the Middle East, resulting in the Arab Spring. Protests favoring democracy broke out across North Africa and the Middle East's Arabic-speaking countries. Protests in Syria, Libya, and Yemen quickly spread over social media, igniting full-scale civil wars. Other governments were unable to maintain their positions of power. Thousands of pro-democracy demonstrators were brutally beaten by Moroccan police. The regime of King Hamad bin Isa Al Khalifa forcibly quashed nonviolent pro-democracy protests in Bahrain that called for the release of political prisoners and human rights improvements (Figure 9.6).

Slim404, a controversial Tunisian blogger with the real name Slim Amamou, was one of those in the #optunisia channel who is a native Tunisian. Amamou and others put their lives in danger by relaying information and software between Anons, the rest of the globe, and the people on the ground. Amamou was taken into custody on January 6, 2011.

Anonymous
Operation: Tunisia

1. Install

TOR-Bundle Package for Tunisians:
http://pastebin.com/ThbE8W4V
Care Package
http://goo.gl/gnd94
Tunisian Proxy servers (may or may not be working):
http://pastebay.com/113527
http://aliveproxy.com/proxy-list/proxies.aspx/Tunisia-tn

2. Join irc.anonops.ru
#OpTunisia

You cannot win,

Ammar 404

FIGURE 9.6   An image of "Operation Tunisia" with directions for installing the digital care package and connecting to the #OpTunisia IRC network.

OPEGYPT

Later, OpEgypt erupted, bringing considerably larger demonstrations and a much more difficult situation. Just as they did on the "Day of Revolt" in Tunisia, Anonymous immediately put up lifeline internet connections and launched DDoS attacks against government servers in Tahrir Square on January 25. Mubarak shut down the internet three days later. Anonymous was shocked and in disbelief. On the other hand, Mubarak was toppled on February 11, a short time after Ben Ali. This was a recurring theme for Anons: they valued feeling like they were a part of history. People throughout the world knew the pranksters became activists by sticking up for those who needed support in their fight for justice, which they found inspiring. The Freedom Ops operatives were spread all around the world during the campaign (Figure 9.7).

Although Anonymous did not overthrow Mubarak in Cairo or raid Qaddafi's compound in Tripoli, they worked tirelessly to support the demonstrators on the ground, especially those who were unable to use the internet due to government firewalls and restrictions. Operation Tunisia and Operation Egypt, which both targeted government websites with DDoS attacks and attempted to help demonstrators better use the

Anonymous
Operation: Egypt

Recruiting starts
23rd January 2011

1. read Bypassing Censorship Manual
http://www.mediafire.com/?9gq8v3eczwfqs12

2. download Carepackage
http://www.megaupload.com/?d=K65QF9NW

3. join
irc.anonops.ru #OpEgypt
SSL Port 6697

FIGURE 9.7   An image of "Operation Egypt" with directions for installing the digital care package and joining the #OpEgypt IRC network.

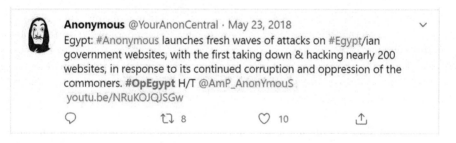

Anonymous @YourAnonCentral · May 23, 2018
Egypt: #Anonymous launches fresh waves of attacks on #Egypt/ian government websites, with the first taking down & hacking nearly 200 websites, in response to its continued corruption and oppression of the commoners. #OpEgypt H/T @AmP_AnonYmouS
youtu.be/NRuKOJQJSGw

💬   🔁 8   ♡ 10   ⬆

FIGURE 9.8   Screenshot of #OpEgypt.

internet for their cause, were carried out by Anonymous in January. Hacktivists may have been a target for struggling regimes to avert a revolution, and they failed miserably. On the other hand, similar actions were taken to support dissidents in neighboring countries like Bahrain and Syria.

That tagline "We never forget" from Anonymous is spot on. Currently, DDoS attacks on government websites are still being carried out (Figure 9.8).

THE HBGARY HACK

HBGary Federal CEO Aaron Barr was the target of an attack in February by Anonymous, a hacktivist collective. Barr had made the blunder of publicizing his

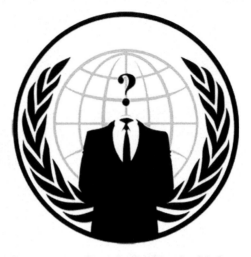

This domain has been seized by Anonymous under section #14 of the rules of the Internet.

Greetings HBGary (a computer "security" company),

Your recent claims of "infiltrating" Anonymous amuse us, and so do your attempts at using Anonymous as a means to garner press attention for yourself. How's this for attention?

FIGURE 9.9   The HBGary Federal website has been vandalized.

infiltration into Anonymous and knowledge of its inner workings in the public domain. He asserted that there were approximately 30 members in the organization, with 10 serving as the group's "core" decision-makers. He used social network analysis to link their internet relay chat (IRC) handles to their real names. Anonymous was enraged, as evidenced by the look on his face. Anonymous replied with the wrath of the defiled after Barr accused them of heresy by claiming the leaderless organization had a secret leader they all secretly obeyed (Figure 9.9).

To get at the 71,000 emails and documents from HBGary, the hackers used an SQL injection, one of the hacker arsenal's most disgusting-sounding but most effective weapons. These emails and documents included information about Barr's private life, a troubling PowerPoint presentation about WikiLeaks, and journalists like Glenn Greenwald who supported the whistleblower organization. It was suggested that more harsh steps may be required to exclude Greenwald from the discussion.

OpBART

OpBART was born out of the tumultuous offline world of racial tensions and police brutality in the San Francisco Bay Area's light rail system. Since the 2009 shooting of Oscar Grant by the BART police in San Francisco, antipolice brutality demonstrations have grown commonplace (Figure 9.10).

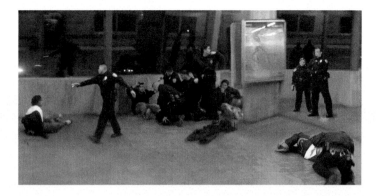

FIGURE 9.10   On December 31, 2009, a homeless man (Oscar Grant) was shot and killed. While one cop has his knee on the victim's neck, the other (Johannes Mehserle) fires a single shot to the back of his head. After being convicted of involuntary manslaughter and serving an 11-month prison sentence, Mehserle was eventually released (https://www.youtube.com/watch?v=nXWSgG-KNng).

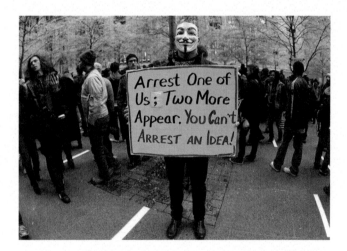

FIGURE 9.11   Zuccotti Park protesters peacefully voice their displeasure. The previous weekend's violence was caught on camera as police arrested 80 protesters and sprayed mace into the faces of female protesters in one memorable episode. The NYPD officers' "cowardly" use of force against peaceful protesters was exposed in the video, which sparked outrage.

OCCUPY WALL STREET

As a result, in late August of 2011, Anonymous came out to support Occupy Wall Street, bringing the movement's plight to the media's attention for the first time. Occupy Wall Street protesters were using the tactics Anonymous had perfected during their time on the streets of New York. When the crowds arrived in Lower Manhattan in September, those wearing Guy Fawkes masks were the first to be approached by the media (Figure 9.11).

There was no Occupy Wall Street in Egypt's Tahrir Square, which attracted Egypt's young heroes who were educated and cutting edge. At Occupy Wall Street, the outcasts were embraced. Rather than the vastly oppressed masses demonstrated elsewhere, many were members of society's neglected and disenfranchised ranks. In September and October, those who had been rejected, as well as homeowners who had fallen victim to predatory subprime mortgages during the financial crisis of 2008/2009 and students who were drowning in student loan debt, began assembling in parks around the country.

10 Hitman for Hire

Despite the presence of con artists and scammers, the world of assassins for hire on the Dark Web remains a frightening place. People acquire various items on the untraceable Dark Web, including pharmaceuticals and exotic animals. Occasionally, reports emerge of someone attempting to use the Dark Web for a different purpose: murder. Most hitman services are unquestionably scams aimed at defrauding people of their bitcoins. Scams are a more convenient, less dangerous, and profitable strategy for marketplace owners. A buyer sends the specifics of what they want to kill and how they want to kill them; a strike that appears to be an accident is always more expensive. Customers pay in bitcoin ahead, which the website's administrator promises to refund if the attack does not occur. The administration promises speedy action but instead delivers excuses and stonewalls the hitman, who was caught for a traffic infraction or unlawful gun ownership. The administrator then states that a more experienced assassin could be recruited; however, doing so would cost as much bitcoin. Some clients keep paying for months after the administrator has determined that there is no more money to be extracted from them (https://mercenaries.pw/).

THE CON ARTIST OF THE BESA MAFIA

Besa Mafia is a Dark Web site owned by the Albanian mafia ("besa" means "honor" in Albanian). It is controlled by a scam artist known only as Yura. Yura boasts, "We have a vast network worldwide." "When you purchase one of our services, we will contact a local member of our mob near the victim and have him offer the services to you. Whether you require a beating, a murder, to scare someone, to burn down a house or a car, or to obtain guns or poison, we can assist you," as shown in Figure 10.1.

On their website, Besa Mafia offers the following services:

We have hitman who are willing to carry out assassinations for a fee ranging from $5000 to $100,000, depending on the personality and manner you like.
Beating, starting at $2500–10,000, we can beat up whoever you want.
Starting around $2500–5000, set fire to cars and houses.
Purchasing Weapons and Poison "We can give weapons and poison depending on your needs."

Consumers should contact Yura via secure email (evelynwmartin@secmail.pro) or Wickr (hitman4hire) to place an order (Figure 10.2).

Yura spent a lot of time and effort defending the website's integrity. A man from California named "Thcjohn2" wrote to the Website advertising his assassin services. "Of course, I'm broke and desperate," Thcjohn2 commented, "and I'm looking for a quick buck." "I served in the United States Navy for several years." Yura had begged

DOI: 10.1201/9781003404330-10

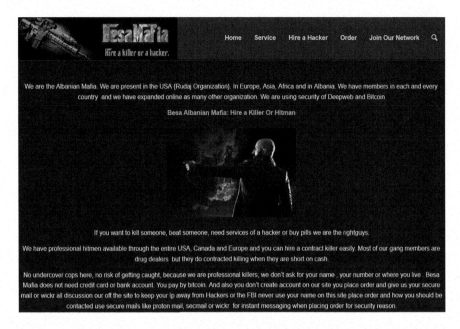

FIGURE 10.1 Mafia website (http://zsyvom262oiaoc6es7bgg66xieyil6nqkh7jn5ntragh-pqgudbcl3vad.onion).

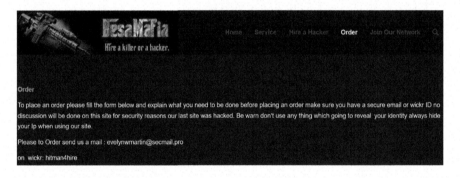

FIGURE 10.2 Order screenshot.

Thcjohn2 to help her instead of accepting his offer. Make films of burning cars to increase the site's reputation. Yura was also curious.

Thcjohn2 is planning a series of fictitious murder videos. Soon after, videos of criminals flashing firearms and articles praising Yura's hitman website began to appear on the internet, such as this one on YouTube:

https:// www.youtube.com/watch?v=KILUsa4crzI

Yura has created a swarm of micro-websites on the surface web to share information on the Besa Mafia while purportedly opposing it. Yura had engaged freelance search engine optimization (SEO) professionals to optimize the sites to show up high in the search engine results for terms like "hitman for hire" and related terms.

People looking for a hitman would stumble across Yura's websites criticizing Besa Mafia's immorality, then proceed to the Dark Web's Besa Mafia website. The site immediately became a highly profitable operation, with consumers willing to pay top dollar to have people murdered.

However, a hacker known as bRspd hacked Besa Mafia in late April 2016 and published vital material online. User accounts, personal communications, "hit" orders, and the website where he advertises his assassin services, including a ZIP file with images of victims from the site's "hit" orders, were all exposed in this hack. The original leak article included 250 accounts with email addresses, usernames, and passwords in the form of orders.csv and msg.csv. There are 38 "hit" orders in the leak and 2,683 personal messages sent and received by site administrators.

An email exchange between Yura and two arsonists was also included in the data dump, as was an exchange of emails between Yura and a Texas investigator seeking information on a hit placed on a Texas woman through the site. Yura allegedly passed over the information provided by the murderer; they stated that they were "willing to cooperate with the FBI."

In June 2016, a second, very identical incident happened. This set in motion a chain of events. To begin, Yura persuaded his customers that the leak was small. "We are not a rip-off, and there are no bitcoins that have been lost." In a message to a customer, Yura said, "Our website was hacked; however, hackers only stole information on a few users." "There was no bitcoin stolen." Certain media outlets also covered the leak. Meanwhile, Yura set about rebranding CrimeBay and developing a new website.

Hackers used information from bRspd's dump to gain access to the website, gaining access to Yura's Gmail. The hackers snooped through his emails and discovered that Yura discussed purchasing a much-needed English course, advertising messages for freelancers, and bitcoin payment information. The hackers obtained the cryptographic keys to get access to Besa Mafia's website domain by combining this information with the content of the two bRspd breaches. The hackers duplicated and saved all of Besa Mafia's content to hand it over to the cops – and then shut down the website, sending users to a site they had created. A picture of a closed, rusted door appeared on the new page shown in Figure 10.3.

Following the Besa Mafia debacle, Yura created CrimeBay, claiming to be a member of the Chechen mob. "For important persons, such as little celebrities who have bodyguards, we provide you skilled ex-military operatives starting at USD 30,000," he said as a new service. They perform the deed with a sniper rifle and can flee quietly." Hackers could continue reading the site's correspondence because CrimeBay and Besa Mafia used the same source code in Figure 10.4.

The Besa Mafia is back today. Yura proudly proclaims, "WE ARE BACK AGAIN, AND MORE SECURED," in the huge text on the homepage.

According to Yura, the hackers acquired access by ordering and chatting directly through the Besa Mafia website. As a result, Yura has issued additional instructions to customers: "In addition, you users no longer establish accounts on our website. To keep you safe from the FBI, you place a purchase and provide us with your secure email or Wickr account. All communication takes place off the site. For security

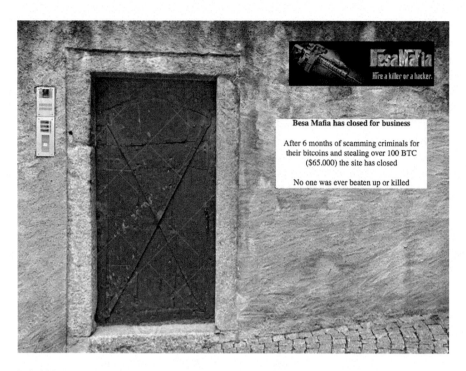

FIGURE 10.3   The website of the Besa Mafia after "Operation Vegetable."

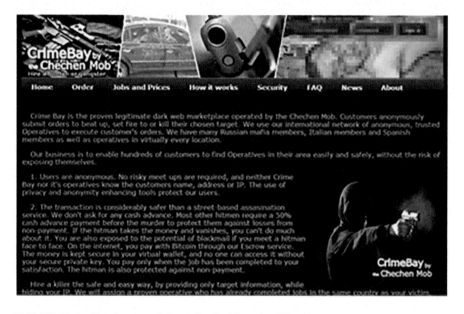

FIGURE 10.4   Yura's rebranded murder-for-hire- site CrimeBay.

reasons, never use your name on this site to place an order or contact you. Instead, use secure mails like proton mail, secmail, or wickr for instant messaging when placing an order."

"BE WARNED DON'T TRY HACKING THIS SITE OR RISK YOUR LIFE," he warns potential hackers.

The conversations showed a "death list" of people whom other people intended to kill when the Besa Mafia website was hacked, which is an interesting result. Clients looking to hire hitman on the Dark Web are far more hazardous than scammers like Yura, who run false hitman sites. The actual evil guys here are the clients who wish to hire an assassin to kill someone they know. Yura didn't have any hitman on hand, but it turns out that some of Besa Mafia's patrons took matters into their own hands and killed their victims.

Customers came from all over the world to visit the website. Some trolls posted funny pleas, but the majority of users were sincere. A user from the Netherlands paid 20 bitcoins to have someone killed in a staged cycling accident. And a Minnesotan man spent four months communicating with Yura about how to have a woman he knew murdered.

Hackers handed over a paper to the cops that detailed the Besa Mafia's multiple hacks and data dumps and a top ten list of the site's most hazardous users.

Dogdaygod, a user who used the moniker Dogdaygod, was one of the "most sought" users. In February 2016, Dogdaygod sent Yura his first communication, and he was itching to assassinate a woman from Cottage Grove, Minnesota. Initially, Dogdaygod offered a hit-and-run or a premeditated traffic crash as a method of assassination but subsequently suggested a more sensible option, such as shooting the victim and setting fire to her home.

Dogdaygod had a ferocious hatred for his intended victim. He wrote, "Please help me kill this bitch." Yura had encouraged him, saying, "Yes, she is a bitch who deserves to die." The discussion dragged on for months until Dogdaygod, fed up with Yura's increasingly ridiculous justifications, demanded a refund for the missed hit.

"Unfortunately, this website has been taken over," Yura stated. He pretended to be a hacker to divert Dogdaygod's attention and possibly extort more money from him: "Unless you send ten bitcoin, we will send all customer and target information to law enforcement," Yura wrote to be a hacker. Dogdaygod did this on May 20, 2016, when he sent ten bitcoins. Operating a phony hitman website and defrauding criminals is profitable.

The Federal Bureau of Investigation (FBI) contacted Amy Allwine, a Minnesota resident whom Dogdaygod had provided to the Besa Mafia. On May 31, 2016, almost a month after the bRspd breach. Someone paid at least $6,000 to murder Amy Allwine, an IT professional and a local church's deacon, on the dark web. Amy, shown in picture 10.5: The Allwines claimed they had no idea who the Dogdaygod persona belonged to.

Amy Allwine died six months later. Her husband contacted 911 on November 13 to report discovering her body in her bedroom. He told the operator, "I think my wife shot herself" (Figure 10.5).

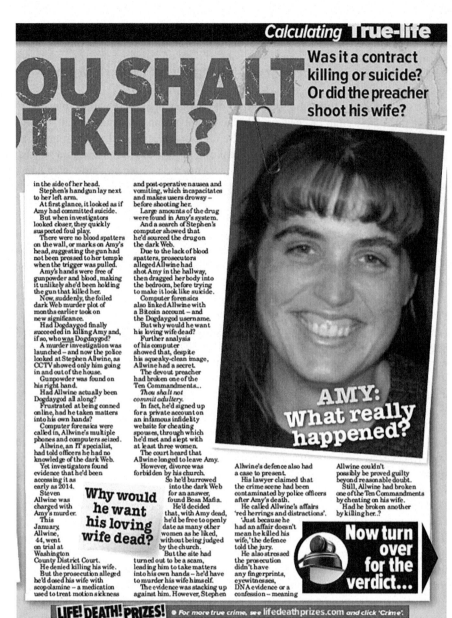

FIGURE 10.5   Amy was murdered on November 13, 2016, by her husband, aka Dogdaygod.

The police discovered evidence connecting Stephen Allwine to the murder, including cookies for dark web-related websites, and bitcoin transactions. Dogdaygod tried to buy scopolamine on the darknet – Amy had high doses of the drug in her system.

Allwine, dubbed Dogdaygod, was arrested in January 2017 for killing his wife. Stephen Allwine killed his wife because he desired a divorce but was afraid of being

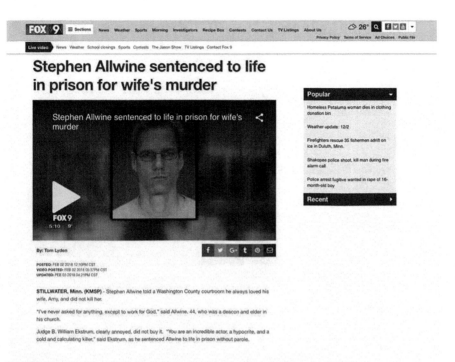

FIGURE 10.6   Allwine was sentenced to life in prison in February 2018.

removed from the severe fundamentalist religion in which he was active. Stephen was a lay preacher in the United Church of God, and his job appeared to be the most important thing in his life, even though he had adulterous affairs and was willing to kill to maintain his public image. Prosecutors cited several affairs as possible motives, and the fact that Amy's life insurance policy is worth $700,000 named Stephen as the sole beneficiary. Allwine was convicted in February 2018 and sentenced to life in prison, as shown in Figure 10.6.

The National Crime Agency (NCA) of the United Kingdom eventually initiated an international investigation into the "death list" hackers collected from the Besa Mafia and CrimeBay websites. They found and charged several Besa Mafia clients with criminal conspiracy. A British doctor, David Crichton, was arrested by the NCA in March 2017 after he ordered the murder of his former financial advisor. Crichton claimed he placed the order out of frustration, but the website never received any money. He was cleared of all charges in July 2018 and is now living happily ever after. An NCA tip led to the arrest and conviction of Emanuela Consortini, an Italian-born user in Denmark, for ordering the murder of an ex-boyfriend.

The NCA and Bulgarian police eventually shut down CrimeBay in May 2017, but not before Yura ramped up his marketing with an attempt to extort money by crowdsourcing a hit on the new President: "Donald Trump is an exceedingly difficult target," CrimeBay admits, "but he is neither a God nor an immortal, and CrimeBay relishes a challenge," as shown in Figure 10.7.

Fund raising to kill Donald Trump

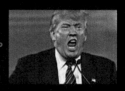

We received many messages from our customers about the cost involved in killing Donald Trump.

Our response is that killing Trump is neither short nor simple: it would cost tens of millions to bring a team of overseas, expert hitmen to kill him who would have the skill to penetrate his security and a chance of escape.

Donald Trump is an extremely difficult target given his public status and the resources now dedicated to protecting his person on a full-time basis. However, he is neither a God nor immortal, and Crime Bay enjoys a challenge.

All of our operatives do jobs for money. We, the cyberteam managing this site retain a commission for each job. There are no operatives that would kill Donald Trump for free. Crime Bay however, will waive its normal commission on account of other intangiable benefits from association with the murder of a controversial right wing US president.

We have several ex-military trained experts who might attempt assassinating Trump, but not without strong incentives. To influence a suitably experienced team to take on what would be a suicide mission for most other operatives we need to offer a significant bounty.

Because the involved costs are so heavy, our visitors asked to donate some amount of money that will help with raising the funds to make an appealing offer to one of our expert teams.

The donated amount will remain in their personal wallets on our site, until Donald Trump is dead. If the hitmen team fails to do the job, the donors gets their money back. Our customers pay only for successful job.

If you want to assassinate Donald Trump, please donate your amount by putting the money in your wallet on Crime Bay. We will calculate the total amount from all contributors, and when the sum is appealing to any of our hitmen teams, they will be assigned to the job.

If the team fails or is arrested, we can send another team. The money will be sent to hitmen only after the completion of a successful hit.

Please signup or login, send any amount of bitcoin to your wallet, and send us a message telling us it is for the Trump assassination.

If you know others who have bad intentions for Mr. Trump share this address with them. Spread the word, raise the funds and he will die.

FIGURE 10.7   Donald Trump fundraising.

RUSSIA'S TOP FEMALE ANTICORRUPTION INVESTIGATOR WAS SHOT AND KILLED IN THE STREET

On the other hand, some assassinations do start on the Dark Web. Take the instance of Lt. Col. Evgeniya Shishkina, a police investigator who was shot and killed outside her home near Moscow on October 10, 2018. She has been researching narcotics trafficking and fraud for the Interior Ministry, as shown in Figure 10.8.

Federal investigators in St. Petersburg reported the arrest of two suspects in Shishkina's case on March 7, 2019. According to an official statement, Abdulaziz Abdulaziz, a 19-year-old medical student, was the one who carried out the killing. A 17-year-old high-school student is the second man. Although the minor's name has not been revealed, his initials are "A.G."

According to police sources, the order was placed on an illicit online platform called Hydra on the Dark Web by the proprietor of a drug-dealing store. Shishkina's assassination is thought to be one of the earliest hit orders placed on the Dark Web. In August 2018, the suspect "A.G." accessed the Dark Web site Hydra and posted in a forum that he was looking for work.

The following month, "A.G." received a message on the messaging platform Telegram from someone who operates a Hydra business, detailing the contract killing in detail. A million rubles ($15,215) were given to "A.G." to organize the assassination of Interior Ministry detective Evgeniya Shishkina. According to police papers, the 17-year-old allegedly split the 1 million rubles he was offered,

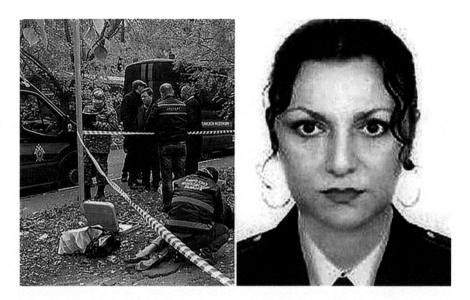

FIGURE 10.8   The murder scene of police investigator Lt. Col. Evgeniya Shishkina in Krasnogorskiy, Bayonetta.

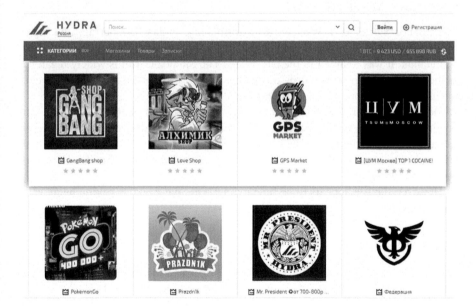

FIGURE 10.9   Hydra homepage (http://hydrarusigitbkpn.onion).

retaining 400,000 for himself and providing 600,000 to Abdulazizov to carry out the murder.

Hydra, which has its roots in Russia's hacker underground, has become the world's largest online drug market. But it's also a one-of-a-kind Dark Web drug operation, as shown in Figure 10.9.

Hydra now has 2.5 million registered accounts and 400,000 active consumers. At its peak, AlphaBay, the largest Western Dark Web market, was reported to have 400,000 registered members. Unlike other markets, where merchants pay a one-time account opening fee, each of Hydra's 5,000 stores must pay a monthly rent. With ads on the top banner, a Trusted Seller account costs $100–$1,000 per month. Trusted Sellers with at least 1,000 transactions should not have more than 7% of their monthly customer disputes.

Hydra's 5,000 shops paid the platform an estimated $1 billion in sales commissions, upgraded shop profiles, and shop rents between 2016 and 2019. This dwarfs its Western Dark Web competitors.

Having learned from previous dark web drug markets, Hydra's administrators have implemented a comprehensive quality assurance system. Each product is tested by Hydra's team of chemists and human guinea pigs, with medics on hand to provide safety advice. These test results, complete with graphs, analysis, and images, are shared in a subforum. The government imposes penalties if the equipment isn't up to par. Anyone who tries to pass oregano off as a high-grade chronic will be banned from the site. Fentanyl and firearms, hitman, viruses, and pornography are prohibited, while drugs, phony passports, shady SIM cards, and counterfeit cash are marketed.

SINALOA CARTEL HITMAN

The Sinaloa Cartel is a Mexican drug trafficking, money laundering, and organized crime syndicate based in the Baja California states of Durango, Sonora, and Chihuahua. It was founded in the late 1980s. The Sinaloa Cartel is widely regarded as the world's most powerful drug trafficking organization, and it is, without a doubt, the most powerful organized crime organization in Mexico.

Despite its claim that "under the shelter and protection of the Deep Web, our hundreds of Sinaloa Cartel members offer you high-quality drugs, guns, and professional assault services at affordable costs," the "Sinaloa Cartel Marketplace" (http://sinaloajbzogpkeu.onion) on the Dark Web is not affiliated with the Sinaloa Cartel, as shown in Figure 10.10.

However, the site appears to be functioning, with many people paying bitcoins to hire an assassin.

DARK MAMBIA

"DarkMamba is a private military company comprised of ex-military and ex-special forces personnel. "We're a global company," as shown in Figure 10.11 shown.

CRIMINAL NETWORK

"Normal charges start from $4,000 and go up depending on killer skills. Although it is a small fee, many gang members do not live and are willing to kill for this

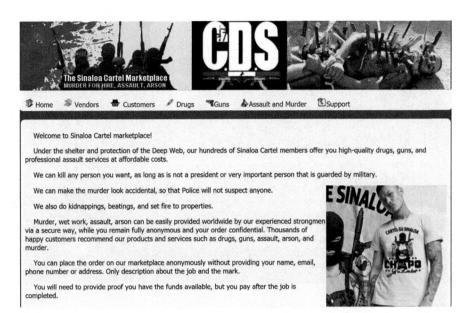

FIGURE 10.10 The Sinaloa Marketplace (http://sinaloajbzogpkeu.onion).

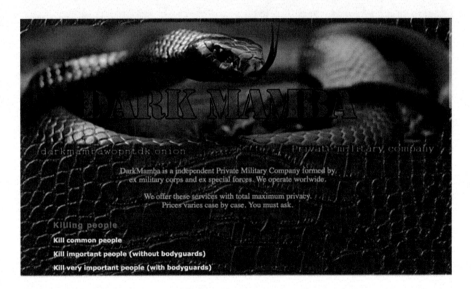

FIGURE 10.11 Dark Mambia website (http://darkmambawopntdk.onion).

money. There is one stipulation for this service. Your victim must be a regular person without a gun, a bodyguard, or any kind of self-defense training," as shown in Figure 10.12.

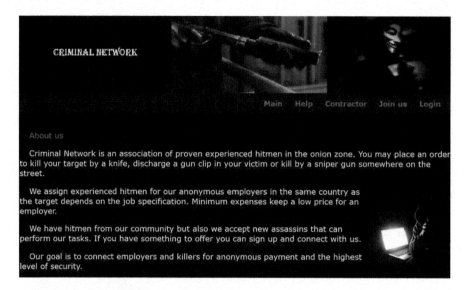

FIGURE 10.12   Criminal network website.

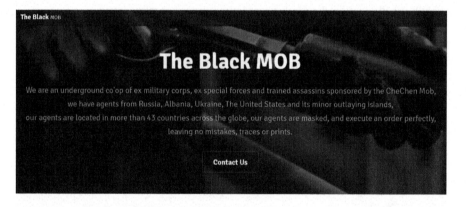

FIGURE 10.13   Black MOB (http://blkmobbzqjhpn232.onion).

THE BLACK MOB

The Black Mob is another hitman-for-hire outfit that looks to be thriving on the Dark Web. The Chechen Mob claims to be funding an underground organization of ex-military personnel, ex-special forces, and trained assassins with operations in more than 43 countries, as shown in Figure 10.13:

> Our agents are disguised and carry their orders flawlessly, leaving no traces, traces, or prints.

The services are vast, and the costs are likely the highest of any hitman-for-hire website on the Dark Web:

Kidnapping ($70,000–$250,000), Personal bio/social life attack ($10,000–$50,000), Personal Financial destabilization ($30,000–$70,000), Family Financial destabilization ($100,000–$200,000), Torture ($20,000–30,000), and Set victims cars on fire ($20,000–$50,000).

At such costs, one wouldn't have to con too many people per year to make a decent life! The site has been up since 2016, and these people may be making a fortune.

MARA SALVATRUCHA

"If you are a weak person who cannot kill or abuse your hated man, you may request that we do it instead. We can do it," as shown in Figure 10.14.

ASSASSINATION NETWORK

Assassination Network offers the most snazzy-looking murder-for-hire site on the Dark Web. It has a chance to win an award for the best-designed website on the Dark Web. Instead of the horrible phony photographs found on other hitman sites, a beautiful slide show is on its homepage. There are no gimmicks or desperate attempts to persuade potential customers that they are authentic. Not only does the site lack the obnoxious spelling and punctuation problems that plague every other hitman website, but the writing is also knowledgeable and persuasive. The site contains links to news reports about unusual and unsolved homicides that its assassin network claims were carried out – effective marketing, as shown in Figures 10.15 and 10.16 below.

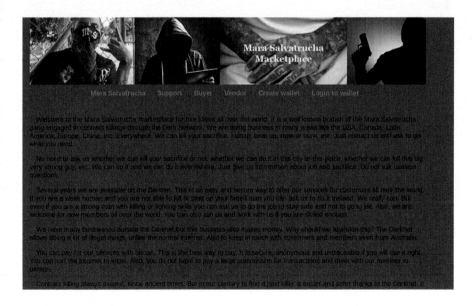

FIGURE 10.14   Mara Salvatrucha (http://marak2vqaeup4ibj.onion).

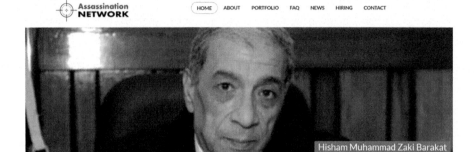

Assassination NETWORK in the Media

Daily Express   Guardian   FOX 5   EL◆MUNDO   Ultima Hora

FIGURE 10.15   Assassination network website (http://assassinuyy7h425.onion).

 Tunahan Keser

† 23 June 2017
Location: Quickborn, Germany
Method: Handgun

 Naim Caliph

† 4 February 2017
Location: San Fernando, Trinidad
Method: Handgun

 Arturo Perez

† 26 January 2016
Location: Ontario CA, USA
Method: Handgun

 Hisham Muhammad Zaki Barakat

† 29 June 2015
Location: Cairo, Egypt
Method: Roadside Car Bomb

 Alberto Nisman

† 18 January 2015
Location: Buenos Aires, Argentina
Method: Handgun

 Jeffery Mark Wiggill

† 19 June 2013
Location: Soweto, South Africa
Method: Handgun

 Amílcar Henríquez

† 15 April 2017
Location: Nuevo Colón, Panama
Method: Assault Rifle

 Pavel Grigorievich Sheremet

† 20 July 2016
Location: Kiew, Ukraine
Method: Car Bomb

 Clinton Elliot Yow Foo

† 1 October 2015
Location: Toronto, Canada
Method: Sniper

 Dominic Newton "The Jacka"

† 2 February 2015
Location: Oakland CA, USA
Method: Handgun

 Gabriel Català Rufino

† 23 August 2014
Location: Mallorca, Spain
Method: Handgun

 Cyril Beeka

† 21 March 2011
Location: Cape Town, South Africa
Method: Drive-by shooting

FIGURE 10.16   Hitman list.

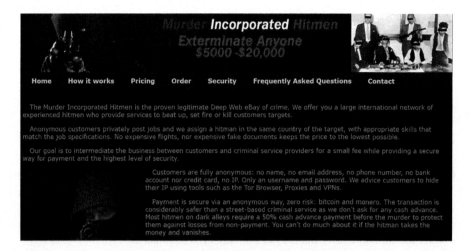

FIGURE 10.17 Murder incorporated hitman.

HITMAN FROM MURDER INCORPORATED

"What's the point of hiring a professional assassin? Because it is inexpensive, safe, and allows you to murder without being caught. When you commit the murder, make sure you're in a public place surrounded by people and friends, and no one will suspect you," as shown in Figure 10.17.

SUMMARY

The evidence strongly implies that hitman websites are frauds, but those who want someone killed aren't paying attention. One thing is certain: they've turned into hotspots for actual people looking to pay to have someone killed. And numerous men and women are in prison due to paying at one of these sites and being detected by the authorities.

Hitman websites are simply a great way to deceive people. What are your options if they don't follow through? Is it time to call the cops and file a fraud complaint against the website? Hardly.

11 The Positive and Evil Side of the Dark Web

We've covered how to access the Dark Web safely and anonymously in the previous chapters by installing and using several security and privacy-focused operating systems, private browsers, and VPNs.

Let's talk about what happens on the Dark Web in this chapter to decide why you want to go there. We'll speak about how the Dark Web is used and the stories (true or not) about what happens there. Some of these examples will be visual and detailed (not for the faint of heart), but they are not my original creations.

I'll repeat stories with which I've heard, read, or had firsthand experience.

Not all of them will be frightening, morbid, or disgusting. Some will be positive, describing how people utilize the Dark Web for whistleblowing, sharing information, marketing, buying and selling, and offering medical assistance, among other things.

In this chapter, we'll discuss the following subjects:

- The good and evil sides of the Dark Web
- Onion websites
- Dark Web black market using Bitcoin

The majority of what we hear in the media is about illegal activities like narcotics, guns, and people trafficking. Yet, the Dark Web may be used for various benevolent and useful purposes.

It's critical to recognize that the Dark Web provides an environment where people can express themselves freely and without fear of repercussion (for better or worse), gain access to knowledge or content that would otherwise be prohibitively expensive (or even illegal) to obtain, and connect with people who share similar interests, subcultures, or hobbies (or any other uniting factor). Like any other tool or technology (and yeah, I'm quoting), the Dark Web isn't intrinsically wicked. Individuals populate the Dark Web, which people use for good or evil. The Dark Web's original aim was to establish an online utopia populated by individuals of all nations, religions, and genders sharing information freely and cooperating for all.

I realize this seems like a science fiction story, but it is a worthwhile aspiration nonetheless. The criminal element introduced itself somewhere along the line (or people simply noticed how easy it was to execute criminal operations anonymously on the Dark Web). The Dark Web has had a terrible reputation since its inception.

The name "Dark Web" does not imply that it is wicked; nonetheless, the media and marketers have attached evil or nefarious aspects to the Dark Web to boost media sales or consumption. The Dark Web is not as accessible as Surface Web sites, which adds

 DOI: 10.1201/9781003404330-11

to its mystique. As I previously stated, you'll need a special browser (such as Tor) to access the Dark Web; you'll need to take extra measures; and, most crucially, you won't be able to find sites or results from the Dark Web using traditional search engines.

These things contribute to the anonymity and privacy that users can enjoy when visiting the Dark Web. So, let's get started. Remember that many of the tales and data on the Dark Web are also available elsewhere; it's simply tougher to figure out who you're dealing with, but human nature will always remain human nature.

ONION WEBSITES

Many businesses have started to create Dark Web websites, primarily to provide access in countries where open use is prohibited. For instance, consider Facebook. In October 2014, Facebook announced a Dark Web version to address access issues when Tor users accessed their accounts through the regular Facebook site. Users in countries with restricted Facebook access can access the social network through the Dark Web version. The following is a screenshot of the Facebook onion site, as shown in Figure 11.1.

Several advertising organizations also set up shop on the Dark Web to cater to individuals who want to view advertisements while maintaining anonymity and security. As you may be aware, many advertisements collect information on us, and some are even classified as malware. One of the reasons why adblockers were created was to address this issue. Adland, for example, curates and presents ads and commercials from all around the world, touting the world's greatest collection of Super Bowl commercials. To safeguard their readers/surfers, they developed a Dark Web portal.

The following is a statement from Adland's founder:

> The target of Adland is concerned about privacy. There are two categories of readers in our group. Numerous individuals work in advertising and numerous individuals who work in technology. such as gamers who already have AdBlock installed.

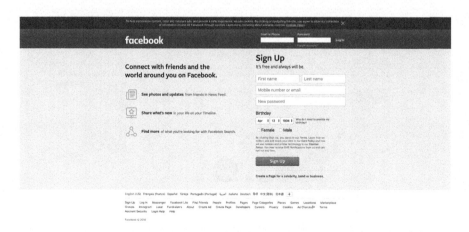

FIGURE 11.1   Facebook onion.

Furthermore, she noted that the current condition of ad networks (on the Surface Web) is nearly indistinguishable from malware. Many third-party calls are being made between the [tracker] and the publication you're reading. She sees the Dark Web as a massive adblocker that prevents cookies from tracking data.

So, hosting an ad site on the Dark Web helps ensure that the ads are legitimate and do not contain malware or cookie-collecting features.

The website Adland is depicted in Figure 11.2.

ProPublica, an independent, Pulitzer Prize-winning nonprofit news organization dedicated to uncovering occurrences and stories that violate the public trust, has now developed a Dark Web website to make it easier for whistle-blowers and others who wish to disclose information anonymously to do so. Figure 11.3 is from ProPublica's website.

Users began looking for a means to keep their search habits private once they started receiving tailored ads based on their web searches. Anonymous commerce is seen as a big threat by Facebook, Google, and others. One of their finest marketing strategies is monitoring and tracking users' searches, followed by tailored ads.

As previously stated, dissidents and activists in oppressive regimes use the Dark Web to communicate to avoid getting into trouble with their government. Unfortunately, some governments still restrict outside communication through traditional channels or report what they are experiencing to the outside world.

Human Rights Watch, a global nonprofit human rights organization, proposes that human rights activists use the Dark Web to communicate safely and secretly.

The Human Rights webpage is depicted in Figure 11.4.

Tor is used in East Asia to protect people's identities when sharing information concerning sweatshops and other labor law violations.

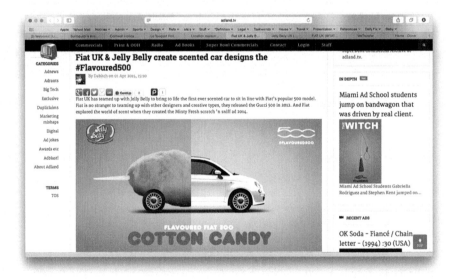

FIGURE 11.2   Adland website.

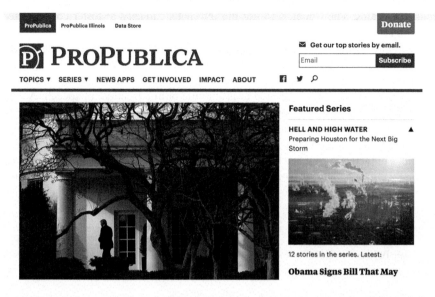

FIGURE 11.3 Propublica website.

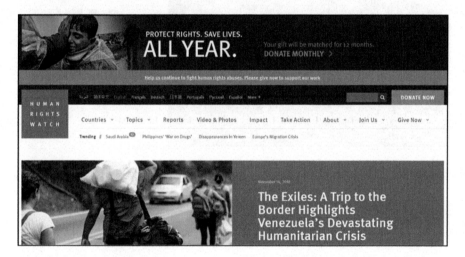

FIGURE 11.4 Human rights webpage.

Many events you hear about or see in movies and TV shows, such as battling a giant corporation's dominance of a small town in the eastern United States, are handled through the Dark Web, with local inhabitants rallying and planning their activities anonymously and confidentially.

Human rights workers utilize the Dark Web to report abuse and avoid arrest anonymously while working in risky regions.

Bloggers use Tor to hide their identities and band together to aid one another and promote free expression. Global Voices, for example, is a multilingual and multinational network of volunteer bloggers, journalists, translators, scholars, and human

rights advocates. Their goal is to use the internet's capacity to foster cross-border understanding.

They have a journalistic team that covers topics rarely covered by mainstream media, and they translate the stories into multiple languages to overcome linguistic obstacles. The Global website Voices is depicted in Figure 11.5.

They also have a team dedicated to promoting online freedom of speech. Advox is a Global Voices organization that reports on threats to online speech and shares techniques for safeguarding netizens' work and words. According to its website, it supports initiatives to change internet policy and practice worldwide. The Advox website is depicted in Figure 11.6.

Another group, Rising Voices, attempts to empower marginalized communities with training, tools, micro-grant financing, and mentoring to share their stories

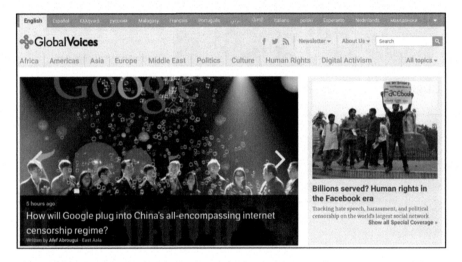

FIGURE 11.5   Global voices website.

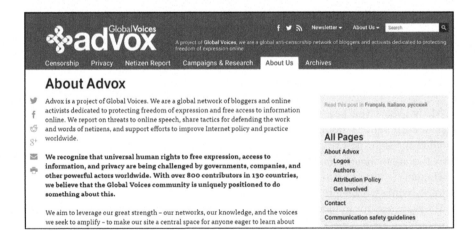

FIGURE 11.6   Advox website.

through media such as blogs, wikis, and media sharing (video/audio/photos), podcasts, and vlogs. Figure 11.7 shows the webpage for Rising Voices.

Many news organizations have lockboxes on the Dark Web, including SecureDrop, the Washington Post, and the New York Times. Users can transmit information and tips anonymously and securely. Reporters Without Borders, which campaigns for freedom and defends journalists worldwide, is an example of a Dark-Web-based journalistic organization.

Lawyers, investigators, and media investigating governments use it to avoid being hacked or prosecuted. The SecureDrop website is seen in Figure 11.8.

Obtaining medical advice and medications is another prevalent use of the Dark Web. Some people are apprehensive about approaching a doctor they know and asking questions, and not having to divulge your true identity can help alleviate that fear. Others inquire about the risks of combining multiple medications and the prescribed

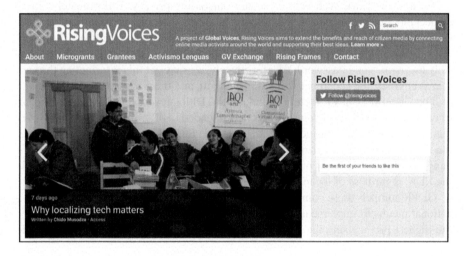

FIGURE 11.7 Rising voices webpage.

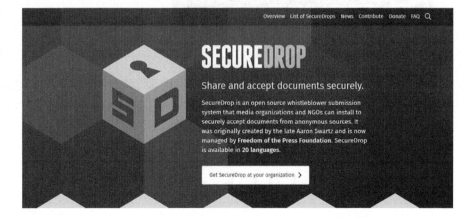

FIGURE 11.8 SecureDrop.

medications, their effectiveness, side effects, and other details. Others attempt to obtain drugs they require but would not obtain otherwise.

Doctors, also known as Dr. Fernando Caudevilla, is a well-known story about a volunteer doctor from Madrid, Spain, who provides medical and medication advice on the Dark Web.

He works as a family physician by day, but he answers over 1,000 drug-related queries in forums on Silk Road 1, Silk Road 2, and The Hub at night. The doctor believes that drug use should be a personal choice and favors legalization.

He works with Energy Control, a Spanish nonprofit dedicated to reducing harm among recreational drug users. The Energy Control webpage is depicted in Figure 11.9.

What about regular people? Many people utilize the Dark Web to find information or media that would be difficult to get across on the Surface Web or too expensive to purchase.

Tor and the Dark Web help us secure our online privacy. Unfortunately, many respectable businesses can have unethical staff who sell our personal information. For example, after apparently anonymizing the data, ISPs sell customers' browsing information and history (including any searches conducted, websites visited, and possibly usernames and passwords). Unfortunately, we may get this information through search engines, the social networks we belong to, and the websites we frequent.

The General Data Protection Regulation (GDPR) governs all EU and European Economic Area (EEA) citizens. GDPR was intended to offer individuals control over their data and provide businesses with standards for handling personal data belonging to their employees, customers, or business partners. GDPR applies to any company based in the EEA or processing personal data of persons or enterprises inside the EEA, regardless of location or citizenship.

GDPR compels these companies to put in place suitable technological and organizational means to implement the data protection principles it establishes and utilize the highest privacy settings by default. This means that the data isn't made public

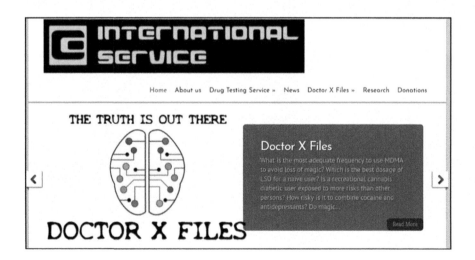

FIGURE 11.9 Energy control website.

without the individuals' explicit, informed consent and that it can't be used to identify them without supplementary information, which is kept separately.

These safeguards are already in place on the Dark Web by default, especially if you use Tor or another darknet. Many people rely on them to protect their personal information.

The vast majority of Dark Web users care about their privacy and anonymity, so unless you provide information yourself, decline to use the standard precautionary measures we've discussed (which is comparable to explicit, informed consent), or are maliciously attempting to collect information about people, you'll be de facto implementing GDPR by taking appropriate measures to protect personal information. The following is a screenshot of the European Union's GDPR website, shown in Figure 11.10.

Tor can also be used to protect minors by obfuscating their IP address and preventing anyone from determining their whereabouts (both on the Dark Web and the Surface Web). Naturally, parents should limit their children's access to the Dark Web to keep them from mistakenly (or purposely) visiting the less-savory and illegal sites, but utilizing Tor on the Surface Web is sufficient.

There's a lot of it because one of the Dark Web's primary purposes is to share knowledge without censorship. Many people research various topics, some of which are sensitive and thus subject to monitoring by the NSA or any other governmental agency throughout the world, simply because they don't want their friends and family to know what they're researching.

Many notable figures have private blogs, forums, or websites on the Dark Web, which allow them to express themselves without jeopardizing their public image. This is true for celebrities, politicians, and everyone in the public eye.

So, how about sharing information? Many communities exchange training and guidance on various topics, ranging from criminal activities, including hacking, falsifying documents, and manufacturing narcotics or other illegal substances, to deepsea fishing and poetry debates.

WikiLeaks is a website known for its political and business disclosures, obtained mostly on the Dark Web and then published on its Surface Web website. The WikiLeaks website is depicted in Figure 11.11.

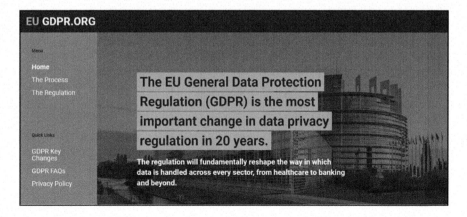

FIGURE 11.10 EU GDPR website.

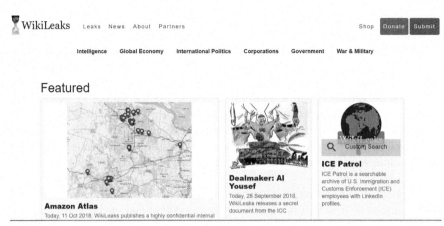

FIGURE 11.11   Wikileaks website.

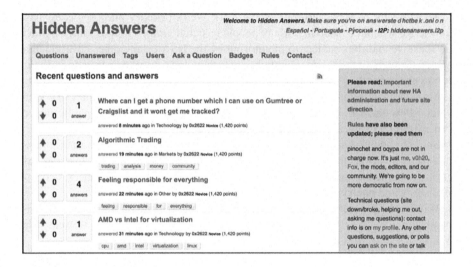

FIGURE 11.12   Hidden answers.

Bibliomaniac, for example, is a site that hosts book clubs and sells books. According to their website, you may locate every book globally, but be cautious and avoid doing anything unlawful, such as downloading copyrighted content.

Music is accessible on the Dark Web in the same way it is on the Surface Web, but to a much greater extent. Almost everything is free.

Some Dark Web websites, such as Tor Kittenz, only offer photographs or slideshows, but others reveal terrible content such as live tortures, murders, and kidnappings, among other atrocities. Some, I've heard, show visuals of injuries and accidents (much like Ogrish or Gorish on the Surface Web, but worse, if that's possible). In general, sites that display dead bodies are not uncommon. Others enable you to get answers to virtually any question. For example, Hidden Answers is the Dark Web's version of Reddit, where you can ask or post anything. The website Hidden Answers is depicted in Figure 11.12.

DARK WEB BLACK MARKET TRANSACTIONS
INVOLVING THE USE OF BITCOIN

The Dark Web's vast potential is only limited by human imagination. I've heard the term "Dark Web" used in various contexts, and one of them is eBay on steroids or eBay for criminals.

The truth is that you can purchase almost anything on the Dark Web, including illegal drugs, guns, counterfeit paperwork, and a variety of other unlawful goods and services. Additionally, you can purchase anything available in legal stores or on legal websites. From carrots and veggies to technological items, some websites sell jokes and pranks such as underage false identification – you can even discover illegal animals for sale.

However, never use your credit card to purchase anything located on the Deep Web. In the shadows of the internet, purchases are made with cryptocurrency (or digital currency), such as Bitcoin (to name the most well-known – there are several others).

Users must first create an account and a Bitcoin wallet to utilize Bitcoin. The purchaser transfers Bitcoin from their wallet to the seller's wallet. The transaction is secured with a private key that enables the seller to confirm that the Bitcoin is genuine and has been successfully sent to their wallet. The blockchain verifies this. A blockchain is a collection of financial records (blocks) that are cryptographically linked together. Consider a blockchain to be a public digital ledger that is not managed centrally, is distributed across numerous computers, and is encrypted.

Each block contains unassailable information (or so it is believed) about the blocks preceding and following it and transaction information. Attempting to edit this information will result in attempts to update the information in the remainder of the chain's blocks, making it difficult to do so without the consensus of the chain's other members.

Personal information is not disclosed, which is one of the reasons for the Dark Web's success with digital currency. Additionally, Bitcoin can be exchanged for conventional official currency in practically every country.

The following Figure 11.13 is from the website of the Bitcoin Organization.

On July 15, 2015, the online dating service Ashley Madison was breached. The hackers sent an email to the website's owners, requesting that they quickly shut down the site. When the demand was denied, the hackers uploaded all the material they had obtained on the Dark Web, including company and personal user data. Ashley Madison, a dating website, was hacked on July 15, 2015.

The Dark Web is a haven for all forms of obscene content, from mundane to nasty or terrifying. A heinous website called the Cruel Onion Wiki has documented animal slaughter. Although it has been closed numerous times, it continues to resurface. Personal information is a particularly well-known offer (passwords, emails, IDs, and bank information). Additionally, some offer to locate specific information for you.

When most of us think of the Dark Web, we instantly think of hackers. There are numerous hackers on the Dark Web, but not all are malicious. Some are only acquiring and disseminating knowledge. On the other hand, others are around to offer their evil services. Numerous organizations create and sell cyberweapons

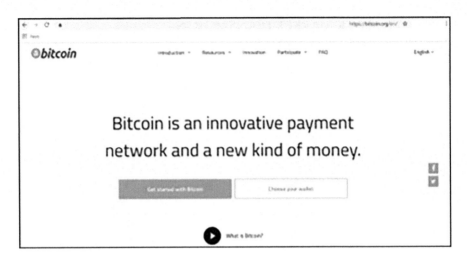

FIGURE 11.13 Bitcoin organization.

(such as general or specific exploits, malware kits, and botnets). Others specialize in cyberattacks (distributed denial-of-service attacks, cybercrime, website defacement, and spam and malware distribution are just a few examples.). With easy access to knowledge on how to exploit vulnerabilities and malware that is relatively easy to use (such as Trojans or ransomware), conducting social engineering assaults (such as spear-phishing) is a simple matter. Additionally, you can rent a botnet for a specified period. Undercover on the Dark Web, unscrupulous individuals can acquire or rent any of these items and others with no technical knowledge required (mainly if they purchase a service).

The drug is a subject that might go on indefinitely if examined in relation to the Dark Web. There is a pharmacy there that sells every medicine known to man. Even extremely novel synthetic medications are sold, but the danger is magnified. Most of these medications have never been adequately evaluated, and Dark Web users are frequently used as test subjects.

Another sector that thrives on the Dark Web is that of hired killers. Numerous professionals promote their services online, with a minimum charge of $20,000. According to reports, most of these assassins are law enforcement officers or con artists.

Human and human-organ trafficking are also covered there; unfortunately, it's a very prolific subject. Many of the stories you may have heard of individuals waking up in ice baths with stitches in their sides are based on this, with enslavement following closely behind.

12 Techniques for Analyzing Dark Web Content

INTRODUCTION

The dark web contains information that is inaccessible to regular search engines. Specialized software is required, and even then, there isn't any guidance on where to begin looking for content on the site. Several websites that can be accessed on the dark web are listed independently. It's possible to find these lists on well-known wikis and social media sites like Reddit. There are still only a few listings because most of the listed websites are no longer active, have switched hosting providers, been closed down by law enforcement, or have long since vanished from view. This is where the average person can find the dark web. The analysis is key for darknets; technical users and law enforcement agencies have their methods. These darknets' content is evaluated with specialized tools and procedures. Traditional search engines' crawling strategies don't work on the dark web because the content there can't be found. Websites that are linked to each other are crawled more efficiently. Crawling the black web, devoid of hyperlinks and thus difficult to index, is thus prevented. In this chapter, we'll talk about analyzing dark web content.

The following subjects will be covered:

- Deep web versus surface web.
- Mechanisms of conventional web crawlers.
- Surfacing deep web content.
- Deep website analysis.

DEEP WEB VERSUS SURFACE WEB

It's helpful to think about how surface web indexing engines work to understand how web content analysis works. Their method of operation is to create indexes of websites that they have crawled. Robots with particular computerized scripts go through the internet organized, known as web crawling. Search engines continue to trawl the internet to expand or refresh their indices. On the surface web, this occurs with little restriction. Search engines won't crawl part-surface websites because crawling uses resources from the crawled sites. Adding commands to the robot.txt file in the root directory of their website will allow them to do this. Because of the enormous amount of data produced on the internet today, crawling is becoming increasingly difficult for search engines. There are still gaps in Google's surface web index, for example.

On the other hand, these search engines cannot explore or analyze the deep web in the same way they can the surface web. Where online pages are hyperlinked,

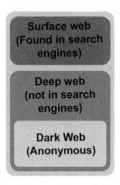

FIGURE 12.1 The surface and deep webs are depicted (See https://blog.knowbe4.com/what-is-the-difference-between-the-surface-web-the-deep-web-and-the-dark-web).

crawling is most effective. A link to another website is created when a crawler discovers an external link. As a result, a web of connections will be created between the various pages. The crawler can access only static pages. Accordingly, dynamically generated content isn't appropriate. However, most of the internet contains secret material that regular crawlers cannot index. As a result, search engines have no information about them. The following is a comprehensive list of deep web data characteristics.

> Users' requests trigger the creation of dynamic content. Specifying certain data characteristics that the user wants to see depends on their inputs. A dynamically generated HTML page is generated and returned as output when an input is provided.
>
> Unlinked—the deep web's pages are not linked to one another.
>
> Non-textual content, including multimedia files and non-HTML content, is extremely difficult to index.

The deep web is predicted to be an overall size is about 500 times greater than the surface web. On dark networks and the deep web, around 200,000 websites exist. Because standard search engines are incapable of crawling them, their contents cannot be retrieved (Figure 12.1).

MECHANISMS OF CONVENTIONAL WEB CRAWLERS

Crawlers that index surface websites are known as traditional crawlers. Yahoo Search, Google, and Bing are a few examples. Their operation is depicted in Figure 12.2.

A URL is the starting point for the crawler. This URL could have been discovered while crawling another website. The crawler will retrieve all of the web pages at that URL. The text and hyperlinks from the retrieved web pages will be extracted.

They are made up of the extracted data that is submitted to an indexer, who organizes it into categories. Keywords, linked pages, authors, and so on are examples that can be included here. A similar process begins with the hyperlinks from the URLs that have been indexed. Crawlers lack mechanisms to distinguish between pages with

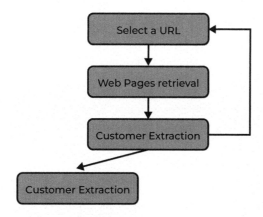

FIGURE 12.2 The conventional web crawlers.

forms and pages with semi-structured data. Data must be collected from forms, so they must use loops to collect it.

SURFACING DEEP WEB CONTENT

It is necessary to access the deep web to study its content. This data must first be surfaced before it can be accessed. The following is an example of a method for surfacing content from the dark web:

1. Locating sources
2. Selecting data from various sources
3. Transmitting selected data to a data analysis system.

Content from databases, internet servers, and dynamic websites can all be found on the black web. Data sources may be combined or integrated into the analysis of dark web information. However, this integration may not be effective in some circumstances due to four factors. First, there's the potential for duplicate data to be entered. In addition, the data repository may be overloaded if the integration system introduces unused data. Because of this, the data integration system's conclusions will be of lower quality. According to the third argument, increasing the amount of data in the integration system may result in the inclusion of low-quality data. Incorporating data into the integration system has a significant price tag. These costs must be incurred to store and integrate data during the collection and processing phases.

DATA EXTRACTION

After the schema match is complete and the appropriate data source has been identified, the data can be retrieved. There are numerous ways to retrieve data from the deep web. Websites aren't downloaded in their entirety because doing so would be prohibitively expensive in terms of both money and time. The data is only culled from the relevant sections of the file.

SCHEMA MATCHING FOR SOURCES

Following the conclusion of the previous phase, the data is uncovered, and the analysis process begins. Schema matching determines the relevance of extracted data by comparing it to a search keyword or phrase. Darknet sites with data matching the schema are retrieved based on the inputted request. Dark web page retrieval and processing are made easier and cheaper with this. Schemas are used to ensure processing resources are allocated to data sources that contain valuable information.

DATA SELECTION

Even with simple online searches, you can find hundreds or thousands of results pages. They're all filled with relevant data gleaned from the search terms. However, not all search results are relevant or of high quality. Some of them may be of subpar quality. The deep web has the same pattern. When a search is conducted using keywords, hundreds of thousands of deep web sources with related information may be discovered. They do, however, differ in terms of quality. Because of this, they must be placed in some sort of order.

For this reason, many websites invest in search engine optimization (SEO) to rank well. Website owners do not expect their sites to appear in deep web search results. So there is no SEO. As a result, figuring out how to index the extracted data is the responsibility of the search engine or search technique. The following are the steps for performing a basic ranking:

> The parameters that are used to determine a search's relevance are defined. Examples include keywords, phrases, headings, and text size, and this aids in the elimination of low-quality search results.
>
> Other quality-determination criteria are outlined in this document. Additional criteria for defining high-quality sources are developed here as part of the quality assessment model.
>
> The retrieved sources are ranked according to the quality dimensions and evaluation model and graded on a quality scale based on a predefined threshold.

DEEP WEB WEBSITES ANALYSIS

The deep web requires a lot of time and effort to analyze, and it entails the following distinct procedures.

A DEEP WEB WEBSITE SEARCH ANALYSIS'S ELIGIBILITY

A well-known issue on the surface web is content replication and duplicate sites. Because recurring search results may contain the same information repeatedly, this can significantly impact the accuracy of the information returned. Websites with duplicate content are penalized by surface-level search engines. Because of this, new content will be ranked lower if a search engine finds that all of a website's content is nearly identical. After scanning its servers, the deep web faces a similar

issue in content analysis. There could be many outcomes, but some of them could be duplicates. The search results must be cleared of duplicates before this can happen. Unique data will then be sent to the next stage of analysis. Once you've verified that the listings are genuine, you can move on to the next step.

Non-HTML content can be found in some deep web results, which contrasts with most of the results found on the surface web. Special access rights are required to access content on the deep web. For the most part, these aren't even websites, and some of their information needs to be deleted entirely. Finally, genuine web pages that come up in search results are discovered. The algorithms used to determine whether a search result qualifies as relevant are constantly updated due to the analysis's inherent complexity and imprecision.

THE NUMBER OF DEEP WEB WEBSITES: AN ANALYSIS

Some people and organizations, such as law enforcement, must monitor the deep web for illicit activity. For example, law enforcement will have to investigate a new drug market or a child pornographic website on the dark web. Keeping track of the total number of darknet websites enables us to determine when additional sites should be inspected. It's not a wild guess when you say there are a lot of deep web pages. There are so many websites in this internet section because of special analysis. Overlap analysis is used to estimate the total number of deep web websites. To perform an overlap analysis, search engines that are already crawling the deep web are used (as well as custom-built search engines).

Based on the coverage provided by the search engines, the approach conducts an analysis. In pairwise comparisons, the number of results from two sources and the number of shared results that do not overlap are considered (Figure 12.3).

For instance, in Figure 12.3, the letters na and nb represent listings from two distinct sources. The estimated total population size, or the total number of websites, is denoted by N.

In this context, the degree of overlap between search result listings is N0. With this information in hand, we can make an educated guess about the overall population of

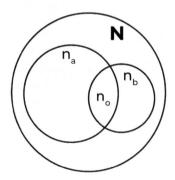

FIGURE 12.3   Overlap analysis depicted graphically.

the deep web. Due to the possibility that this could be interpreted as ambiguous, we should consider another option. Assume the total population is 100, and we wish to determine whether the overlap analysis yields the same result for us. If two sources each have 50 items in their overall population and both share an average of 25 items, indicating that they are both unique, then neither should list 25 items. As a result, they should offer a total of 25 unique products. The following steps must be taken to determine the total population: 50/(25/50). The final result is 100, corresponding to the previously stated total population. The overlap analysis and division produced an identical figure. However, this is more difficult to accomplish on the deep web due to the procedures involved in determining the listings from two sources and the volume of listings shared or unshared by them.

During this form of examination, there are two things to keep in mind. The first is that determining the number of listings from a source should be precise. The success of the entire investigation hinges on this. The accuracy of the entire analytic technique suffers if the number of listings is incorrectly calculated. The second point to consider is how the listings will be generated, and they should come to their own conclusions. Our study, in this case, breaks the second criteria, resulting in a lower outcome. The listings used are search engine listings, which does not imply independence. Because most searchable databases are linked to one another, it is debatable whether dark web search engines are self-sufficient. When these two factors are combined in a real-world setting and several pairwise comparisons are performed, a more precise estimate of the deep web's site count can be calculated.

DEEP WEB SIZE ANALYSIS

It may appear unusual that estimations of the extent of the deep web are smaller than those of the surface web. The deep web makes up 95% of the internet, with the surface web accounting for only 5%. As a result, the deep web's actual size must be enormous. On the surface, web search engines like Google have already indexed billions of documents on the internet (web pages are also considered documents), representing less than 5% of the internet. According to some estimates, the deep web is 3.4 TB in size. However, given how difficult it is to determine the number of documents on the deep web, it would be interesting to learn how this estimate was made. A form of analysis is used to get at such data, primarily estimations.

Averages are used to get the approximate overall size of this internet section. The typical document and data storage sizes are used. The projected size of the deep web is then calculated using a multiplier. Because the figures are so large and calculating average sizes is difficult, evaluating sample site sizes takes a long time. There were two people in our last scenario.

A total of 100 sites made up the population. We multiply the average population size of a sample by a factor to get the overall population size of all 100 sites.

If the population of the darknet is believed to be 17,000 sites, this method can be used to determine its size. First and foremost, we must identify potential sample sites. With a 95% confidence interval, we can choose 100 websites at random. We can calculate the record or document count for each location using the 100 samples. The average page size for these sites could be calculated using the total number and size of documents. The total page size of a darknet site can be calculated using the average page size of the site. An average can be derived after establishing the overall size of each darknet site. The dark web is displayed in its entirety. Multiply the total number by the average size of a darknet site.

Darknet size = Average site size * no of darknet sites

ANALYZE THE TYPES OF CONTENT

The media has been chastised for portraying the deep web in a skewed light. They frequently portray it as a hazardous area of the internet where crimes occur. In their opinion, this is the region of the internet that no one should seek to enter for fear of being hacked or having their IP addresses stored and kidnappers led to them. Their skewed perception of the dark web originates from the fact that they only cover it when law enforcement authorities shut down drug markets, jail founders of illegal activity-related dark web websites, or shut down weapon-sale websites. They are rarely going to cover this facet of the internet in any other way. The dark web is, in fact, a large realm with a diverse range of content. It would be unjust to judge it solely based on media opinion. The dark web facilitates various activities; when reporting on this under-reported section of the internet, the media is either unaware of or deliberately overlooks several of them.

Finding out what kinds of content are available on the dark web, on the other hand, is a difficult undertaking. This is because the content is designed to be hidden. It is required to conduct some analysis to determine the content available on the dark web. Because the darknet is vast and no exact figure can be given, some cost-effective procedures must be employed to discover the many sorts of data and services available. Sampling is the most cost-effective method of examining the deep web's numerous content categories. If an estimated 17,000 darknet websites exist, a sample of 700 can be evaluated. The sort of data on each site may be evaluated using the samples, which can then categorize the darknet.

ANALYZE THE POPULARITY OF THE WEBSITE

The number of visits, page views, and references that a darknet website has can all determine its popularity. Alexa is a web-based system that regularly monitors page visits and evaluates dark websites. Alexa analyzes up to 71% of deep web pages and maintains their popularity. This is possible via an internet-based universal power function that can track page visitors (Figure 12.4).

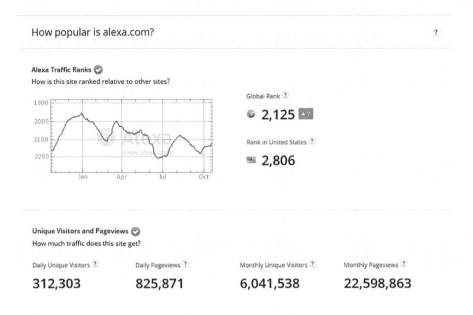

FIGURE 12.4   The user interfaces for Alexa.

LOG ANALYSIS

On the other hand, deep web analysis does not stop data retrieval. For nefarious purposes like hacking communication networks, the analysis is sometimes done. Contrary to popular belief, the link between Tor clients and darknet servers is not safe. It's possible to look at dark web traffic that comes in and goes out. The use of logs to help with deep web analysis has seen some conceptual advances.

The NetFlow protocol can theoretically be used to look into the shadow web. An attacker can look through the NetFlow logs of routers that function as direct Tor nodes or are close by to see what information they contain. It is possible to conduct dark web investigations using these logs, which are available within the Tor network and contain a wealth of information. Figure 12.5 shows the information found in NetFlow records:

Netflow analysis, which can look at and analyze traffic to and from Tor, may be able to deanonymize as many as 81% of dark web users. Cisco, the world's leading networking equipment and service supplier, commonly employs NetFlow technology. Network traffic entering and exiting Cisco routers is logged using NetFlow, and administrators primarily use NetFlow to monitor router congestion. Other than Cisco, many other companies use NetFlow as a networking device standard. There's a good chance you'll run into this technology while surfing the dark web.

In Chakravarty's research, NetFlow was used for darknet traffic analysis in the lab and in the real world. The study was the first of its type, and it used an analysis tool to learn about users who were viewing certain content on the dark web.

- Record number;

- Protocol version number;

- Time of stream head and stream end;

- Interfaces for inbound and outbound network traffic;

- Address of source and destination;

- The stream's bytes and packets count;

- IP protocol number;

- Port of source and destination;

- All flags observed during TCP connections;

- The value of Type of Service;

- Subnet masks for the source and destination networks.

- Gateway address;

FIGURE 12.5 NetFlow data types that can be accessed. A darknet is a place where anonymity ends, according to https://securelist.com/uncovering-tor users where anonymity stops/70673/

The investigation started by creating a disturbance on Tor's server side, then seeing where a comparable perturbation would appear on the client side. A statistical correlation was used to make the observation. The research yielded a 100% success rate in the lab, but when the same analysis technique was used in tge real world, only an 81% success rate was obtained. The study showed that the dark web isn't completely secure because it may be studied to deanonymize people and their consumption of material. The study found that a persistent Tor network attacker could cause disruption and observe traffic at the entrance and exit routes, respectively, to undertake an endless number of traffic analysis runs. This traffic analysis technique is depicted in Figure 12.6.

The investigation was carried out using a deep web server and website. A large file was downloaded from the server by website visitors. Injecting code on the server gave the researcher access to the router's NetFlow. The darknet server was relaying data over Tor's anonymous network when it fetched the NetFlow logs.

Correlation analysis would be useful in this situation. For several minutes, the end-user would continue to receive data from the server over the Tor network. Also, the router's NetFlow logs, through which the data was traveling, would be scrutinized during this time. Using the NetFlow logs of one router, the researcher could then connect traffic directed at an anonymous client. This would show the client's departure node and the kind of content they were attempting to access. Below is an additional illustration of how darknet research is done, as shown in Figure 12.7.

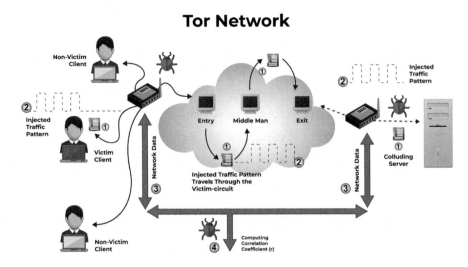

FIGURE 12.6 Analysis of Tor traffic using NetFlow data. While the server generates a typical traffic pattern 1, the client is compelled to download a file from it. Adversary gets server-to-client traffic flow data 3 and computes their coefficient four after the connection is terminated.

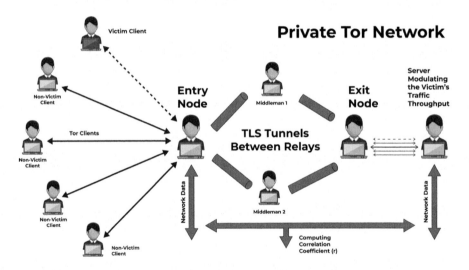

FIGURE 12.7 The log analysis is depicted as a diagram.

SUMMARY

Analyzing the deep web has been the subject of this chapter. Indexing and analyzing the deep web is difficult because of the differences between the surface and deep webs. This chapter has discussed how a typical web crawler, such as the kind used by surface web search engines, works. The basic nature and hyperlinked structure of surface web pages have been demonstrated to make them crawlable.

Once a crawler has finished crawling the current page's content, it will look for any linked pages and proceed.

In contrast, there is no hyperlinking on the deep web. As a result, darknet pages are difficult for standard search engines to analyze and index. As a result, research is done methodically. This is the first step: bringing the hidden content of the web to light. Finding it will require a thorough search and the extraction of relevant data, then selecting the most relevant data for analysis. This chapter covered a wide range of analysis methods used on deep websites. This includes looking at the content and popularity of a site, its size, the total number of websites, and even things like logs. Because log analysis is a unique method of investigation, it has received special consideration. To compromise darknet websites, this technique is used to break into them. According to the investigation, the compromised routers' NetFlow log files were used to conduct the investigation. Using an anonymous network, researchers could determine who was using it and what kinds of content they were accessing. On the dark web, these types of analyses are the most popular.

13 Information Extraction from Dark Web Contents and Logs

INTRODUCTION

Unstructured and semi-structured material abounds on the dark web, making analysis difficult. Traditional data analysis systems cannot handle unstructured data, and extracting information from this data type has historically been impossible. However, technological advancements have developed tools to analyze and extract usable information from unstructured data. This chapter will cover the following subjects and technologies, as well as their guidelines:

- Examining web contents and logs
- Policy guidelines for log analysis
- Log analysis tools
- Analyzing files
- Extracting information from unstructured data.

EXAMINING WEB CONTENT AND LOGS

The deep web has piqued many people's interest due to its hype in the past few years. Recent media coverage of security services shutting down darknet sites selling illegal goods has sparked renewed interest in the deep web's contents. As a result of the shutdowns, security agencies have set aside resources to prevent the re-emergence of known criminal sites on the dark web. Most researchers are working to decode the dark web and analyze its data. From blog posts to e-books to images, content analysis can decode the web's structure and meaning. Data can be text, images, audio, or short video clips. This investigation revealed data that can help both scientists and lawyers. Assessing the web's societal and economic relevance is also aided by it (Figure 13.1).

Content-wise, the deep web is more diverse than the surface web. Content analysis of deep web data helps categorize data for later research or application. Content analysis can reveal trends, usability, and data reliability.

Content analysis can be done manually or using specific technologies. This chapter will look at technologies used for deep web content and log analysis. We'll now examine the various ways in which extracted deep web data can be analyzed.

DOI: 10.1201/9781003404330-13

```
[Thu Nov 07 18:04:13 2019] [warn] RSA server certificate CommonName (CN) `bee-box.bwapp.local` does NOT match server name!?
[Thu Nov 07 18:04:13 2019] [notice] Apache/2.2.8 (Ubuntu) DAV/2 mod_fastcgi/2.4.6 PHP/5.2.4-2ubuntu5 with Suhosin-Patch mod_s
sl/2.2.8 OpenSSL/0.9.8g configured -- resuming normal operations
[Thu Nov 07 18:10:19 2019] [error] [client 192.168.254.1] File does not exist: /var/www/favicon.ico
[Thu Nov 07 18:10:19 2019] [error] [client 192.168.254.1] File does not exist: /var/www/favicon.ico
[Mon Nov 11 18:29:02 2019] [warn] RSA server certificate CommonName (CN) `bee-box.bwapp.local` does NOT match server name!?
[Mon Nov 11 18:29:02 2019] [notice] FastCGI: process manager initialized (pid 6815)
[Mon Nov 11 18:29:06 2019] [warn] RSA server certificate CommonName (CN) `bee-box.bwapp.local` does NOT match server name!?
[Mon Nov 11 18:29:06 2019] [notice] Apache/2.2.8 (Ubuntu) DAV/2 mod_fastcgi/2.4.6 PHP/5.2.4-2ubuntu5 with Suhosin-Patch mod_s
sl/2.2.8 OpenSSL/0.9.8g configured -- resuming normal operations
[Mon Nov 11 19:03:25 2019] [warn] RSA server certificate CommonName (CN) `bee-box.bwapp.local` does NOT match server name!?
[Mon Nov 11 19:03:25 2019] [notice] FastCGI: process manager initialized (pid 6652)
[Mon Nov 11 19:03:27 2019] [warn] RSA server certificate CommonName (CN) `bee-box.bwapp.local` does NOT match server name!?
[Mon Nov 11 19:03:27 2019] [notice] Apache/2.2.8 (Ubuntu) DAV/2 mod_fastcgi/2.4.6 PHP/5.2.4-2ubuntu5 with Suhosin-Patch mod_s
sl/2.2.8 OpenSSL/0.9.8g configured -- resuming normal operations
[Mon Nov 11 19:04:52 2019] [error] [client 192.168.254.1] File does not exist: /var/www/favicon.ico
[Mon Jan 06 17:01:59 2020] [warn] RSA server certificate CommonName (CN) `bee-box.bwapp.local` does NOT match server name!?
[Mon Jan 06 17:01:59 2020] [notice] FastCGI: process manager initialized (pid 6980)
[Mon Jan 06 17:02:05 2020] [warn] RSA server certificate CommonName (CN) `bee-box.bwapp.local` does NOT match server name!?
[Mon Jan 06 17:02:05 2020] [notice] Apache/2.2.8 (Ubuntu) DAV/2 mod_fastcgi/2.4.6 PHP/5.2.4-2ubuntu5 with Suhosin-Patch mod_s
sl/2.2.8 OpenSSL/0.9.8g configured -- resuming normal operations
```

FIGURE 13.1 A website log file.

WEB CONTENT ANALYSIS

The dark web provides an abundance of data, making it difficult to discern what is significant. The dark web lacks search engines, which are essential for evaluating web content. Comprehensive dark web analysis via search engines is impossible, even with current content crawling techniques. The internet's diverse data types, especially the dark web, necessitate more powerful content analysis techniques. A website log file is shown in Figure 13.1.

Intelligent technologies will analyze dark web content for study or legal purposes, interpreting domains and user statistics. The dark web's data can be accessed if user statistics are identified. Users prefer sites with appealing content, indicating that the dark websites they visit have something to offer. Further analysis of the most visited sites' logs may reveal a classification of the dark web's most popular sites. Thus, the analysis includes extracting information from data such as documents, web pages, user statistics, and deep web crawling. Analyzing unstructured data can turn it into structured data, and data dumps from the deep web can be collected and analyzed to make them more useful.

Deep web content analysis also includes usage. Consumption will increase on sites that interest them. Legal agencies can learn about new sites selling illegal substances using programs that track site visits. Even if the analysis does not immediately identify the location of visitors to a darknet site, it is vital for further action. For example, if a malware-selling website receives a lot of traffic, authorities can compromise it to arrest the site's administrators and users. Usage research can also help those building dark websites. Many services are available on the dark web, and as more people want to use them, they may prefer the busiest sites. They can use design elements from these websites to attract new customers. One of the dark web's most popular drug businesses, for example, had a fully customized layout similar to Amazon's. The site's rapid user acceptance led to other sites with similar aesthetics. Despite the sites being taken down by authorities, this is a good example of usage analysis on the dark web.

Deep web analysis can look at web structure, content, and usage. Web structure analysis examines a website's links that allow users to access additional information or move between web pages. It can use link analysis to compare data.

BENEFITS OF CONTENT ANALYSIS

Content analysis is frequently used to aid in forming opinions and conclusions. Researchers and law enforcement agencies, for example, conduct the research. Once the analysis is complete, useful patterns can be discovered and analyzed. These can assist law enforcement in determining which darknet domain names warrant further investigation. It's possible to identify fraudulent websites and content, anti-terrorist propaganda, illegal online stores, virus peddlers, and child pornography. For example, they could find out who is selling what and if they are cyberterrorists or virus sellers. Web content analysis reveals illegal content, while web structure analysis reveals the communication networks of dark web interest groups. Law enforcement can listen in or intercept communications if these networks are identified, leading to the capture of terrorists, drug traffickers, or other criminals. The content analysis framework is shown in Figure 13.2.

Analysis of web content can also assist researchers in locating new dark web research hotspots. Using content analysis to look for stolen data on the dark web may also be helpful. The dark web is where hackers resell or use the stolen data they've obtained. Deep web content analysis can help investigators find stolen data by identifying patterns in the website's content. Several companies already offer this service, which involves searching the dark web for stolen client. Solving larger problems like sensitive data being sold to criminals could be easier if this information is discovered early. The Swedish firm News Monitors is an example of this type. The company uses an artificial intelligence system to watch the dark web for signs of stolen personal information being sold there. When a match is made, the company notifies customers that they may have been affected by a data breach and encourages them to look into it. Using AI instead of traditional analysis methods makes monitoring and analysis easier (Figures 13.3 and 13.4).

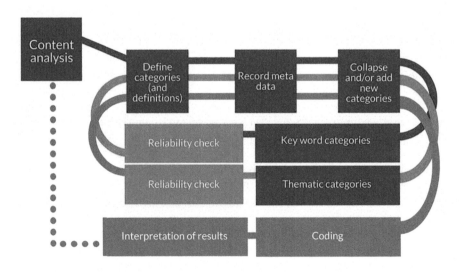

FIGURE 13.2   Content analysis framework.

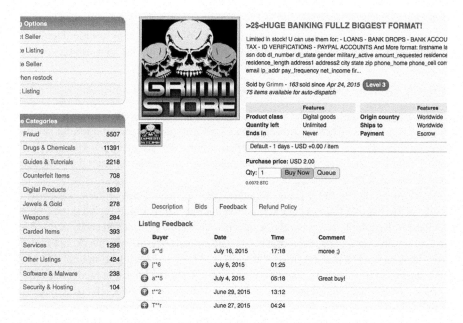

FIGURE 13.3   A dark website is offering access to a stolen bank database.

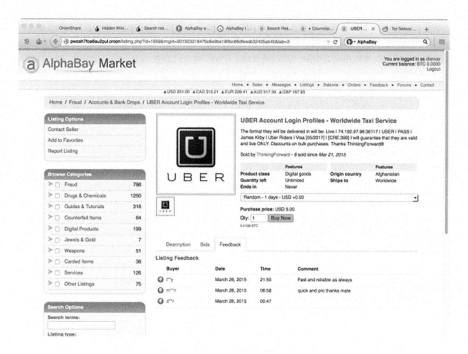

FIGURE 13.4   On the dark web, people are trying to resell allegedly stolen Uber records.

As a result, deep web content and log analysis can help reduce illicit deep web usage while uncovering new deep web services. When searching on the deep web, search engines only have access to a small portion of the total data available.

POLICY GUIDELINES FOR LOG ANALYSIS

An in-depth examination of data collected, processed, and stored in information systems is called log analysis. In this case, the dark web gathers information for several reasons. Educational, security, and informative purposes are just a few of them. Web content and log analysis are required because the information gathered for the reasons above must be fit for use.

We think it's fair to judge things based on their fairness. Each of these is described briefly in the list that follows. The terms "availability" and "reliability" are used interchangeably. Reliability refers to relying on a resource to be current and easily accessible. The dark web's data constantly changes because most logging systems do not update their databases. In contrast, automated tools make it challenging to update dynamic content. It must be manually maintained to keep most of the logged content accurate.

An authentic web record shows that the claim has been verified to be true. Because of the lack of this feature, It's challenging to develop systems or technology that can quickly validate dark web data. By definition, the deep web jeopardizes web content's integrity. However, there is content on the dark web intended to inform other users and the general public. This data is only helpful if the system fully confirms the source.

An item's accuracy and completeness as measured by the web record, log, or another piece of material. On the dark web, weblogs are likely to have inconsistencies and gaps in their content. On the other hand, a Weblogging strategy must accurately record all data accessed and collected.

Logs and web content that can be used have been gathered, processed, and interpreted with a specific end goal in mind. Dark web data analysis and exploitation would primarily aid in developing effective security techniques for computer systems. Using website content logs, the corporation should defend its systems better and make investment decisions.

RISK ASSESSMENT

Getting access to, mining, and logging dark web website material requires a careful risk assessment. The use of outdated, incomplete, incorrect, and erroneous information on the dark web poses a risk. Additionally, new landscapes must be examined when management contemplates a new product or service line. Because of risk analysis, the management is better equipped to deal with any surprises. Ensure that secure systems will be utilized to mine, analyze, and store data. The company must first conduct a risk analysis and mitigation procedure. The risk assessment framework is shown in Figure 13.5.

Gathering and analyzing data from the dark web carries several concerns, including gathering and analyzing data from the dark web carries several concerns, including:

- The legality of the data gathering and use.
- As a result, there has been a backlash and a loss of support from key stockholders.

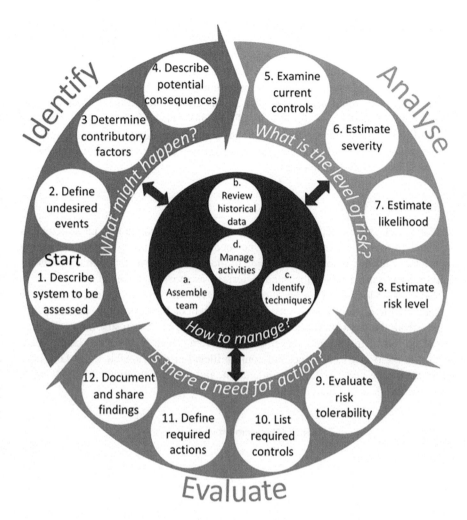

FIGURE 13.5   Risk assessment framework.

- Information that is false or untrustworthy is gathered.
- Expenses incurred as a result of a malware infection in the system.
- Negative media coverage.
- Collection of potentially malicious content that could bring down the systems that process the data.

RISK ASSESSMENT AND MITIGATION DUTIES AND RESPONSIBILITIES

When analyzing deep web information, the following are some of the methodologies that should be used:

Only those designated and educated to handle dark web content should scrape it from the web. Identifying and training users of dark web content scraped from the

organization's network is critical, as is providing a detailed description of what information was collected and stored about the dark web content scraped.

Taking care of the site, include who is in charge of site upgrades, removing old content, and ensuring that all data collected is accurate. The chief information officer is usually in charge of the company's information systems. When it comes to an organization's informational needs, this person is in charge. When using the dark web, she is solely responsible for the security of any information she obtains.

The legal department handles a company's legal requirements. There should be a team of lawyers in this case who are specifically trained to deal with legal issues relating to information technology.

RISK MITIGATION

This approach entails taking the required actions to guarantee that identified risks are handled and that these events do not occur in the future. The risk mitigation approaches outlined below address some of the main concerns listed in the previous section. Risk mitigation is illustrated pictorially as shown in Figure 13.6.

Retained for long-term storage on company systems with proper logs and website content documentation. The vast majority of content on the dark web is alive and will only be available for a short period before being removed. As a result, data collectors should be forced to take pictures of websites from which they scrape data as legal proof that the organization does not contain illegal or questionable data. The timestamp should be given special consideration, and this information should be saved alongside the recorded data for easy retrieval.

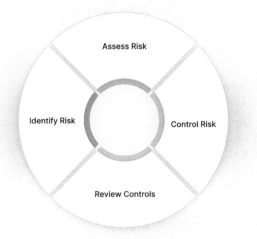

Risk Management Process

FIGURE 13.6 Risk mitigation.

Having legal mechanisms for scraping, collecting, processing, and storing information obtained on the dark web. Therefore, it is necessary to protect the systems used to access these dark websites by updating their security regularly to close any vulnerabilities and avoid the collection of harmful tools such as malware while scouring the area.

A continuously updated database is strongly recommended because of the industry's tremendous dynamism. A retention schedule that specifies a reasonable frequency for updating the database and adding new content would be acceptable. This should be done frequently to ensure that the system has the most up-to-date and accurate data.

There should be staff training to ensure that those in charge of gathering data can manage the operations from the dark web while gathering and storing the data.

WEB CONTENT LOGS ARE THE RESPONSIBILITY OF THE PERSON IN CHARGE OF THEM

Accessing and using content on the dark web carries several risks that must be managed with caution. If the information that has to be obtained is considered positive and useful to the organization, a specific team of authorized persons should be created to carry out the operation. Individuals will receive specialized training that is tailored to the organization's needs. Individuals using the dark web use the tools provided by the chief information officer to reduce their risk of being exposed. The tools will be pre-approved and vetted to ensure that they are perfect for obtaining information and safely transmitting it to storage systems. This team will teach the rest of the personnel outside their direct obligation to gather this material from the dark web.

The chosen team will be in charge of keeping the databases up-to-date and ensuring the accuracy and integrity of the data. This team should be composed of people from the information technology department, notably security officials. The strategist lowered the attack vectors, and by restricting who has access to the dark web on the company's behalf, risk factors can be reduced.

LOG ANALYSIS TOOLS

Clickstreams, IP addresses, deep web resources, and user profiles are extracted from blogs to better understand user behavior and hidden patterns. The deep web makes it difficult to access a wide range of logs for analysis. Because deep web users are anonymous, accessing and analyzing logs is difficult. However, a deep web page's popularity and content can reveal its user base. To know where deep web users are located, gather a representative sample to evaluate deep web users by language. Data from https://dnstats.net/ and other deep web tracking sites can also be used. This data can be used to identify popular deep web resources or activities. You can also collect deep web domains and look up their protocols to see their host resources.

Big data and standard database and data analysis technologies can't handle it. The deep web collects a lot of data, and new data analysis technologies are required. The new data-processing tools should allow concurrent access to data sets of varying sizes and complexity. To make better decisions, users should drill down into the source data.

MapReduce is a distributed data-processing framework that can handle enormous amounts of data. MapReduce implementations provide typical data analysis and calculations on computing clusters, and Hadoop is frequently used in conjunction with the MapReduce data analysis model. To evaluate unstructured data, the model employs mappers and reducers, and data collection and analysis are the responsibilities of mappers. The mappers then generate intermediate data, which is delivered to the reducers, who aggregate the data before understandably presenting the results.

MapReduce is a processing algorithm and program architecture that uses the Java programming language to allow distributed computing. MapReduce's algorithm is divided into two parts. The first goal is to convert data files into tuples composed of key/value pairs from a separate data set. The second task is to make the map's output and combine the data tuples into a smaller group (Figure 13.6).

It's easy to scale data processing across many nodes when using MapReduce to deal with large amounts of heterogeneous data. This can speed up the processing and analysis of large amounts of data.

Massive amounts of unstructured or structured data found on the deep web can be processed and analyzed using a variety of Hadoop-based solutions. Apache Pig, Apache Hive, Apache Flink, Jaql, Zookeeper, and Apache Flume. Apache Pig is a distributed computing solution for big data analytics. The Pig Latin programming language is used in this program, making it easier to do parallel programming, optimize it, and add functionality. In addition, Pig Latin is operating system-independent.

As a result, Apache Pig provides a high-level Hadoop language that makes the MapReduce framework easier to use. However, Apache Hive, part of the Hadoop ecosystem, can be used for data warehousing. It can store, query, and manage massive amounts of data. HiveQL, a querying language similar to SQL, is used to accomplish this. Thanks to the inclusion of Apache Hive in the ecosystem, Hadoop is now a data warehouse capable of processing SQL-style queries.

Apache Flink is a streaming data engine. This tool allows for distributed processing. A variety of Application Programming Interfaces can be used to feed data into Flink. Additionally, Flick uses its machine learning and graph libraries when working with stream flows. Apache Flume uses Apache Kafka, a Hadoop-based distributed and dependable system, to collect and deliver massive amounts of log data from applications. Flume, which collects, aggregates, and moves a lot of log data in and out of Hadoop, is used to move log data in and out of Hadoop (Figure 13.7).

Jaql is a declarative, functional language used in the Hadoop framework. Integration of the language into the Hadoop framework speeds up massive data processing. To take advantage of MapReduce's capabilities, the framework uses the language to break down high-level queries into low-level queries that can be processed simultaneously. This section will cover the final component of the Hadoop framework.

The Zookeeper, a centralized architecture with various services is provided by this component in the framework, allowing synchronization across a cluster of machines. The Zookeeper's services are vital for managing a large cluster of devices.

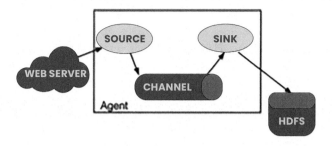

FIGURE 13.7   Apache flume as seen from above.

USING THE HADOOP FRAMEWORK HAS MANY BENEFITS

The Hadoop ecosystem offers several advantages for processing and analyzing deep web data. Hadoop sounds like a distributed database on a cluster of machines. This makes it possible to add or remove servers at any time. So the framework can detect and fix any hardware or system issue, allowing it to process and analyze large volumes of heterogeneous data confidently and efficiently. Existing data-processing systems can benefit from using Hadoop in conjunction with them to increase their processing power. This is due to Hadoop's versatility in dealing with a wide range of big data problems. For example, transaction processing can be carried out using existing systems such as relational databases, but Hadoop systems can take in data from various sources. Using Hadoop, you can combine and aggregate data from numerous sources to analyze it in depth. The lack of indexing and linkages means existing systems can connect to Hadoop systems for efficient data storage and processing. When data is saved in the Hadoop system, it doesn't matter how it is later analyzed because the system can manage it.

No matter how useful Hadoop may be for processing bid data, it can be a pain to set up, implement, and maintain. There is also a shortage of available job opportunities for qualified Hadoop specialists on the market today. Furthermore, Hadoop systems frequently require many computational resources, notably servers and other hardware. A final note on the computing overhead of Hadoop systems. The systems must support massive amounts of inter-node communication and synchronization to process and analyze large data.

ANALYZING FILES

For example, law enforcement can use deep weblogs to make strategic decisions. The most difficult thing is analyzing large amounts of unstructured or semi-structured data efficiently. These data types can be found on the deep web in various places, such as blog posts, chats, and social media feeds. Different Hadoop distributions can analyze this type of data. It is possible to process and analyze deep web data by utilizing Apache Flume to collect, combine, and move it into or out of the Hadoop distribution. Hortonworks Data Platform (HDP) and Amazon Elastic MapReduce are two commercial Hadoop distributions that analyze deep weblog posts.

Most Hadoop distributions, such as HDP, include Apache Flume, which collects log data from multiple applications and delivers it to the Hadoop framework. Flume is a resilient and fault-tolerant Hadoop distribution that is used by the majority of Hadoop distributions. Furthermore, the system is compatible with major operating systems like Linux, Windows, and OSX. There are three key parts of Apache Flume.

Amazon's Elastic MapReduce data analytics tool can analyze data. MapReduce queries can be handled quickly because they are built on the Hadoop's Distributed File System (HDFS) architecture. For example, the data analytics tool could be used for data warehousing or online indexing. Adopting Amazon Elastic MapReduce has the primary benefit of allowing users to lease cloud servers. As a result, configuring and using the tool will be a breeze. Furthermore, by renting the tool, a firm avoids the expense of purchasing fixed information technology assets.

Hadoop HDP uses YARN's centralized design for security and stability. The platform can deliver big data analytics on data-at-rest or real-time applications. Massive amounts of structured or unstructured data pulled from the deep web can be deployed, integrated, and dealt with using HDP. The HDP platform's key benefit is its open software development strategy. As a result, users can tailor certain platform features to their needs. There are no limitations to the use of the data analysis platform. In the HDP, the most important components are YARN and HDFS. The platform can allow users to handle multiple workloads simultaneously by using YARN. YARN manages resources and provides a pluggable architecture for data access. The platform relies on HDFS for scalable, fault-tolerant, and cost-effective data storage.

The following diagram shows how Teradata Aster, a commercial Hadoop solution, analyzes weblogs. For example, emails and weblogs are collected by Apache Flume, a Hadoop component shown in the diagram. For example, flume can collect data from email systems before storing it in a Hadoop-centric central data area. After being collected and stored in a centralized location, the data is analyzed. Getting the data ready for analysis is critical because it enables you to focus on the most important aspects of the study while also removing items that aren't of interest. Once the data has been cleaned, you'll have the information you need. It's important to choose features carefully when working with log files because they often contain information that's not useful when performing analysis. This process entails identifying the essential features and reducing the number of nonessential features to a manageable number. It'll be easier to analyze log files because they typically contain a lot of data and thus require a lot of processing resources.

HDFS is used to swiftly load and store any file format. HDFS is a component of Hadoop. This means that HDFS will be the foundation for widely disseminated file storage. Using Name Node and Data Node, we can accomplish this goal. The Name Node is responsible for delivering data services to collected data, while the Data Node provides distributed storage. HDFS enables parallel computing, which is necessary for large-scale data analysis and processing. The HDFS file system works by breaking up large files into smaller ones that can be studied more easily. After that, the data is dispersed among the cluster's nodes in small chunks. They are copied to each node, and in case of server failure, at least one duplicate is saved on a separate server.

The files are then processed to obtain the data and structure needed for analysis. SQL-MapReduce routines enable tokenization, email parsing, text analysis, and other processing. The MapReduce component detects patterns, correlations, or links between files. MapReduce employs computers to transfer data to DSS. Map, shuffle, and reduce are the next steps in processing the data. At the map stage, mappers process data, using software tools. The data is then stored in HDFS. The mapper function receives the input files line by line before dividing the data into smaller parts.

A new set of output files is created in HDFS from the input files during the reduction stage. Throughout the MapReduce process, Hadoop sends various MapReduce tasks to relevant computers in the cluster. There are a variety of data-passing operations that Hadoop manages. These operations include allocating task work to servers, confirming job completion, and moving data between server clusters after various data transfer duties; the data is gathered, processed, and sent to the Hadoop server. As a result, the MapReduce component of the Hadoop ecosystem is extensively used for text extraction from files to facilitate in-depth research.

UNSTRUCTURED DATA ANALYSIS AND INFORMATION EXTRACTION

Any information that doesn't conform to a specific format is unstructured data. There's a wealth of unstructured data on the deep web, such as logs, documents, photos, and videos, all stored in various repositories. Machines on the internet generate massive amounts of unstructured data. According to estimates, companies have about 20% of their data structured. The rest of the internet's content is completely random. Unstructured data analysis was previously impossible due to a lack of technology. A manual evaluation was the only option because of the limitations of human speed and processing power.

Thanks to technological advances, unstructured data may now be converted to structured data. When organized data is available, it can be used for various other purposes. It's critical for law firms, researchers, and even businesses to extract value from unstructured data. Extraction methods come in a wide variety of flavors, with varying degrees of success. You can also use text analytics, which concentrates on unstructured text because it is the most valuable type of data.

The advancements computing technologies that have enabled natural language processing (NLP) have made text analytics viable. Humans were frequently used to extract information from unstructured data because past technology could not. Their ability to grasp and synthesize natural language may extract some value from this data type. As a result, they could interpret the meaning of data in various formats and lengths. Computers now have this ability thanks to NLP. As a result, several jobs that formerly required a human to complete, such as data analysis, can now be automated. NLP was created to allow computers to understand natural language. NLP is widely employed today as evidenced by the several voice assistants that have been developed. Text analysis uses NLP and statistical approaches to extract information from unstructured data. As a result of NLP, computers can better understand who did what, when, why, and how.

Text analytics can look for connections between seemingly unrelated pieces of data. NLP is commonly used in the software and hardware industries to promote their wares, to give you an idea. For example, it is possible to use NLP to determine the connection between declining sales of a program and user feedback. There is no direct link between the two datasets, but NLP can identify negative customer feedback and link it to error reports and declining sales. Unstructured data dumps can contain various types of data that text analytics can match to create a well-organized and useful piece of deep web data.

Even though NLP excels at processing unstructured data, it still requires some human input. As a result, it can't work completely because human intelligence is required for some procedures. For example, a human must set up the unstructured data characterization settings. In some circumstances, a person must define the associations that NLP will search for. A taxonomy is embedded into text analytics. It functions as a word dictionary, assisting NLP in comprehending better words in data chunks. To include more categories for analysis, the taxonomy can be tweaked. If the unstructured data dump contains medicine names and buyer remarks, the NLP can be given a taxonomy that includes common buyer comments such as "this is nice stuff," "I trust this vendor," and others. They can help NLP analyze data streams and extract bits that include taxonomic ideas and their relationships. The buyer and seller, for example, could be mentioned in remark metadata.

After NLP or other similarly capable tools have completed their analysis, human intelligence must interpret the data. It is believed that the outcomes of unstructured data analysis should not be taken as 100% accurate. Even if there are certain concerns with accuracy, NLP can produce highly accurate results.

Be employed in decision-making. Structured data outputs, on the other hand, can be changed by humans to improve accuracy. Negative sarcasm, which hides a negative meaning beneath a funny comment, is one of the things that humans excel at understanding.

Text analytics is popular outside the deep web. Companies that mine social media data have used it extensively. This app collects and analyzes social media posts and comments that mention a company. A company's brand benefits from real-time data collection and analysis. If a negative comment is received, the business may investigate the matter. Politicians and corporations may benefit from social media mining, particularly during election seasons. Social media analytics companies can assess public opinion on a politician's candidacy and chances of winning. Customers' feedback is also analyzed using text analytics.

Given that humans cannot read all comments, NLP is commonly used to sort them into positive and negative responses. A company's brand benefits from real-time data collection and analysis. If a negative comment is received, the business may investigate the matter. Politicians and corporations may benefit from social media mining, particularly during election seasons. Social media analytics companies can assess public opinion on a politician's candidacy and chances of winning. These examples show how NLP can be used to analyze unstructured data. Unstructured social media streams Website feedback is also unstructured. Insurers collect semi-structured or unstructured data from various sources. However, NLP can make sense of all of these data. It shows how to evaluate unstructured deep web content.

A company's brand benefits from real-time data collection and analysis. If a negative comment is received, the business may investigate the matter. Politicians and corporations may benefit from social media mining, particularly during election seasons. Social media analytics companies can assess public opinion on a politician's candidacy and chances of winning.

SUMMARY

This chapter focuses on extracting meaningful information from unstructured data, which makes up a large portion of the deep web. Background: Traditional analysis methods failed to analyze the dark web's unstructured content. This chapter examined how NLP tools analyze web content. Human-like text software for synthesis, as a result, they can link data sets that appear to be unconnected. Web content analysis, deep web usage, and web structure have been explored. In addition, policy requirements for harvesting and analyzing unstructured content from the deep web are discussed in this chapter. Because the information kept on the dark web is supposed to be concealed from public access, extracting and analyzing it may have legal implications. This chapter examines the risks and mitigations of handling deep web data. This chapter examined powerful systems for analyzing large amounts of data, including big data and log analysis tools. Structured, semi-structured, and unstructured data all make up big data. As a result, big data tools can deal with unstructured data. The process of analyzing unstructured data has been clearly outlined. Finally, the chapter examined unstructured web content using text analytics. The NLP-based tool can analyze large amounts of data for the deep web. The following chapter will look at deep web forensics and various methods used to perform forensics on the deep web.

14 Dark Web Forensics

INTRODUCTION

The well-known dark web is linked to various illegal and terrorist activities. Given Tor's mostly anonymous design, a cybercriminal's base of operations and communication is likely to be on it. Everything from drugs to weapons to hitmen, hackers, malware, stolen data, and terrorist communication has been sold on the dark web. The notion that law enforcement will not detect criminal activity on the dark web is widely held. There are no regulatory bodies to prevent criminal activity and illegal goods on the dark web. Businesses are still concerned about the dark web's existence and the theft and sale of sensitive data.

However, it is an exaggeration to claim that the dark web is beyond the reach of the law. The dark web is also not completely anonymous, which is a myth. Several illegal dark web marketplaces have been shut down recently, demonstrating that law enforcement is still catching up with darknet criminals. Ross Ulbricht, the suspected inventor of the Silk Road 2 marketplace, is a good example. Ross Ulbricht was sentenced to life in prison for his dark web activity. This indicates there is no such thing as perfect anonymity or a lack of accountability in this internet section. This chapter will address the forensic investigation features of the dark web and strategies for defeating them. It will do so in the following areas:

- The basics of forensic.
- The dark web's crypto market and cryptocurrencies.
- Forensic investigation scope and models Forensic toolkits (FTKs) anti-forensic techniques.

THE BASICS OF FORENSIC

The dark web may be unregulated due to all of the illegal activities. While this is somewhat true, law enforcement authorities are more successful in investigating and apprehending the major suspects behind the unlawful goods and services provided on the dark web. By 2015, 312 people had been arrested for darknet market crimes. The sale of drugs, guns, child pornography, and malware was unlawful. The following chart shows the number of people arrested in each market (Table 14.1).

There were 162 people arrested in total, 162 of whom were buyers and 116 of whom were sellers. Ten black market workers and four market owners were also detained. This arrest of dark web purchasers shows that law enforcement is interested in those who are selling illegal goods and those who are purchasing them. When using darknet marketplaces to buy weapons from a seller in the United States, four people were arrested in Australia. Denmark's cops claim to have taken down two infamous dark web drug traffickers. The same drug sellers exploited Silk Road

DOI: 10.1201/9781003404330-14

TABLE 14.1
On the Dark Web, Users Have Been Arrested

Marketplace	No. of Arrests
Sheep	3
Utopia	5
BMR	9
Hydra	1
Agora	6
Evolution	27
Silk Road 1	140
Silk Road 2	85

1, 2, and 3, and Agora and Evolution. According to the European Union, around ten people who bought weapons in the region have been arrested. After being caught making and selling fake currency, an American man was extradited to the United States.

He had relocated to the African country, where he was arrested and deported to face charges in the United States due to an undercover sting operation.

An increase in the number of high-profile arrests has recently occurred in the United States. In the middle of 2014, Weaponsguy, a well-known online seller of weapons, had many unhappy customers who complained that their orders had not yet arrived. According to media reports, authorities in the United States were able to apprehend him and use his account to investigate the activities of other sellers and buyers. Most of the arrests involving weapons were made due to police departments using his account to set up traps. After being found buying and peddling drugs on the dark web, a college student was arrested in May of 2015. Seizures were discovered in his accounts, where his deposits were being used mainly to purchase cryptocurrency, resulting in his arrest after suspicious activity was discovered.

Since the publication of this article, more people have been arrested. As a result, the underbelly of the dark web has been exposed. It emphasizes the importance of forensic evidence in dark web criminal investigations and lawsuits. Dark web forensics demands more complicated techniques to collect evidence or track criminals. As a result, most darknets made it difficult to track who used them and what sites they visited. Since the introduction of cryptocurrency, following money trails has become more difficult. Investigators are forced to work longer hours to find or track down criminals operating on the dark web.

Dark web forensics is difficult due to the inability to locate and track dark web users. Despite its insecurity, the dark web will remain anonymous. As a result, the anonymity barrier must be broken to reach the intended recipients. If you wear this cloak, no one will know where you are or what you are doing online. Legal agencies must first establish jurisdiction to conduct an investigation, which can only be done without a physical location. The crimes committed by darknet market targets may be known to law enforcement, but locating them is difficult.

Law enforcement authorities such as the National Security Agency (NSA) and the Federal Bureau of Investigation (FBI) took their time to discover vulnerabilities in the dark web's architecture that allowed them to collect data on dark web users for forensic investigations. Even when criminals try to break the law, despite the displeasure of dark web users, it is necessary to enforce the law. The FBI and NSA have utilized browser weaknesses to acquire evidence and capture offenders. Legal authorities have devised new data collection methods to collect information on individual users and the traffic flowing through dark networks to their computers. Security agencies have set up rogue entry and exit nodes on the dark web to collect traffic entering and exiting. Criminals can now be tracked down on the dark web by law enforcement. Users of the dark web can no longer assume that their actions will go unpunished because of their location.

Even if police departments lack the essential equipment, the dark web can help identify criminals. They have the resources, and professionals are willing to work for a fee to alert law enforcement to criminals operating on the dark web. Individual hacker groups also target darknet websites believed to be involved in criminal activity. Because they let child pornographic sites use their servers, vigilantes recently attacked websites hosted by Freedom Hosting. For example, all it takes is finding willing hands to perform digital forensic analysis to gather evidence about dark web criminals.

THE DARK WEB'S CRYPTO MARKET AND CRYPTOCURRENCIES

You'll find the criminal if you follow the money. For law enforcement agencies, this has been standard operating procedure. When banks were the primary means of transferring funds, this was especially effective. Because banks are regulated and supervised, law enforcement agencies can simply seek court orders asking for more information about the accounts that received the money in a money trail. As a result, the task was to determine who had been paid the money, which would reveal a great deal more about the crime (Figure 14.1).

However, in 2009, the introduction of digital money Bitcoin has transformed the criminal justice system. Using this coin ensured the privacy of every user. If money is converted to Bitcoin and swapped, no one will know who do it. Criminals may return stolen money to avoid getting caught. As a result, the dark web's favorite money, bitcoin, was born. Around this time, many new websites surfaced, many of which offered questionable goods and services in exchange for Bitcoin. Even today, the dark web's financial transactions are conducted entirely in bitcoins. Cryptocurrencies have been used in global strikes in the past. The ransomware attack of 2017 encrypts it and requests a ransom payment to decrypt the machine. The ransom demanded Bitcoin as a payment method. Other types of ransomware encrypt systems and demand payment in Bitcoin or other cryptocurrencies.

Many criminal underground markets on the dark web only accept cryptocurrency payments. For example, to obtain fake IDs and passports, the customer must pay the supplier in Bitcoin. You can do more than just this, and no one uses cash in these markets for fear of being identified by cops (Figure 14.2).

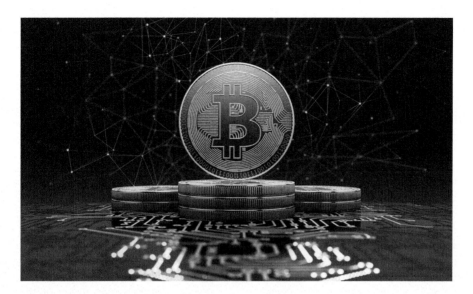

FIGURE 14.1   Bitcoin logo.

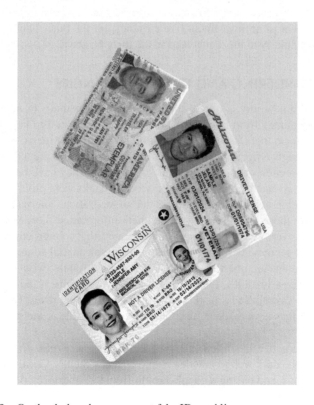

FIGURE 14.2   On the dark web, you can get fake IDs and licenses.

The dark web loves cryptocurrencies for a variety of reasons. The first thing to consider is anonymity. Cryptocurrency relies on blockchain technology to conduct transactions using each user's wallet. The FBI cannot raid particular servers and acquire evidence to incriminate users who have given or received money using cryptocurrency. The transaction's parties' names are not recorded. Money is simply taken from or added to a cryptocurrency wallet without any parties involved. Second, money transfers made with cryptocurrency cannot be reversed. As a result, unlike with the transfer of actual money through services like PayPal, a seller is protected to the extent that a rogue buyer will not be able to reverse a transaction.

The ease with which cryptocurrencies can be laundered is the third reason for their widespread use on the dark web. We'll cover this in more detail later. Fourth, bitcoin transactions do not incur the same fees as bank transfers, and customers are drawn to them because the fees are kept to a minimum.

Sellers prefer cryptocurrencies to fiat currencies, last but not least, because the value of fiat currencies fluctuates. When the value of cryptocurrencies increased to the point where ordinary people began to invest in them, it was considered a breakthrough. As a precaution against future price increases, they could convert their fiat currency to cryptocurrency in advance. The value of most cryptocurrencies, on the other hand, began to decline in January. Since then, the value of bitcoin, the dark web's preferred cryptocurrency, has fallen from $20,000 to $9,000 and continues to decrease. Payment in an investment-like currency, on the other hand, is extremely appealing, particularly to those involved in the dirty business.

MONEY LAUNDERING AND CRYPTOCURRENCIES

Cash collected unlawfully is one of the most common methods of money laundering. Acquiring money from overseas banks or businesses used to be a hassle. This gave the impression that the funds were not obtained through illegal means. Money laundering through Swiss banks is prevalent. Swiss banks are known for their secrecy and protection of foreign accounts. As a result, they have been used as tax havens and money-laundering hotspots. Previously, banks were prohibited from disclosing information about their customers due to legislation. International pressure has been put on these institutions to make client information more transparent and compliant. However, Swiss regulations are adamant that foreign clients be treated with the utmost secrecy. Foreign clients depositing substantial sums of money into Swiss bank accounts are questioned less. Tax evasion through Swiss banks has been around since the early 1900s. During WWI and WWII, affluent individuals sought to relocate their cash to Swiss bank accounts to avoid paying taxes. However, Swiss financial authorities have made money laundering impossible or much more difficult (Figure 14.3).

The best alternative has filled this void and is now accessible to everyone. It is possible to use the dark web to launder cryptocurrency money. Criminals, terrorists, corrupt politicians, and business people benefit from these services. Various types of money-laundering activities will be discussed in this section.

When cybercriminals collect their stolen money, the first laundering service is offered. For example, the WannaCry ransomware developers got $300 or $600 from

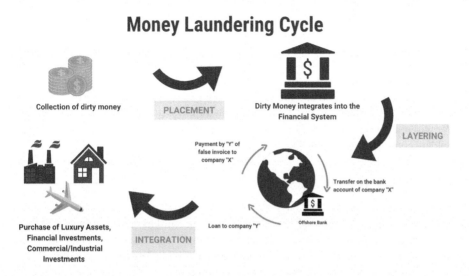

FIGURE 14.3 A conventional method of money laundering.

victims who paid the ransom to recover access to their data. These hackers are cautious by delaying the withdrawal of any Bitcoin payments they've received. Contrary to popular belief, Bitcoin transactions are not anonymous. Finding them won't be difficult; getting them will be. These hackers are likely to be tracked down, given the attention from law enforcement agencies worldwide. As a result, they were compelled to go to greater lengths to obscure their identities. Darknet websites provide cybercriminals with money-laundering services. Hackers have used them to improve their heisting skills because they are a part of the shadow economy. The final step in the underground economy is laundering as a service, in which dirty money obtained through criminal activity is sanitized and made usable without the risk of being apprehended.

Laundry is a service that cashiers can provide. On behalf of cryptocurrency holders, these are the people who exchange cryptocurrencies for fiat currencies. They are believed to have large sums of money, which they will return to "dirty" cryptocurrency holders. They can give cash, luxury cars, and valuable objects that can be sold to recoup funds. Cashiers can collect huge sums of clean cash through covert methods. They may, for example, have contacts in legitimate banks who can set up phony accounts to deposit and withdraw money. False identification papers can also be used to open bogus bank accounts. If they accept filthy cryptocurrencies on any website that converts them to real money, they can send the converted amounts to the fake bank account. If a trail is successfully followed from one cryptocurrency to another, the fake account will be the only thing visible at the end of the day.

In the second category, the person is in charge of everything. But it's riskier due to the money trail's proximity. As a result, someone uses a series of cryptocurrency converters to perform anonymous transactions on the dark web. These items will be delivered and resold in person or on the cryptocurrency market via a separate account and wallet. You can buy things on the dark web or at physical venues that accept

Bitcoin. They can then resell these items and deposit the proceeds into an unrelated cryptocurrency wallet, Y. As a result, tracing the dirty money will be difficult and time-consuming. Due to the decentralized nature of these transactions, records are scarce. Some people prefer to convert their cryptocurrencies in bits to fiat currency and believe they will not be traced. On the other hand, those who launder money are very good at what they do and are rarely caught unless they make a mistake.

A few other options are available to people looking to clean up their dirty money. We will not categorize them as types of laundering because innocent cryptocurrency holders could still use them. The following are some of them:

ATMs FOR BITCOIN

These are Bitcoin ATMs that are privately owned and that Bitcoin holders who want to remain anonymous prefer. These ATMs function similarly to traditional ATMs in that they exchange Bitcoins for cash without requiring the user's personal information. Their objective is to keep customer information as private as possible. Most Know Your Customer (KYC) laws are disregarded to accomplish this. Notably, it is more expensive than other Bitcoin exchangers, at roughly 15% of the money traded.

BITCOIN MIXERS

Examining transactions on the public ledger is one way to track Bitcoin transactions. If wallet X received $5,000 while wallet Y lost $5,000 in a short time, the owners of wallets X and Y were transacting. As a result, more investigation into these transacting parties may be possible. To fill this void, Bitcoin mixers have arrived. They're used to hide transactions from outsiders, making it nearly impossible to figure out who's doing what. For example, if wallet X held $5,000 in Bitcoin, the recipient might not get it all at once; the Bitcoin mixer can split the funds, convert them to other currencies, buy new currencies, and sell them before distributing them gradually. As a result, the source and receiver of funds are not connected. However, Bitcoin mixers are expensive, costing up to 15% of the amount combined.

MONERO

Concerns regarding Bitcoin transactions' privacy and distributed ledger technology arose after the arrest of Silk Road 2 creator Ross Ulbricht. As a result, money launderers opted for more anonymous cryptocurrencies. Monero has seen a surge in popularity on the dark web, owing to its built-in tumbling/mixing feature. As a result, Monero transactions are more anonymous than Bitcoin transactions. Monero has been accepted alongside Bitcoin on several exchanges. As a result of this growth, Numerous anonymous cryptocurrencies have been created and will continue to be created. Like DASH and Cryptonite, other anonymous altcoins might reassure users of their privacy by making it harder to trace a logical money trail. These present substantial challenges to forensic investigators, especially when utilized for criminal objectives.

BITCOIN PROPERTY EXCHANGES

As a result of the increased public adoption of cryptocurrency, many businesses now accept Bitcoin as a form of payment. Amazon.com was expected to adopt Bitcoin shortly, but hopes have been dashed due to the e-commerce giant's lack of confirmation. Those hopes were entirely speculative, based on the assumption that widespread adoption would significantly increase Bitcoin's value. However, other businesses do not intend to accept cryptocurrency as payment. Purse.io is a platform where users may trade Bitcoin for items. Amazon uses the internet service to take Bitcoins from customers who want to buy something with Bitcoin. For example, a buyer who wishes to pay with Bitcoin for a $2,000 television will be unable to do so. Purse.io, on the other hand, will accept Bitcoin and conduct Amazon transactions with real money rather than Bitcoin. The buyer ships or collects the items after purse.io completes the transaction. The Bitcoin will not have been sent yet by the buyer. Purse.io continues to sell Bitcoin. As a result, they will obtain the Bitcoin buyer's address(es) and provide them to the Amazon buyer to transfer the cryptocurrency.

As a result, once the Amazon customer receives the goods, purse.io will ensure that Bitcoins are sent to a willing buyer. A fee will be charged to the willing buyer for receiving Bitcoin anonymously and without having to visit a Bitcoin exchange platform. This is a cost-effective business model because it allows Bitcoin owners to purchase without converting their currency to fiat. On the other hand, a money launderer could take advantage of this. They could make a wish list and send it to purse.io, knowing that they would be reimbursed. The laundering process will be nearly complete once the items are delivered and the funds are transferred to cryptocurrency buyers. Reselling Amazon items on other platforms, such as eBay, is all that is required.

SCHEMES FOR LAUNDERING CRYPTOCURRENCY EXPOSED

BITCOIN-LAUNDERING ARRESTS

In 2016, an arrest warrant was issued for a gang of early-twenties men on suspicion of money laundering. They were found to have laundered up to $22 in Bitcoin from darknet websites as the proceeds of drug deals. As a result, darknet sellers are likely to trust these cashiers to clean up their dirty money. During their arrests, cops confiscated luxury cars and substantial sums of cash, which they used to launder money. What makes them even more intriguing is that they were discovered due to a mistake. They used to deposit large sums of money into their bank accounts and then remove them quickly. As a result, they were discovered due to their sloppy deposit and withdrawal practices rather than a cash trail. Police would be notified, and suspicious account holders would be arrested if they created fake bank accounts using forged identification documents, but that would be the end of the matter. No one could be arrested since the purportedly suspicious bank accounts were registered in the names of nonexistent people. However, they were imprisoned at such a young age due to careless mistakes (Figure 14.4).

Ten men have been arrested in the Netherlands on suspicion of laundering money from criminal sales on the Dark Web using Bitcoin.

The Dutch Fiscal Information and Investigation Service and the Public Prosecutor's Office raided 15 houses around the country, arresting ten young men in their early twenties.

After banks reported big cash deposits swiftly removed via ATMs, police recovered cash, expensive cars, and ingredients to produce ecstasy.

FIGURE 14.4 Two young men were arrested for a Bitcoin-laundering operation (https://zdnet.com/article/arrests-made-over-bitcoin-laundering-scheme-dark-web-drug-deals/).

BTC-e

A Russian guy faces up to 55 years in prison if convicted of large-scale Bitcoin laundering. A Russian was identified as the brains behind a lucrative Bitcoin-laundering scheme that netted criminals involved in computer hacking and drug trafficking $4 billion. A Greek beach hotel was where the man was arrested while conducting business. Founded in 2011, the BTC-e website is now a major Bitcoin trading platform run by Vinnik. But BTC-e was secretly laundering money for dark web clients. From one point of view, the exchange platform was an ideal business because it served as a hub for exchanging digital and fiat currencies. As a result, the owner of this site had the opportunity to provide laundering services using the currencies that his customers had already given him. According to reports, most of the sites' revenues came from money laundering rather than cryptocurrency exchanges.

Money laundering is a two-step process. Thus, investigators couldn't link BTC-e to it. BTC-e became a victim in two steps. Step 1: Get money from the dark web to launder. These were stolen from drug dealers, child pornographers, and cryptocurrency users. These were deposited into Mt. Gox's account, under Mr. Vinnik's control. It's possible Mr. Vinnik hacked Mt. Gox, another exchange platform, and took control of it to launder money. Mt. Gox would exchange cryptocurrencies for cash for BTC-e customers through a series of transactions with BTC-e.

With the assistance of Greek authorities, forensic investigators gathered evidence against Mr. Vinnik before apprehending him. This August, Mr. Vinnik is accused of money laundering and financial fraud. Prosecutors said cybercriminals regularly utilized Mr. Vinnik's platform to launder money. There was supposed to be a chat platform on the website where people could openly discuss how to make money in business, and customer service would offer advice on how to get their money started. In this case, the police can interpret the false websites and accounts, bringing the actual criminals to jail. Contrary to popular belief, these cases demonstrate that forensics teams can penetrate the anonymity provided by cryptocurrencies and uncover criminals.

MODELS AND SCOPE OF FORENSIC INVESTIGATIONS

Collecting evidence is crucial in forensics. In some cases, it could be used to track down and prosecute a deep web cybercriminal or child pornographer. On the dark web, gathering evidence is much more difficult and time-consuming than in other places. Law enforcement agencies will be unable to act until they can verify a criminal's real-life identity, regardless of how well-known they are on the dark web. They will arrest the suspect once they have enough evidence to convict him. If law enforcement has broken into an illegal market, it will not be shut down immediately. They have no limit on how much time they can spend gathering evidence or revealing the identities of other marketplace participants. Some vendors may even be able to participate in drug sales. They can spend a lot of money on the dark web to find a wanted suspect's real name or location. The forensic investigation model is shown in Figure 14.5.

Consider Ross Ulbricht's arrest, alias Dread Pirate Roberts, the infamous founder of Silk Road 2. The US Drug Enforcement Administration initially connected him to Dread Pirate Roberts through a Silk Road case under investigation. Criminal justice investigators were tasked with tracing the distribution of illegal drugs to many people and determining who was responsible. On the other hand, Ulbricht's association with the Dread Pirate Roberts was not gratuitous. Due to Tor's anonymity, investigators had

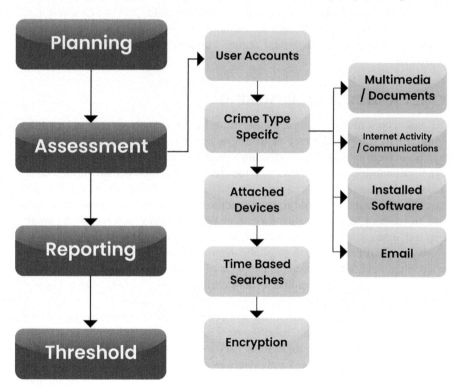

FIGURE 14.5 Forensic investigation model (abstract).

difficulty cracking the Silk Road case. They located a Silk Road 2 user named Altoid. As a result, the argument for determining who used this username was compelling. When they could not locate it elsewhere, they turned to a programming forum, where the user had posted a request for coding assistance. Fortunately or unfortunately, Altoid disclosed his true identity in this forum post via his email address. The investigators sought to locate Altoid, who had revealed his true identity as Ross Ulbricht. His actions on the Silk Road website, where he was the administrator, were monitored. According to Ulbricht's defense in court, the Dread Pirate Roberts admin account was shared and passed down by several individuals. This claim could have been fatal to the prosecution's case had additional evidence not been gathered. Ulbricht was, however, connected to Dread Pirate Roberts via forensically gathered digital evidence.

Forensic investigations used to successfully prosecute offenders hiding on the dark web can be learned from Ross Ulbricht's case. The parts that follow elaborate on the forensics and processes.

SCOPE

A wide range of digital forensics techniques is available on the dark web. It is necessary to include forensics in all aspects of the investigation, including policies and processes, evidence collection, assessment, analysis, and reporting. As a result, the scope of a forensic inquiry dictates the methods to be followed. The flowchart below depicts the general procedures used during a forensic inquiry. It is not meant to be exhaustive.

POLICY AND PROCEDURE MAKING

The dark web forensics exercise entails examining extremely private and confidential information. This data may be irretrievable if lost. Therefore, forensic exercises must be treated individually to guarantee proper evidence collection and handling. As a result, most forensics begins with the creation of comprehensive guidelines and procedures that investigators can use as a starting point. To ensure the validity of the data, these procedures should recover specific evidence and document their activities. Prosecutors frequently turn to seasoned cybersecurity experts when pursuing deep web cases. It's up to these experts to decide whether they go along for the ride or just provide training on how to go about gathering evidence on their evidence collected in the field, where untrained people may be present, is useful in this situation. When collecting evidence online, cybersecurity experts are still useful. They can provide a list of programs that can be used to gather evidence.

Policies and procedures should include codifying evidence construction actions, such as looking for and safely handling retrieved evidence. Before the investigation can begin, it is necessary to understand the case's facts and the permitted investigative actions. Only warrants and authorizations can be used to collect certain types of evidence. In the absence of such evidence, a defense lawyer may persuade the judge to dismiss the case. When Ross Ulbricht's case was appealed, his defense team used a similar strategy. They claimed that the seizure of Ulbricht's internet traffic was unconstitutional because it was carried out without a warrant or any other evidence

of probable cause. The defense had high hopes for the appeal, even though it was denied. Before beginning an investigation, make sure warranties and authorizations are understood to avoid wasting important evidence.

EVIDENCE ASSESSMENT

Any forensic investigation should begin with a review of the evidence that may be collected. It is critical to comprehend these types of case specifics. Detectives must anticipate collecting and evaluating evidence from hard drives, emails, social media, and other data storage sites to prove that person X committed crimes like identity theft. Their responsibility must also include analyzing whether the information received from such sources can perpetuate the specific crime. Before investigators can persuade people to give personal information, they must first determine the type of evidence they seek. They must also know how to protect such evidence. The sources' integrity is also examined to prevent inappropriate collection or storage from being thrown out of court.

Investigators in Ross Ulbricht's case discovered crucial evidence on his laptop. It was necessary to locate him while he was connected to the Silk Road site. That's why they pretended to be members to ask for favors. Ils pounced on him when he was logged into a Silk Road member account. Then they could gather and preserve the proof they needed. They did a thorough evidence review before collecting with surgical precision.

EVIDENCE ACQUISITION

Because evidence is acquired here, it's a crucial step in the forensic procedure. Preventing evidence destruction during purchase is accomplished through diligence and extreme care. To put things in perspective, consider the Ulbricht case's evidence-gathering strategy. He had already been pulled out of a library by investigators. He registered on the Silk Road website a short time later. The investigators might either make a huge discovery or lose everything at this critical juncture. If they charged at him, he might have set the auto-erase feature on his laptop. That would defeat the purpose of the investigations, which is to bring him to justice and teach others a lesson. As a result, they acted like a feuding couple inside the lab. It took Ulbricht some time to grasp the gravity of the situation. Not without erasing everything on his laptop, including his information. A flash stick containing special software was used to extract data from Ulbricht's computer as soon as he was apprehended. We think that was an excellent illustration of how evidence could be acquired.

Whatever the case may be, the purchasing procedure has been meticulous. Additionally, paperwork is required for judicial purposes and acquiring proof. Evidence collection necessitates documentation at every stage. Do not forget to keep track of the gear and software you're working with. Data must be obtained from sources using proven procedures to avoid data loss or destruction. The guidelines for evidence reservation should be followed once the evidence has been received. Evidence theft can be prevented by taking extra steps like immediately copying and forwarding evidence to investigators.

The most important thing is to ensure that all evidence is gathered legally. For example, a court will throw out data obtained through illegal means. This is why it's crucial to have proof on hand to show the judge how each item was found.

EXAMINATION OF EVIDENCE

To ensure the success of possible evidence investigations, retrieval, copying, and storage must be standardized. Whenever possible, data collected during investigations is archived. There's also a list of data analysis methodologies. Software is a strategy. Before apprehending Ross Ulbricht, authorities would have been required to recover deleted material from his computer. Even if he had his computer locked, they could have accessed it without his password. Fortunately, there is software that can help you avoid this. Investigators don't always have to rely on software to find critical information. Look for recent data in the file metadata, such as authors and last modification dates. Even though this case has nothing to do with the Dark Web, it is extremely relevant to today's discussion. Mr. Higinio Ochoa was a member of the anonymous hacker group in 2012. His hacker alias was Cabin Cr3w, and he was well-known for his work hacking police databases. He once posted a bikini photo of his girlfriend on a police database and claimed to have pawned her as payment for their time. Regrettably, he was unable to scrape image metadata. The police later used this metadata to track down and arrest Mr. Ochoa, the hacker. He is not allowed to use the internet as a condition of his release. This example shows how easily accessible data, such as file metadata, can be used in court as evidence. The chances of discovering useful information are high because criminals frequently leave traces of their activities.

Investigators can use various techniques to locate specific data on various media types. For example, Dread Pirate Roberts and Ross Ulbricht were only linked by the username Altoid. They looked for Altoid's usage on the internet and found a forum post with his email address and true name. Use one of the search techniques available on Google to find a specific information. Investigators can use certain techniques to search for relevant files or programs hidden on a computer.

Investigating file names can also aid in the analysis of evidence. Analyzing the files on a server can reveal the directories on the internet or dark web where the data is stored. This makes it easier for investigators to locate other relevant files in the same folder as those under investigation. For example, here's a link to a PDF document:

"www.domainname.com/files/secret files/hacking/stolen passwords.pdf"

Researchers can learn more about hacking and secret file directories from the domain name. If the hacking directory contains credit card numbers, stolen identities, and bank account information, the hacker may access additional information.

Downloaded files also leave a digital footprint, indicating where they came from. They can go straight to the source with this information and see what is available. In some cases, a suspect may also be accused of the additional offense of content distribution. In this case, detectives must link the suspicion to files on a website. As a result, they may need to confirm that the file names on the suspect's computer match.

Investigators frequently collaborate with lawyers and other investigators to properly handle evidence. The students can also learn how to prepare evidence for a court hearing.

DOCUMENTATION AND REPORTING

The ultimate purpose of forensic evidence gathering is judicial use. As a result, forensic investigations end with documentation and reporting. During the evidence collection, the importance of documenting the exercise was emphasized. This paperwork needs to be double-checked for accuracy and completeness. All methods for retrieving, copying, and storing evidence and subsequent examination and assessment must be documented. This is extremely useful when it comes to courtroom integrity issues. Serious cases have been dismissed because judges couldn't tell whether the evidence presented to them was true or false due to investigators' inability to document how they gathered evidence. Due to the ease with which digital data can be forged, thorough documentation of all processes is required. Digital data documentation can also be used to verify data extraction and analysis. Allowing the court to select its experts helps.

Investigators frequently hire cybersecurity experts to assist with data preparation for reporting. If the information is presented in a readable format, judges and other laypeople must comprehend it. Even if the judge and jury have no experience with information security, the experts must simplify their explanations for them to understand.

MODELS FOR DIGITAL FORENSICS

Digital forensic investigators must conduct their investigations correctly. A judge can easily disregard digital evidence because it can be tampered with easily. As a result, law enforcement agencies have been developing digital forensic investigation processes and procedures since 1984. This section will examine some of the models designed to help investigators. It's best to first review the computer forensic investigation method. The flow is consistent, and all models share the same abstract structure. The earliest approach for obtaining and preserving digital evidence dates back to 1984. This is the foundation of all digital forensic investigation models. The investigation process includes the following steps:

- Acquisition
- Identification
- Evaluation
- Presentation

When we discussed the steps involved in digital forensics, we covered all of the above stages. Since law enforcement uses digital forensics models, we'll jump right in. These models are built on top of the above-described four-step investigation process.

DIGITAL FORENSICS MODEL (ABSTRACT)

The DFRWS paradigm was stretched into nine steps to form this forensic investigation methodology. The model is shown in Figure 14.6.

In this strategy, identification comes first, followed by preparation. This paradigm incorporates an exploratory preparation phase. Examples include search warrants, tool acquisition, monitoring of questionable authorizations, and management support. The Approach Strategy follows, which is a new introduction as well. The model allows for more evidence to be collected while causing the least amount of harm to the victims. A defined strategy can be used during this phase. During preservation, data is segregated and secured. During collection, data is moved from sources to investigators. This phase requires duplicating evidence. The evidence is thoroughly examined during the examination phase to extract tiny details. The analysis phase aids in determining the importance of the derived details in the context of the case at hand. The process is summarized in a report and then presented. Finally, concealed evidence such as laptops and servers is returned to their owners. This model accounts for pre- and post-investigation processes, which DFRWS takes responsibility for.

INVESTIGATIVE MODEL FOR DIGITAL FORENSICS

This is the DFRWS (Digital Forensics Framework), created in 2001. As shown in Figure 14.7, it has six phases.

A common digital forensic investigation model. Due to its uniformity and standardization, it was readily accepted in court. Each step described the techniques investigators could utilize. Techniques like crime prevention, signature resolution, anomaly detection, and system monitoring were used to watch for potential problems. It vastly improved the identification procedures' accuracy and security. A case management guideline for preservation was also provided to assist investigators in storing various data formats. Imaging technologies were developed to retain accurate evidence. The model discussed a software and hardware solution for extracting precise details from evidence during collection. Data could also be recovered after it had been deleted using various methods. Following that, the testing and evaluation phases began. Data tracking, pattern matching, and discovering previously unknown

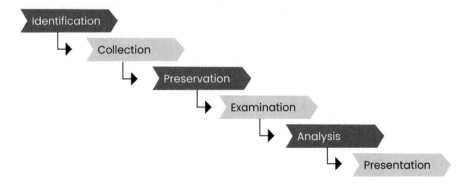

FIGURE 14.6   Forensic investigation model (Abstract).

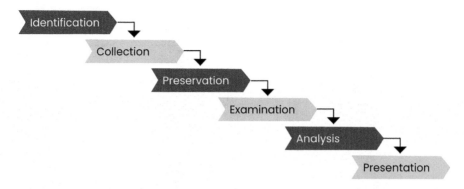

FIGURE 14.7 Phases of digital forensics.

information were all done in this area. The final step was to give a presentation, including all previous materials and expert advice.

PROCESS OF INTEGRATED DIGITAL INVESTIGATION

This model from 2003 combines the various available models. The goal was to develop a model that incorporated physical and digital investigations because they frequently overlapped. It's a big model, with 17 different phases divided into five groups. Figure 14.8 lists the five groups that make up the entire model.

Investigators check to ensure they have all necessary training and equipment throughout the methodology's preparation phase. Acquiring any necessary information is part of the preparation process. The next set of people is being deployed. This is the location of the systems used to identify and verify events. To conduct a forensic investigation, you must go through four phases: detection, notification, confirmation, and authorization. After that, we'll discuss the forensic analysis of the crime site. Of course, at this point, tangible evidence is gathered and analyzed. This technique involves gathering and documenting evidence and then doing digital investigative phases to look for additional evidence. A crime scene recreation follows this, and finally, a theory is offered. This can be seen in Figure 14.9.

The digital crime scene investigation is the final set of phases. The digital component of the investigation is the focus of this phase, and it performs a thorough examination of every device in the vicinity.

A separate investigation is carried out as if the scene were a separate crime scene to obtain information from it. The digital phase is divided into six stages, just as the physical phase is divided into six, as illustrated in Figure 14.10.

The final phase is the review phase, designed to help the model improve over time. During the review phase, it is necessary to examine all of the procedures used during the investigation to identify areas for improvement.

Other models exist, but these are consistently utilized by law enforcement. The newest models focus on specialized technologies like cloud computing, Internet-of-Things, and data mining, and they cannot be used for other forensic investigations due to their limited application.

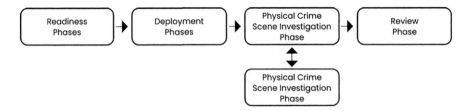

FIGURE 14.8 Integrated digital investigation.

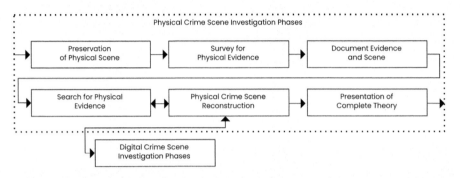

FIGURE 14.9 Recreation of a scene.

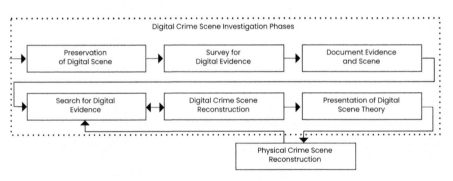

FIGURE 14.10 Physical phases.

FORENSIC TOOLKIT

Forensic investigators may need to employ specialized tools to boost productivity. Along with assisting them in collecting evidence more quickly, these toolkits automate certain processes. This can be accomplished using a few readily available tools. Investigators frequently substitute the FTK for the FTK, and AccessData developed the FTK as specialized software for investigating and analyzing digital forensics.

According to this claim, FTK enables faster data searches and analysis. The most critical technique for accomplishing this is to index data in advance, eliminating the delays caused by other search tools and strategies. According to the tool's creators, it is the most efficient and accurate method for extracting small details from large datasets. FTK is shown in Figure 14.11 below. Forensic investigators should consider the FTKs following characteristics.

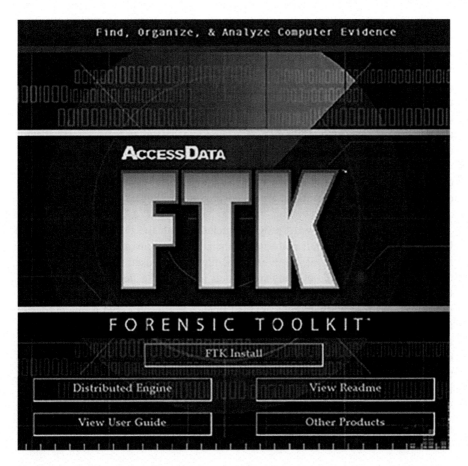

FIGURE 14.11 FTK installation.

Users rave about how stable it is, even at high speeds. It is the only forensic program to utilize a computer's numerous cores. Because it makes full use of the computer's resources, it is significantly faster than other tools. With pre-indexed data, the tool can do rapid searches and filtering. In this way, it reduces the need for duplicate files. FTK is database-driven, storing data in a central location that is easily accessible to all users. FTK will centralize all of the investigators' data, allowing for more efficient analysis. As a result, combining data sets within the same investigation is no longer necessary. Researchers who are not physically present will also benefit, as they will all have access to the same data.

Apart from searching for data, you can do numerous other things with FTK. This program makes it simple to crack passwords. Investigators may come across password-protected files containing critical information during their investigations, and they can use this tool to decrypt the file and open it. Even if a suspect is unwilling to cooperate by opening files on his computer, this method can be extremely beneficial in certain circumstances. Additionally, the tool can be used to examine emails. The tool can use the email dump as a source to extract the data you need. The utility will extract a word, number, or phrase from the data dump. Each of the elements listed below contributes to the FTK:

This toolset is great for email data. As previously indicated, FTK will allow investigators to examine bulk emails for specified characters, phrases, or numbers. Analyzing message IP addresses is enabled by parsing emails, which the tool does. While conducting investigations, investigators frequently come across encrypted files that they must decrypt to continue. According to the program's developers, decryption is now the most popular feature. The password cracking capabilities of FKT allow for the decryption and cracking of password-protected files. The FTK includes a sophisticated file search system. They can be located using various criteria, including their sizes and pixel count.

This feature is primarily used to ensure that all legal requirements are met in court. Additionally, attorneys have access to a web-based view of the analyzed evidence. If any of your operations are discovered to be illegal, you may require the assistance of an attorney.

Cerberus is an anti-malware program included with the Free Tools Kit (FTK). Certain suspects may install malware on their laptops to avoid being harmed during the analysis or retrieval. Virus-infected files can be used to disrupt a process. Cerberus can also sniff out malware, which prevents file deletion attempts. The FTK Imager is a component of FTK that enables the viewing and editing of image files recovered from suspect devices. Investigators frequently obtain image files of the systems under investigation and analyze those images rather than the devices themselves. AccessData charges an additional fee for FTK, a premium product. In contrast to other products, the FTK toolkit and imager are available for a free trial through the company. While the imager is free to use forever, the toolkit requires a license key. Firms engaged in forensic investigations should consider investing in streamlining the process.

ANTI-FORENSICS ANALYSIS

Certain techniques designed to make investigating specific files and programs significantly more difficult can obstruct digital forensic investigations. The techniques are as follows.

SEARCH ENGINE CHARACTERISTICS

Some suspects make data dynamic to prevent search engines from discovering certain data. As a result, it is generated only in response to specific inputs. If analysts are unaware of this, they will search for information on a website and empty it. Simultaneously, Visit the same webpage. And enter some information, prompting the generation of data. It's a good way to hide sensitive information, such as evidence that could be used against you.

DETECTION OF VIRTUAL MACHINES AND SANDBOXES

Techniques such as virtual machine (VM) and sandbox detection are frequently employed to avoid detection. To put things in perspective, a ransomware attack dubbed WannaCry infected 150 countries in 2017, according to the FBI. According to the researchers who discovered it, a sandbox or virtual environment caused WannaCry

to stop running. Because the malware stopped working, analysts could not ascertain how it had acted in the past. It was still subjected to static analysis, which directly examined the code rather than a behavior analysis. Some suspects are armed with tools that can perform the same function as those in question. When investigators gain access to these tools, they simply suspend operations in VMs or sandbox environments until the investigation is completed. It is only possible to debug the tool on a sacrificial system or inspect the raw code.

SUMMARY

These activities aid in the gathering of the evidence needed to convict criminals. The owner of the prominent dark web market Silk Road 2 was caught as an example of similar forensic work. Cryptocurrencies have impeded digital forensic investigations on the dark web, and they've destroyed the money trail utilized to track out suspects. The chapter also looked at how fraudsters have exploited bitcoins to help with money laundering. The forensic investigation, as well as the models, were presented in great detail. The steps of a forensic investigation are discussed in this section. Following that, it looked at a variety of common forensic investigation models. The FTK is a forensic investigation tool that is frequently utilized. Finally, evasion methods used by investigators were explored.

15 OsInt Opensource Intelligence

INTRODUCTION

Organizations are unsure of their security status due to the rise of cybersecurity threats, especially since even large organizations have been victims of cyberattacks. Data has grown in popularity and value on the dark web, and hackers are primarily interested. Security firms' job is to keep an eye on the dark web for listings of stolen corporate data. They use various methods to gather intelligence on the dark web to protect their clients. Combining data from open-source platforms can identify cybersecurity risks associated with underground markets. Open-source intelligence from the dark web can be difficult to obtain because of its obvious anonymity. This chapter will go over how to use open-source methods and platforms to gather intelligence.

OPEN-SOURCE INTELLIGENCE

Publicly available information is referred to as open-source intelligence. It is not classified or restricted, and it makes no difference how such information is generated or presented. The information is thought to be unrestricted and accessible to all. However, this definition falls short of defining open-source intelligence on the dark web. Open-source intelligence on the dark web refers to openly available data. However, because special software is required to access the information on the dark web, there are some challenges. The dark web requires the creation of user accounts to access certain types of data. The OsInt life cycle is shown in Figure 15.1.

Freely available information is not always easy to use. The reason for this is due to the content. There is so much of it that finding useful information without further analysis is nearly impossible. As a result, a variety of tools have been developed. To aid users in deciphering open-source intelligence, researchers, penetration testers, and legal agencies, among others, use these tools to gather open-source intelligence on the dark web is openly available data. Data collection is the first step in the intelligence-gathering process. When open-source intelligence is thoroughly analyzed, it can yield useful information. Many digital footprints can be left and used to one's advantage in the public domain. Security authorities, for example, tracked down the originator of Silk Road 2 using open-source intelligence. It is possible to utilize one's digital footprints. Ross Ulbricht, the company's founder, left his genuine email address on the platform while soliciting assistance. Law enforcement agencies were able to conduct additional investigations after determining his identity. Ross Ulbricht would certainly not have been linked to Silk Road 2 if it hadn't been for open-source intelligence gathering. Even if agencies used sophisticated tools to break into the Tor network, they would get no results.

DOI: 10.1201/9781003404330-15

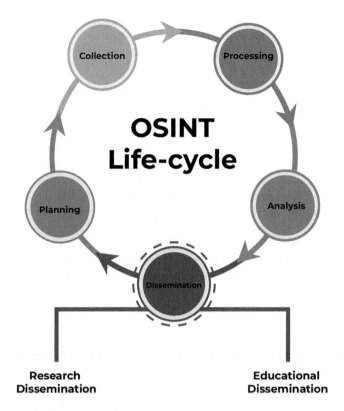

FIGURE 15.1 OSINT life cycle.

SECURITY INTELLIGENCE AND ITS CHALLENGES

The number of threats to which organizations are vulnerable has grown. As a result, organizations' defense mechanisms have had to diversify. The putative founder's account was linked to a Bitcoin chat platform where he asked for coding help, proving that this strategy is ineffective. Furthermore, the human element in organizations has resulted in a general weakness in all of them. Even without using a hacking tool, many companies can be breached by attackers who have refined their social engineering skills. An attack could be as simple as sending an email to a member of the organization's staff. Therefore, businesses are diversifying their investment portfolios and focusing on two areas. Cyber resilience is the first. This should help a corporation endure an attack without being overrun. For example, organizations can invest in additional processing resources to support normal clients while a denial-of-service attack is being dealt with. Security intelligence is the second security mitigation that firms are investing in. Organizations do not want to be sitting ducks; instead, they want to be aware of their threats and avoid them before they happen. This explains why some companies have a perfect track record for cyberattacks. They've spent money on threat intelligence for dangers that haven't been deployed yet.

The dark web is one of the most important places for threat intelligence. Because most of the threats originate here, it is prudent to acquire information from here.

The dark web has become a refuge for malevolent programmers and malware used in attacks. Worse, malicious code for sale on the dark web doesn't require coding genius. These are the most typical issues on the dark web.

DARK WEB SECURITY INTELLIGENCE COMPANIES

For example, SurfWatch charges clients to gather dark web intelligence and does not notify them when something unexpected is discovered. These firms aid businesses in many ways. They can help a company's reputation. Examples include Yahoo's reputation being harmed by its hacking and subsequent sale of consumer data. In the face of more secure competitors like Gmail, only a small percentage of people still use Yahoo email. Customer loyalty is negatively connected with the reputation that these intelligence firms claim to preserve. It's that simple: if a company hasn't been hacked, customers are less inclined to abandon it for fear of losing personal data. Protecting a company's intellectual property is another area of concentration for security intelligence gathering services. These businesses will search the dark web for anyone who has placed data for sale, even if it was stolen due to a hack. There's still a potential that the data will be unlawfully disseminated if it's discovered.

CYBERCRIME-AS-A-SERVICE

To become a cybercriminal on the dark web, all it takes is $10 to acquire distributed denial-of-service (DDoS) botnets and start an assault against a company. Ready-to-hack groups offer varied rates to break into other people's businesses on the dark web. As a result, a disgruntled employee might easily travel to the dark web and gain insider knowledge about hacked companies. The hackers would then be compensated. As a result, technical expertise is no longer required for hacking; expert cybercriminals may execute it for a charge. This has caused alarm among many firms. Hired cybercriminals have been seen to be ruthless and steadfast in their commitments. This is due to their desire to establish a name on the dark web to obtain more lucrative hacking gigs. As a result, they'll launch a volley of attacks, including social engineering and distributed denial-of-service attacks. Other hired cybercriminals just resell their malicious malware to youngsters. Script kiddies are on the rise, and they're just average folks who don't know how to hack and rely on pre-made exploits instead. Script kiddies can threaten businesses because they can obtain various exploit tools and use them against various businesses until they find something valuable.

DDoS attacks appear to be the preferred method based on the incidents reported thus far. According to a dark web investigation, hiring a botnet to launch a DDoS attack costs as little as $10 for an hour, and a single day may set you back $200. These botnets are hired for several days by ruthless hackers. For example, Kaspersky reported that a DDoS attack against an organization lasted 12 days in the first quarter of 2018; it's the longest assault in years. According to cybersecurity experts, DDoS attacks appear to be taking longer than in prior years.

Finally, hacking has become more accessible due to cybercrime as a service. More hackers will advertise their services for hire on the dark web to earn quick money. It's comparable to Uber's taxi service, which allows individuals to pay a fee to use their

cars as taxis. Because hackers are in high demand, the number of cybercrime-as-a-service hacking incidents is almost certain to increase. For businesses to survive, It's critical to know what hire services are being sold and prepared.

INCREASING THE RETURN ON INVESTMENT (ROI) FOR CYBER WEAPONS ON THE DARK WEB

The dark web's increased ROI for cybercrime weaponry is another source of concern for businesses, magnifying the security danger. Cybercrime weapons are comparatively affordable compared to conventional weapons, and a botnet for DDoS assaults costs only $10, according to the section above.

The $10 attack's consequences could be disastrous for a business that processes a high volume of requests at any given time, as all of them will be ignored. The DDoS attack on DynDNS, a market leader in DNS resolution, is a good example. The attack lasted only a few hours and had global ramifications, some websites were unavailable. The ROI of cyber weapons is increasing due to several factors on the deep web. The first is the low entry threshold. As previously stated, being a hacker today does not require technical training. To launch an attack, no sophisticated software is required. There are even free tools available for conducting attacks.

Additionally, today's low-risk, high-reward hacking contributes to the rising ROI. Due to the widespread availability of hacking tools, Cybercrime has evolved into a lucrative business for some thanks to the cloaking methods used by the services for hacking revenues and money laundering. The maturing cybercrime market also aids hacking's increased profitability. On the dark web, everything is set up, from hacking tools to markets for selling hacked personal data, bank records, and other information. Businesses should be prepared for any eventuality resulting from cybercrime's increasing ROI. This is why cybersecurity intelligence is important for focusing efforts on current threats.

INTELLIGENCE-GATHERING FOCUS

When gathering dark web intelligence, several factors are taken into account. These elements will be discussed further down.

HACKING-AS-A-SERVICE

Dark web hackers hired to do work concentrate their efforts in this web area. Finding out what hacking tools and methods are being used is the goal, and this data will help a business decide what defenses to put in place.

STOLEN INTELLECTUAL PROPERTY

Numerous dark web intelligence-gathering organizations and law enforcement agencies are interested in this area. Firms have been hired to monitor stolen data listings on the dark web, where the data was stolen. If and when the hackers decide to sell it, the hacked organization will be notified. A business can be unaware that some of its sensitive information has been leaked to the dark web until it is stolen. Other hackers appear to be motivated to obtain sensitive company information, exploiting it to

profit financially from it. If a company such as X steals a competitor's trade secrets, it's easy to see how that company might use those secrets against the competitor.

Additionally, a company in another country that steals a company in the United States' design prototypes may use the prototypes to manufacture and sell counterfeit versions of the original products. This is referred to as intellectual property infringement. The US-based company will discover far too late that counterfeit copies of its genuine products are costing it money and tarnishing its reputation. For example, numerous footwear manufacturers, including Nike and Adidas, have complained that counterfeiters have plagiarized their shoe designs and are selling their knockoffs at a lower price than the original thing.

FOR SALE: EXPLOITS

Hacking exploits are notoriously sold on the dark web. These are purchased by hackers who lack the technical expertise to construct their exploits. They do, however, pose a significant threat to organizations once they obtain these exploits. As a result, identifying specific exploits for sale on the dark web will be part of the intelligence-gathering process. Knowing what tools hackers have access to can help a company's information security team prepare for such attacks.

VULNERABILITIES FOR SALE

According to reports, the National Security Agency reportedly uncovered a weakness in Windows in 2017 that might allow programs to run commands with administrative privileges. This flaw could be exploited. WannaCry, a ransomware that used the same vulnerability, was released before Windows patched it completely. The dark web sells various vulnerabilities for various programs and operating systems. Fees increase proportionately with the length of time since a vulnerability was discovered. Vulnerabilities that are sold for zero-day exploits are the most expensive. These are exploitable flaws that have not yet been discovered or patched. Numerous zero-day exploits, for example, were used in the Stuxnet attack on the Iranian nuclear facility. This, experts believe, was a tell-tale sign that Stuxnet was sponsored. Because it would have been prohibitively expensive for an individual hacker to use multiple zero-day exploits in a single attack when they could sell the vulnerability on the dark web for a much higher price, using multiple zero-day exploits in a single attack would have been prohibitively expensive. Buying vulnerability intelligence allows companies to start preparing for such attacks immediately.

Dark Web threat intelligence gatherers are tasked with identifying new vulnerabilities in cybercriminals' hands. The National Vulnerability Database published a list of 12,517 vulnerabilities in 2017. One study found that 700 of these had been sold on the dark web before publication. The most vulnerable merchants were found to be 91 dark web vendors. These actors possessed several flaws, and if thoroughly investigated, they could have provided law enforcement agencies with information about their sources.

When a vulnerability is advertised on the dark web for sale, cybercriminals and security professionals responsible for developing and deploying patches compete to be the first to exploit it. The race is depicted diagrammatically in Figure 15.2.

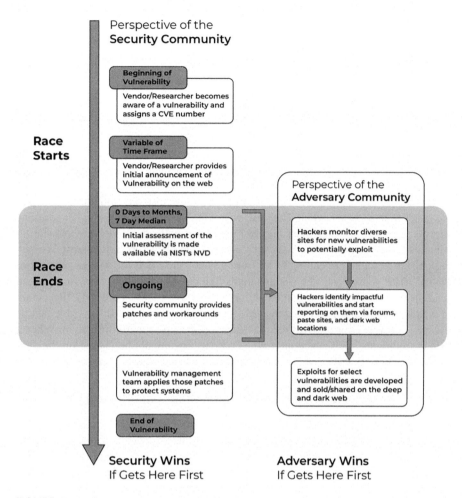

FIGURE 15.2 Stolen personally identifiable information.

Legislators have enacted stringent legislation governing this type of information collection and storage. Sensitive data like social security numbers and medical records are examples of data classified as personally identifiable information (PII). Hackers have been able to steal PII data despite enforcing strict laws for organizations that collect and store it. This type of information is sold for a high price on the dark web. It can be used for various criminal activities, including tax evasion, identity theft, and extortion, especially if the target is a famous person who does not want some of their personal information exposed.

STOLEN FINANCIAL DATA

It's a delicate situation when financial information about its customers is stolen. The victim will invest significant resources in protecting this information, but it will be a major disaster if the worst-case scenario occurs and it is compromised. It's difficult

to estimate how much money a company will lose due to fines, lawsuits, and lost customers. Many intelligence-gathering firms monitor financial data available for sale on the dark web.

CAMPAIGNS FOR SPAM AND PHISHING

Phishing is a method of attack that was previously not considered a serious threat. This is a good idea because phishing emails are quickly identifiable by spelling problems and a lack of formal style. Because it had been used so many times, the Nigerian Prince scam only managed to catch a few people. However, a new breed of phisher has emerged, and it is ruthless. Phishers have scammed many people in the United States when filing tax returns. These new phishers have also targeted users of internet financial systems like PayPal. The dark web is to blame for today's higher phishing success rates. On dark web markets, phishing emails with corporate logos and similar content are sold as perfect duplicates of corporate emails. Users have reported receiving phishing emails pretending to be from PayPal, such as those sent by the FBI or PayPal. With no experience utilizing emails like these on the dark web, a hacker can send them to multiple recipients and defraud them. Let's look at the 2017 IRS email, in which an Indian sent US citizens well-formatted attachments. It's possible that he hacked government or medical records to obtain their personal information. When a firm accumulates intelligence on scams and phishing emails purchased on the dark web, it can alert its staff to these easy social engineering attacks ahead of time.

THREAT INTELLIGENCE ON THE DARK WEB AND ITS VALUE

Data from the dark web can be easily applied to cybersecurity operations. It may be used for various things, including preventing crime and improving cybersecurity tactics for corporations. If a hospital detects that some of its patient data has been compromised, it can search the dark web for stolen medical data. If it discovers a seller with such data, it can take mitigation measures. Historically, organizations have implemented successful mitigation measures. For example, a software corporation recently put an end to the dark web sale of the source code for its enterprise resource planning software. Hackers might browse through this source code, looking for flaws that could be exploited to access the companies that utilize it. According to an inquiry into the incident, the program was being sold by an insider eager to earn quick money. Because it came from a well-known global software corporation, the source code was listed at $50,000.

Other businesses have contacted intelligence and law enforcement agencies to prevent stolen data from being sold on the dark web. Any data that has been stolen is now routinely discovered on the dark web, which acts as a ready market for it. As a result, it has become a critical source of web threat intelligence.

SECURITY INTELLIGENCE'S CHALLENGES

Cyber threats are currently abounding in cyberspace. There are more threats on the dark web that need to be monitored. However, deciding which threats to focus on is one of the most difficult challenges organizations face. They will never be able to protect against all of the threats listed on the dark web due to their limited resources. They may allocate a sizable portion of their resources to threats that never materialize.

Additionally, phony threats and false positives exist. Because sellers are not required to be accountable, it is unsafe to purchase items on the dark web. As a result, they may falsely promote vulnerabilities and exploit toolkits. As a result, it can be challenging to locate actual threat intelligence or its references. Typically, those discovered are among the hundreds of thousands of dark web messages shared. Researchers and law enforcement agencies cannot access some of these chat rooms. There is a lot of content to scan when visiting open chat forums. Additionally, the information may be useless, resulting in resource waste.

It's extremely tough and time-consuming to gather threat intelligence from the dark web. Each untapped market's depths must be probed. Certain markets may require an invitation or membership. At this point, some organizations may choose to abandon the effort, necessitating the employment of paid intelligence analysts. Employees with little or no experience may jeopardize their employers. One reason for this is that some markets operate by having customers request items and determine whether they are available. In one unfortunate incident, a novice researcher inquired about penetration testing options for a system that only a few companies used. In as little as 3 hours, his target organization had received a barrage of malicious requests, all requesting the same data as he was.

This demonstrates that even collecting threat intelligence from the dark web can be dangerous. Researchers avoid disclosing as much information as possible when gathering intelligence from the dark web. Rather than directly interacting with sellers and buyers on these platforms, it is preferable to read and listen. It is possible to amass significant intelligence.

Without the assistance of dark web actors, Individuals who understand how to approach dark web actors without confronting them or directly questioning them can be compensated for threat intelligence gathering.

Finally, due to the vastness of the dark web, communication can be difficult. Those who sell stolen data may not be from the same country as the victims on the dark web, and there is a possibility that they do not understand one another. For example, Chinese hackers could hack into a US company and sell the stolen data on the Chinese dark web. However, the hackers listed the stolen data in a language other than English and made keyword searches in that language. As a result, searches may give no results even if the sought-after material exists on the dark web but is presented in a different language. As a result, conducting searches across all languages on the dark web is nearly impossible.

MONITORING TOOLS FOR OPEN-SOURCE INTELLIGENCE

The following are some tools for analyzing open-source information:

RECON-NG

Open-source intelligence analysis tool. It uses Linux and contains Kali Linux. Recon-Ng is made up of modules comparable to Metasploit, as shown in Figure 15.3.

The image above is from Recon-Ng. Modules vary in size and shape. Some of these are new. These modules help you find specific files or content. Modules can be classified as part of the exploitation category. These are meant to unblock data previously protected by security measures. The tool's import module can handle large

```
recon/contacts-contacts/mailtester
recon/contacts-contacts/mangle
recon/contacts-contacts/unmangle
recon/contacts-credentials/hibp_breach
recon/contacts-credentials/hibp_paste
recon/contacts-credentials/pwnedlist
recon/contacts-domains/migrate_contacts
recon/contacts-profiles/fullcontact
recon/credentials-credentials/adobe
recon/credentials-credentials/bozocrack
recon/credentials-credentials/hashes_org
recon/credentials-credentials/leakdb
recon/domains-contacts/pgp_search
recon/domains-contacts/salesmaple
recon/domains-contacts/whois_pocs
recon/domains-credentials/pwnedlist/account_creds
recon/domains-credentials/pwnedlist/api_usage
recon/domains-credentials/pwnedlist/domain_creds
recon/domains-credentials/pwnedlist/domain_ispwned
recon/domains-credentials/pwnedlist/leak_lookup
recon/domains-credentials/pwnedlist/leaks_dump
recon/domains-domains/brute_suffix
recon/domains-hosts/baidu_site
```

FIGURE 15.3   Recom-Ng interface.

amounts of data. The last category on the list, Recon, is the most critical. If you're looking for open-source intelligence, start here. The Recon modules would have pursued Ross Ulbricht if this tool had been used. The Recon module covers sources such as Who. Is, Github, LinkedIn, and purchase contacts. According to reports, a LinkedIn user named Ross Ulbricht was linked to an email found by law enforcement. His profile mentioned Silk Road 2 and his dark web activities. Using this tool, an email address can be linked to a LinkedIn account.

Recon's work is focused on a single target, while Ng's is split up. Recon-Ng collects data from URLs. When a user creates a workspace, they should specify the domain name of the questionable content. Modules can collect information from and about the entire domain. The application can also leverage search engines like Bing to obtain domain information. Emails from a certain domain and the LinkedIn social network can be cached using the Bing LinkedIn cache. Using open-source, other modules can learn more about a target.

MALTEGO

Paterva created this tool, which is widely used in the cybersecurity field. It's a built-in program in the Kali Linux OS variant that runs on Linux. Maltego has a reputation for performing surveillance on targets. Before creating machines to run transforms, a user must first register with Paterva. Before a machine can run, it must be configured and then started by the software. Maltego looks at its footsteps.

It's possible to utilize a domain name or an IP address. The software recognizes phrases in a wide range of publicly available data sources. Maltego is a natural at learning everything there is to know about a particular target. It can scour the internet for a phrase that matches. For example, if users want to search the internet for stolen data, they can type "Stolen data XYZ bank" into the search box. The software will flag any listings on the internet that contain such a name. The Maltego interface is shown in Figure 15.4.

THE HARVESTER

It's a tool for gathering data on a certain target. It's likewise based on Linux and comes preloaded with the Kali Linux operating system. The program excels at gathering information on email addresses and domain names. A screenshot of some of the choices accessible in the harvester is shown in Figure 15.5.

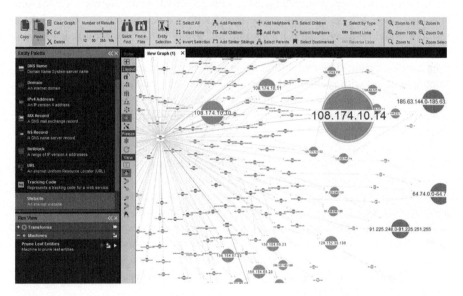

FIGURE 15.4 Maltego interface.

```
Usage: theharvester options

        -d: Domain to search or company name
        -b: data source: google, googleCSE, bing, bingapi, pgp, linkedin,
                         google-profiles, jigsaw, twitter, googleplus, all

        -s: Start in result number X (default: 0)
        -v: Verify host name via dns resolution and search for virtual hosts
        -f: Save the results into an HTML and XML file (both)
        -n: Perform a DNS reverse query on all ranges discovered
        -c: Perform a DNS brute force for the domain name
        -t: Perform a DNS TLD expansion discovery
        -e: Use this DNS server
        -l: Limit the number of results to work with(bing goes from 50 to 50 results,
            google 100 to 100, and pgp doesn't use this option)
        -h: use SHODAN database to query discovered hosts
```

FIGURE 15.5 The harvester interface.

As a result, the tool can be used with various data sources and even social media platforms to gather information about a target. Hackers have leaked data from social media sites and searched popular social media networks like Twitter with this tool to find such data. Users appreciate this tool's ability to extract data from open sources and its other features for analyzing that content.

SHODAN

For a reason, this search engine has been dubbed a "hacker search engine." Shodan is a useful tool for tracking people's, organizations', and data's digital footprints. Because of its ability to search the dark web, Shodan outperforms other search engines. Webcams, servers, and other internet-connected devices were found using the search engine. While running in the background, this program collects a lot of information about the devices and services connected to the internet. As a result, we have a fantastic open-source threat intelligence tool. Traffic lights, CCTV cameras, and other IoT devices can all be found with a quick search on Shodan. As a result, it could be dangerous if it falls into the wrong hands. As a result, it's known as a hacker's search engine. Users have discovered water parks, gas stations, and even a crematorium. The tool directed them directly to these internet-based systems. Intelligent users with specialized knowledge may locate nuclear power plant control systems. When security access controls are missing from a system, any user can gain direct access and manipulate the system. The following article goes over a few of the discoveries made possible by Shodan.

The default password on many printers, servers, and system control devices is "admin," which can be found by searching for "default password." All you need is a web browser to connect to other connected systems.

Independent penetration tester Dan Tentler used Shodan to find control systems for evaporative coolers, pressurized water heaters, and garage doors during a presentation at last year's Defcon cybersecurity conference.

He discovered an automatic vehicle wash and a defrosted ice hockey rink in Denmark. With a single command, a whole city's traffic management system may be switched into "test mode." At a hydroelectric project in France, he designed a control system for two 3-MW turbines.

Source: http://money.cnn.com/2013/04/08/technology/security/shodan/

There is a reason for this search engine being dubbed a "hacker search engine." Shodan is a useful tool for tracking the digital footprints of individuals, organizations, and data. Shodan outperforms other search engines due to its ability to search the dark web. The search engine was used to locate webcams, servers, and other internet-connected devices. While this program is running in the background, It gathers a lot of information about the devices and services linked to the internet. As a result, we now have a fantastic open-source threat intelligence collection tool. Traffic lights, CCTV cameras, and other Internet of Things devices may all be found on Shodan with a simple search. As a result, it could be hazardous if it gets into the wrong hands. As a result, it has earned the moniker "hacker search engine." Users discovered water parks, petrol stations, and a crematorium. The tool directed them directly to these web-based systems. Intelligent people with

specialized understanding may locate nuclear power plant control systems. Any user can obtain direct access to the system and influence it if security access rules are not in place. Shodan was instrumental in finding several objects detailed in the following article.

Many printers, servers, and system administration equipment use "admin" as their default password. Simply use a web browser to connect.

According to Dan Tentler, a security researcher, Shodan was used last year to locate the control systems for evaporative coolers, pressurized water heaters, and garage doors.

Denmark's defrosted rink and self-service vehicle wash Using a single command, the traffic control system for an entire city can be put into "test mode." A hydroelectric plant with two turbines was also built in France.

GOOGLE DORKS

This isn't a completely new search engine; rather, it's a modified version of Google. This happens when you utilize advanced operators in a search query to request specific or hidden results from Google. These advanced operators can refine a search query or inform a search engine about the type of results to deliver. If it falls into the wrong hands, it can be quite dangerous. The utility of advanced operators has been demonstrated through hacking. The operators can be used to compel Google to reveal information about a domain's hidden systems and services. This is the kind of data that a typical Google search would normally miss. Table 15.1 contains several real-life Google Hacking queries. Shodan is a search engine that shows the results of a search query for Virtual Network Computing viewers on the internet (Figures 15.6 and 15.7).

It's possible that running these queries is pointless because they'll only show the login pages. However, many IT departments do not change their default passwords, which is fortunate. As a result, one can try common default username-password combinations for each of these pages; for example, the username is "admin" and the password is "123456." According to password profilers, the most commonly used password is still "123456."

More harmful queries that can be used to find more sensitive authentication details in domains include the following:

"Logname=" "authentication failure;" "authentication failure;" "authentication failure;" "authentic ext: log - Looks for log files with usernames and login paths for failed logins.
inurl:/profile.php?lookup=1- On most websites and forums, this will assist in finding the administrator's name. When brute-forcing, this is a huge help.

Google Hacking, also known as Dorking, has been used to locate open-source intelligence for a long time. This method of gathering intelligence is reliable because it uses an already powerful platform, Google Search. It excels at locating files that are hidden on the internet. For example, we can utilize Google Hacking

to find Mark Weins' physical address, email address, phone number, associations, and even his CV if we're looking for information on him. As a result, it is extremely effective. Hackers use this strategy to track down misconfigured internet equipment such as servers, printers, and surveillance cameras. In rare

TABLE 15.1

You'll Find Examples of Google Hacking Commands in a Table

Date Tested	Command	Types of Expected Outcomes
04-06-2018	`inurl:/CMSPages/logon ext:aspx`	Pages containing login portals
04-06-2018	`"Powered by Open Source Chat Platform Rocket.Chat."`	
04-06-2018	`nurl:/index.php/login intext:Concrete. CMS`	
25-5-2018	`allintitle: "Flexi Press System."`	
04-06-2018	`intext:2001.-.2018.umbraco.org ext:aspx`	
04-06-2018	`inurl:'/blog/Account/login.aspx'`	
29-5-2018	`AndroidManifest ext:xml -github- gitlab -googlesource`	Files containing sensitive information
04-06-2018	`inurl:'listprojects.spr'`	Sensitive directories
04-06-2018	`inurl:composer.json Codeigniter- site:github.com`	Web server detection

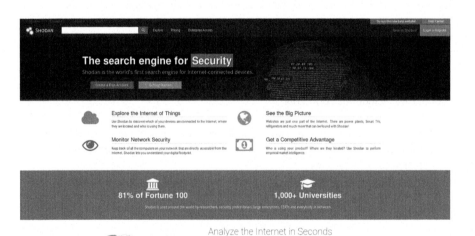

FIGURE 15.6   Shodan displays the login screen for a Windows-based server connected to the internet.

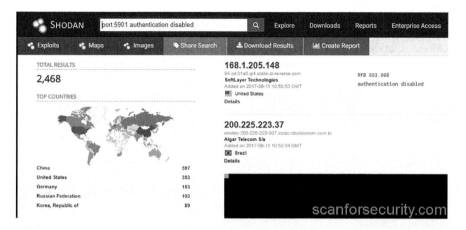

FIGURE 15.7 Shodan is a search engine that shows the results of a search query for VNC viewers on the internet. (For more information, go to https://exploit-db.com/google-hacking-database/2/ for more open-source community-created examples.)

circumstances, this approach can be used to recover login credentials that have been saved insecurely on web servers, notepads, or SQL databases.

DATA GATHERING

Collecting data from the dark web is a difficult task, and organizations often require the cooperation of third parties to access data on the dark web. Open source and dark web data collection methods are covered in this section.

DIRECT CONVERSATIONS

On the dark web, direct conversations with actors can gather information. However, because the actors may force you to reveal sensitive information, this is a risky venture. Law enforcement agencies have used this tactic, especially when collecting information to use as evidence in court against dark web criminals. As a result, this is a very useful data collection method. A researcher only needs to know who to contact. On the dark web, there are well-known usernames for selling extremely powerful malware. These are fascinating connections. As a result, you should approach them as someone interested in purchasing the most up-to-date and powerful malware.

When contacting these actors, however, caution is advised. If they notice that the customer was simply utilizing them, they can track them down. For example, a less-experienced researcher asked an unknown threat actor about a vulnerability that was only present on one particular system made available to a small number of organizations. A wave of malicious activity was unleashed against the organization when the threat actor tracked it down.

On the dark web, threat actors are professionals in their specialties, so exercising extreme caution when dealing with them is essential. They also have a lot of important information on them. They can be used to identify new malware that has been discovered or is being developed. Because they have insider information, they can also locate the targeted organizations. Speaking with a few of these people could yield a plethora of information useful for security purposes, such as spotting potential business threats. If a customer appears to be highly serious, threat actors will not hesitate to share critical information, such as vulnerabilities they are planning or have already produced. As a result, it's an ideal location for gathering intelligence information. Direct conversations with threat actors have the advantage of being quiet. As a result, filtering through the conversation to extract useful information will not be difficult. This is a problem that people face in chat rooms, where they have to sift through a lot of noise and irrelevant messages to find the ones that contain useful information.

CHAT ROOMS

The major goal of researchers, law enforcement agencies, and corporations is usually to achieve this. For intelligence-collection reasons, the information provided in chat rooms is particularly useful. This information can be used to conduct further research. Physical observation is beneficial, but automated analysis is far superior. The majority of companies hire firms to keep an eye on these forums for mentions of their products, executives, or even the company's name. When this happens, you have several options. The first possibility is that dark web users discuss security flaws discovered on a company's system. The subject of discussion could be a security flaw that enables hackers to gain access to Amazon or data theft. They might also be planning an attack on the firm mentioned above. Attackers have asked for help launching an attack against a specific company in online forums. Phishers frequently advertise for expert HTML email creators with Photoshop skills to create phishing emails. The chatter on the chat platform provides enough evidence to alert a business to an attack following the discussions. Another possibility is that users on the dark web are selling the company's data. They may be selling a database dump that has been stolen from a company. When the name of a high-ranking executive is mentioned, hacking plots are almost guaranteed to follow. For example, hackers could access an executive's email account and use it to send money transfer requests to junior accounting or finance department employees. If the name of a company executive is mentioned, an attack against them is almost certainly in the works.

ADVANCED SEARCH QUERIES

Earlier, we provided Software that can be used to collect the data listed below. Google Dorking and Shodan were two tools that were search engines. These are extremely useful tools for data collection. When it comes to tracing people's identities, Google Dorking, also known as Google Hacking, is effective because it encompasses all of the data indexed by the world's most powerful search engine. Critical data buried on the internet will be churned out by the appropriate operators. The typical Google

search engine does not return results on the surface of the web and does not imply that it is shallow. It has crawled many resources on the internet and can quickly identify where a specific name or username has been mentioned. The problem is that Google Dorking isn't very good at finding information on the dark web. This is where Shodan comes into play. Shodan is a search engine that indexes data from the dark web. As a result, the developers have set a limit on how many results can be returned to users.

MARKET LISTINGS

After Yahoo's user data was revealed on dark web markets, media outlets determined it had been stolen. Yahoo had not publicly acknowledged that it had been hacked and that personal information had been stolen. As a result, this is a critical market data source. The issue with markets is that some of them are closed to newcomers. They operate based on invitations, which require a member of the market's administrator to invite someone to view items for sale. On the other hand, many dark web black markets continue to operate without these restrictions.

They have vendors who have everything for sale to the general public listed on their website. The term "public" refers to all users on the dark web. Businesses might utilize these underground markets to track down data that has already been stolen. When Yahoo's data was discovered on the dark web, it was too late to prevent it from being sold. Even though three purchasers had expressed interest, the listing was still accessible. The data was initially sold for $300,000, and each of the three early customers paid that sum. The stolen user data was still on sale after the theft was revealed, although at a decreased price. Yahoo initially disputed that the information listed came from its data centers but later admitted it did.

Businesses could save their data before it was sold to third parties in certain circumstances. Companies pay third parties to look for their data listings on the dark web, a typical monitoring technique. Law enforcement agencies are notified when a listing is made to recover the data before it is sold to a dark web customer.

Market listings can learn about circulating viruses and stolen data on the dark web. On the dark web, most malware is created and sold to cybercriminals. As previously stated, cybercriminals do not need to be programmers. Malware can be purchased on the dark web for a variety of prices. As a result, a researcher on the dark web can find a lot of information by impersonating a cybercriminal looking for malware. The malware, as well as the systems it can attack, will have been described by the sellers.

THE DIFFICULTIES OF COLLECTING DATA FROM THE DARK WEB

Collecting data from the dark web is more difficult than it first appears. Organizations prefer to delegate this difficult task to specialized third-party firms because of the risks involved. A wide range of problems and complexities arise that necessitate the combined use of human expertise and sophisticated technology. Choosing to use their employees to collect data often fails in organizations for the following reasons.

The dark web isn't just for English speakers in terms of linguistic and cultural expertise. Users come from all over the world, including Russia, China, and many others. The majority of these users should be closely scrutinized because they are the most powerful or pose the greatest threat. As a result, a wide range of languages, including Chinese, Russian, and Arabic, will need to be monitored. Researchers may also need information about the cultural background of those they are studying from time to time. They need to be familiar with the terminology and social mores of the area. Data gathered from chat rooms or direct contact with threat actors requires extra caution when using this protection method. If you don't understand the slang, you might miss something important. The threat actors' ignorance of cultural norms may frighten the target population. Organizations face a significant challenge because they don't take this into account when conducting their dark web research or gathering data.

Discovering useful information resides on the dark web, but it won't be handed over to researchers on a plate. It will frequently be obscured under a thick layer of noise and irrelevant information. If you've never used the dark web to gather data before, you risk squandering money on inconsequential waste. When investors lose faith in the dark web data collectors, they will stop collecting data from the dark web altogether.

Some markets are better than others at penetrating trusted environments. Because the FBI and other law enforcement agents are infamous for impersonating buyers and vendors, no one should expect a warm welcome. Markets, which are hotbeds of criminal activity, are well-guarded. Only a small number of people are allowed in, and the people around those with access have learned to trust them. Vetting can include how much time someone spent on the dark web or what kind of posts they made. Those unfamiliar with the dark web or with suspicious accounts will have difficulty gaining access to these markets. As a result, some individuals will have limited capabilities, and organizations seeking intelligence for the first time will discover that their new usernames aren't accepted in trustworthy environments.

To get useful information from the dark web, you'll have to put in effort and money. This will require a significant investment of time and money. It may take a long time to collect data from this part of the internet. It's not uncommon to need specialized software and highly trained workers. On the dark web, professional intelligence gatherers work full-time with actors. While an organization may spend more time and effort on intelligence gathering, this is unlikely.

Compared to the experts' expertise, employees will put in minimal time and effort for a nine-to-five job. Some places, such as marketplaces or meeting rooms, must be constantly inspected to ensure no miscommunication. There are some markets where participation is restricted because of the need for trust. Sellers and buyers on the dark web go through checks to keep law enforcement agencies and researchers out.

This makes putting together their dark web intelligence scouting teams extremely challenging. Data collection is a time- and resource-consuming process in and of itself. Businesses that specialize in completing tasks like these for other companies may appear to be in a better position than others. Although I may be mistaken, they may have needed to keep a dark web account open for years to gain the actors' trust and access to the most secret marketplaces. They probably developed dark web

alliances and relationships to keep up with current events. Therefore, employing third-party experts to keep an eye on the dark web and gather threat intelligence is highly recommended. They also take care not to put their employees in danger due to their actions. Instead, they'll rely on dark web experts with extensive experience and established relationships with potential threat actors on the underground. These people should be doing the heavy lifting when gathering data and information to aid in decision-making.

SUMMARY

The focus of this chapter was on dark web open-source intelligence. There are examples of open-source intelligence's utility in the real world and its definition. The chapter then moved on to security intelligence and how the dark web can collect threat data. A slew of new businesses has sprung up to collect dark web security intelligence and alert their clients when something interesting happens. We've talked about how security intelligence works throughout this chapter. Hacking services, exploits and vulnerabilities for sale, intellectual property theft, financial data theft, theft of PII, and phishing campaigns for sale are just a few examples. In terms of their importance, these topics have already been discussed. This is usually where you'll find useful information about potential threats. There is a lot of information regarding current and forthcoming threats that organizations must be aware of while selling hacking-as-a-service. Organizations can exploit stolen IP, financial data, or PII to prevent further harm. Rarely can corporations prevent the sale of stolen data. The amount of information obtained regarding the phishing con game is increasing.

Phishers use phishing techniques such as cloned emails and websites. The main challenges of gathering security intelligence were discussed in this chapter.

A free and open-source intelligence gathering and analysis tool has been featured in this article. For example, there are six different tools mentioned in the chapter: Google Dorking, Maltego, Recon-Ng, the Harvester, Shodan, and Maltego. Each of the six tools has been explained in detail including open-source intelligence-gathering search engines like Shodan and Google Dorking. We've provided advanced Google Dorking queries as proof of concept, which can be used to uncover private information. The chapter comes to a close with a discussion of open-source intelligence data collection. There have been different areas identified where data can be collected. Chat rooms, direct conversations, market listings, and search queries are examples of this type of communication. Each of these data collection methods has been discussed in detail.

Additionally, the difficulties that can arise when collecting open-source data were discussed. When there is a lack of language competence, access to a trusted environment, and resource limits, determine actionable intelligence. The chapter advises leaving data collection to professionals familiar with the dark web and actual threat actors.

16 Emerging Dark Web Trends and Mitigation Techniques

INTRODUCTION

The dark web has become a source of increasing security concerns; so, understandably, some people wonder why it exists at all. According to the founders of the most well-known dark network, Tor, numerous additional applications are supported by the darknet. As a result, it has become a necessary evil on the internet. The dark web has undergone a radical transformation since its inception. Cybersecurity changes sparked most of the alterations to systems. New crime patterns emerged during the height of legal agencies' interference in shutting down darknet markets. When well-known black markets close, there's always a reaction. Cybercriminals have developed new and more effective methods of attacking organizations due to changes in the cybersecurity tools used by many people. Because of the shifts and developments, the dark web has spawned a criminal economy. Even though law enforcement has extricated prominent criminals from it in the past and continues to do so, the dark web's evolution, trends, and some mitigation measures will be covered in this chapter.

RECENT DARK WEB EVOLUTION

The dark web has grown based on two fundamental pillars: security and privacy. Users concerned about spying on the open internet flock to the dark web. It has enabled spies to work undetected in risky areas and countries where the rule of law exists. Thanks to the dark web, whistleblowers now have a secure place to go. WikiLeaks, which received some leaked information via the dark web, has brought to light several high-profile incidents. The dark web is still mostly used for illicit activity such as cybercrime and the demise of well-known online marketplaces such as eBay. On the dark web, what's new? Here are a few things to consider.

ENHANCED SECURITY, PRIVACY, AND USABILITY

Freenet was one of the first darknets established in 2000 to protect dissidents from repressive governments. The dark web was slow and unusable. However, many users on the dark web were willing to make this sacrifice for increased anonymity. The dark web has improved in terms of privacy and security over time. As a result, their

DOI: 10.1201/9781003404330-16

accessibility has increased. Tor, for example, has upgraded to a newer version of Firefox from an older one. Tor's most recent version looks very similar to the most recent version of Firefox.

Additionally, Tor has been patched for several security flaws. The Federal Bureau of Investigation (FBI) broke into the dark web's Tor network to determine who was exploiting a security flaw in the Tor browser at the time. Tor responded by upgrading to the most stable version of Firefox available at the time. The use of Tor has increased security.

In 2017, a significant evolutionary leap was accomplished. Before the Alpha release of Tor, rogue nodes could monitor network traffic. Security agencies may have identified and apprehended users through rogue nodes. In 2016, the FBI allegedly used a zero-day vulnerability in Tor browsers to gain Tor users' private data. An attacker could exploit this vulnerability to execute any code on a victim's system, including malicious JavaScript code. The malicious page sent MAC addresses, IP addresses, and hostnames to 5.39.27.226. The most serious threat to Tor-connected computers came from malicious JavaScript and SVG. A hacker (in this case, a member of the FBI) could use this code to steal personal information from a Tor user while leaving no digital traces. Rather than that, memory would be loaded and JavaScript code executed. Malwarebytes discovered and patched the zero-day vulnerability. Tor users now have access to Malwarebytes' Anti-Exploit tool.

According to the researchers, the following flaws also enabled them to spy on and steal users' identities.

The Tor windows and screen's size posed a significant security risk. All Tor browsers now expressly discourage increasing the size of a Tor window. Users were advised not to alter the default width and height of the software. The version of Tor in use puts users' traffic at risk of being monitored.

Mac OS users were forced to accept a flaw in their unique user profiling, which was based on the size of the Mac OS window. Tor's initial release featured a $1,000 \times 1,000$-pixel resolution, and the window should be 200 pixels wide or 100 pixels wide for smaller screens. On Mac OS X, a bug in the Tor browser caused the browser's window to take up the entire height of the dock. Search browsers with a window width greater than 200 pixels but less than 100 pixels. By determining which Tor browsers users are using, the flaw could gather personal information about them.

Due to Tor browsers' lack of a default viewport size, it was easier to incorporate revenue-generating scrollbars. Subtract the area occupied by the scrollbars from the window's size to determine their thickness. The scrollbar size provides information about the user's operating system and computer. Tor made use of 15-pixel-thick Mac OS X scrollbars and 17-pixel-thick Windows scrollbars.

The Tor Project revealed that it would now run on Rust code created by Firefox developers earlier this year. Tor was included by default in new versions of Firefox, and Tor exploited the browser's secretive features, such as those found in Firefox. Tor was previously written in C and C++ and utilized that programming language, and Tor's developers have warned that using C will jeopardize its users' security.

On the other hand, Freenet has seen improvements in security and performance. As a result, the Freenet network can support millions of concurrent users without experiencing any performance issues. Users on the dark web can limit the number of peers they interact with to maintain their privacy. On the other hand, other darknets allow peer-to-peer connections, and Freenet users' darknet activity is no longer traceable. For Freenet, law enforcement faces significant obstacles due to the network's robust security measures.

IMPROVEMENTS IN USER INTERFACE DESIGN

There have been increased efforts to make the dark web more user-friendly. Even novice users can now easily access and use several darknets, thanks to improvements in user interface design. Observed user interface designs fall into two categories: basic and advanced. Level one consists of the darknets surrounding each individual. As previously mentioned, Tor has been upgraded to have the same look and feel as the latest Firefox browsers, and Tor has reused Firefox underlying code. Because Firefox is so widely used, it has become more appealing to users and more user-friendly. The darknet's services have improved their user interface design to a second-level standard. For example, user interfaces on the black markets of the Tor darknet have gotten a major facelift. This site is similar to popular surface web retail sites like Amazon and eBay in the user interface (Figures 16.1 and 16.2).

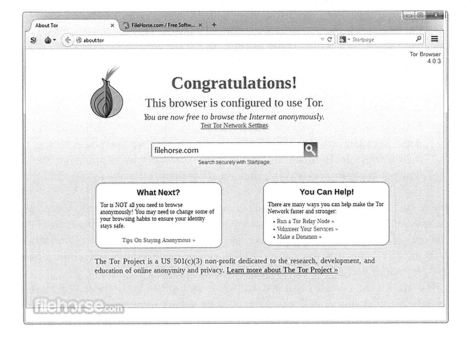

FIGURE 16.1 Tor browser interfaces from the past.

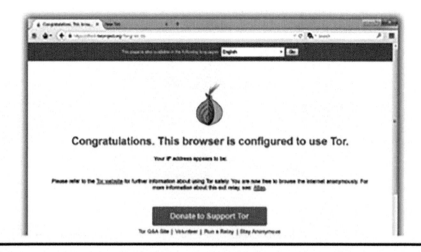

FIGURE 16.2   A new Tor browser interface has been released.

TRUST-BASED MARKETS

Police have allegedly infiltrated the dark web, according to Tor users. With the help of darknet buyers and sellers, they hope to gather evidence against a suspected criminal. Due to this new market trend, trust is increasingly being incorporated into transactional processes. Some markets only allow buyers to invite the market organizers to enter and purchase products. This filtering eliminates any accounts belonging to law enforcement agencies and implicates sellers of illegal goods like drugs. In addition to these safeguards, access controls are in place to ensure a customer's trustworthiness. It's important to consider the age of their darknet accounts, how many people are familiar with them, and how they communicate. Normal law enforcement organizations will either have new and unfamiliar accounts with other users or be curious in their communication to learn more about how things work. It has become more difficult for law enforcement to access markets based on trust. As seen in markets, sellers have tried to reduce the number of dishonest sellers (Figure 16.3).

Customers used to be easy prey for sellers. Cryptocurrency transactions cannot be reversed, so customers who sent money to bogus sellers lost it. On the darknet, there were also police officers posing as vendors. As soon as the marketplaces were shut down, law enforcement began targeting sellers who had registered on the hacked sites. While customers believe they're doing business with the same sellers as before, they're doing business with police officers. Law enforcement officers apprehended several buyers after employing this strategy. A trust-based system, like the one used by Amazon.com, has therefore been implemented in some markets.

After making a purchase, buyers can leave feedback here. A negative review can stifle a seller's business by discouraging potential customers from purchasing this part of the internet. After sending money and not receiving the goods, a buyer complains. They can write a negative review of the shop to warn other buyers. Trust-based trading appears to be the best option for many buyers and sellers. As a result, law enforcement agencies will find it difficult to pose as buyers or sellers.

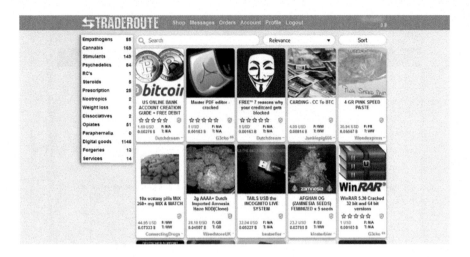

FIGURE 16.3   A marketplace uses a five-star rating system to incorporate user reviews.

CONTINUITY

Severing the head of the mythological monster Hydra would be likened to taking down a darknet marketplace. According to Greek mythology, if a Hydra's head were cut off, two more would grow in its place. Hercules defeated the Hydra by sealing its chopped heads with a specific material that stopped new ones from developing.

> The Hydra was a gigantic water snake with several heads near Lerna in Argos. There have been reports of anywhere from five to over one hundred heads.
>   http://mythencyclopedia.com/Ho-Iv/Hydra.html

On the dark web, users reported seeing the same pattern of head regeneration. When authorities shut down one darknet market, another will inevitably emerge. Because of this, it will be difficult to put an end to all illegal activity on the dark web. In 2011, Dread Pirate Roberts' Silk Road set off a wave of continuity. The FBI took down Silk Road in 2013. They went so far as to put up a banner informing users that the site had been taken over. The black market for illegal drugs appeared to have been shut down on the internet. It wasn't like that at all.

The media pounced on the closure of an advanced, anonymous drug market. Unintentionally, this heightened interest in illicit drug sales by making them more accessible. Demand increased as a result. Drugs, fake currency, driver's licenses, and other forms of identification would require a new market.

There have been two new underground markets created. Hansa and AlphaBay are two of the most popular options. Increasingly popular, AlphaBay now has the greatest number of buyers and sellers. Doing so made it possible for the world's largest darknet market to be built. The market was up and running normally until July 2017, when US and EU authorities decided to close it. They were able to detain Alex

Caves, the company's 25-year-old founder. According to reports, he had a team of ten assistants working with him to keep the site running smoothly. US officials claimed AlphaBay was a dangerous drug supplier, with numerous overdose deaths reported. Overdosing on illegal drugs purchased from AlphaBay was the cause of death for one young lady. Authorities uncovered a market for 250,000 products. There were 200,000 registered buyers and 40,000 registered sellers on the website. Sellers and buyers have transacted in 50,000 transactions since the marketplace began keeping track of internal activities in 2013.

Ten times as many transactions on AlphaBay as on Silk Road were taken down four years earlier. The website servers were located in Lithuania, Canada, the United Kingdom, and France, possibly as a precautionary measure, and seized. During this time, the Hansa market was reportedly taken over by investigators. Users of AlphaBay were migrating to Hansa, which they observed. Hansa's traffic increased eightfold after AlphaBay's demise. Unaware that the website was already regulated, many buyers and sellers created accounts (Figure 16.4).

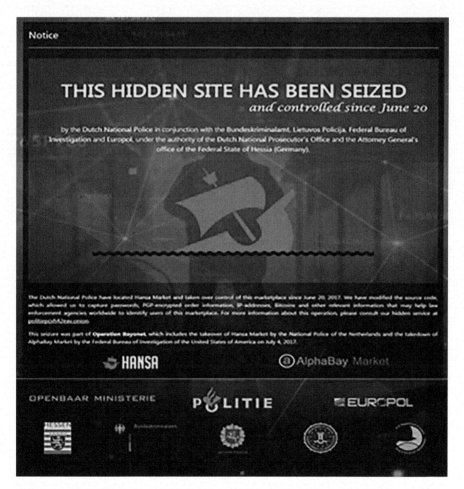

FIGURE 16.4   On the now-defunct AlphaBay marketplace, a notice has been posted.

Many were shocked to learn the amount of money transacted on the website. AlphaBay was linked to the theft of up to $4 million in Bitcoin (at the exchange rate in July 2017). An additional user reported moving $10 from their AlphaBay wallet to another one. Because it's difficult to track Bitcoin, we can only estimate how much was made on AlphaBay between May 2015 and February 2017. Up to $6 trillion is estimated to have been exchanged.

A more successful marketplace emerges whenever a smaller and less successful one closes. It is unlikely that buyers and sellers from the closed market will vanish. This is the market of your dreams. Many marketplaces were shut down in 2017, but Dream Market appears to have survived.

On the other hand, its future is uncertain, as users have reported that the market appears to be under the control of some sort of law enforcement agency. Users are being redirected to a large number of mirror sites. Authenticated users claim that the mirror links do not recognize their login when redirected. There appear to be multiple markets in operation, some regulated by authorities. But it's been a long time since 2013, and the market has survived while all others have closed. The Dream Market appears to be a continuation of the closed markets.

There's also the issue of trying to get better all the time. Traffic analysis and Ross Ulbricht's arrest were made possible because of faults in Tor's code. Some bugs used to work against Tor, but they've since been patched. Cops may be providers or clients to other darknet users until then. Certain markets can only be entered with certain invitations. The faults of previous site administrators have also been erased. Both Silk Road's and AlphaBay's founders passed away in the first week of January. Ross Ulbricht of Silk Road offered Alex Caves' real email address when he asked for coding assistance on AlphaBay. Regardless of who runs the site in the future, no one will ever know your real email address. As a result, it will be more difficult to shut down the next big market.

CRIME PATTERNS

On the dark web, a new kind of crime has emerged. As new patterns emerge, the dark web becomes a hub for cybercrime innovation. There have been numerous patterns found on the dark web, some of which are listed below.

TERRORISM ON THE DARK WEB

Terrorists have shown a growing fascination with modern technology since the 9/11 attacks. ISIS and Al Qaeda, for example, both had social media accounts where they shared videos of their activities. On the other hand, most businesses went to court and had their social media accounts deactivated. As a result, the dark web became their new focus. According to researchers, the dark web is an ideal environment for terrorists. Law enforcement can't keep track of what's going on in the shadows because it's anonymous. Terrorists have discovered that the dark web is a great place to get money for their plots. On the dark web, some websites solicit donations from the general public to aid terrorists in their mission. These sites provide crypto wallet

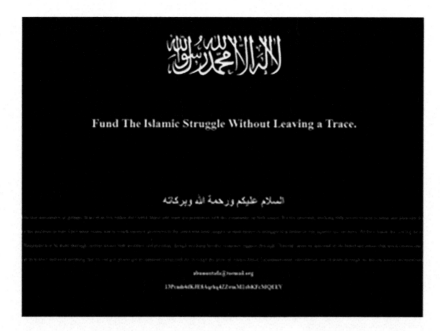

FIGURE 16.5 The dark web has a donation request page for ISIS.

addresses, sending money directly to terrorists. Singapore authorities discovered a dark web page asking for Bitcoin donations (Figure 16.5).

MONEY LAUNDERING VIA CRYPTOCURRENCIES

Money laundering is the process of cleaning up dirty money. Illegal money comes from ransomware, drug trafficking, child pornography, and ivory sales. The money raised by these events must be collected. The money may prompt law enforcement agencies to investigate the robbery or extortion. Until this decade, money laundering was limited to fiat currencies. Switzerland's banks, for example, have strict customer privacy policies. The dark web has become a money-laundering hub since the advent of cryptocurrencies. The perceived anonymity of cryptocurrencies made them initially acceptable evidence-containment measures. However, some cryptocurrencies were weak, and their owners' identities could be easily determined. Mixers are now being used professionally to launder money on the dark web (Figure 16.6).

Due to the volume of transactions made by mixers, authorities cannot locate their owners. You can also use gambling sites. Cryptocurrency owners only need to deposit once, then play and win at a gambling site. A gambling company's involvement in a money-laundering scheme is almost certain. When a player credits funds to the casino, they are combined with other players' funds. After the game, the winner receives a lump sum of mixed coins from all players. A lucky bet can be explained to the authorities if they ask.

MIX MY COINS

Unique code ❓

| ✳ | PLc4HZKSUqS2 |

Bitcoin Address

| B | your_address_1 |

Bitcoin Address #2

| B | your_address_2 | 🗑 |

Add new address

Delay in hours

6 hours

Service fee

1.196%

Start Mixing   Send 1 ฿ receive 0.98604 ฿

Includes address fee

FIGURE 16.6 An example of a Bitcoin mixer on the dark web.

Now let's get down to business. AlphaBay has been linked to USD 4 million in Bitcoin, but only the beginning. The wallet allegedly houses around $10 million in Bitcoin and has seen over $6 trillion flow. Sheep Marketplace, which went silent in late 2013, stole approximately $40 million and Evolution, another darknet market that went offline in 2015, took $12 million with it.

During AlphaBay's exit, an article was written about estimated figures.

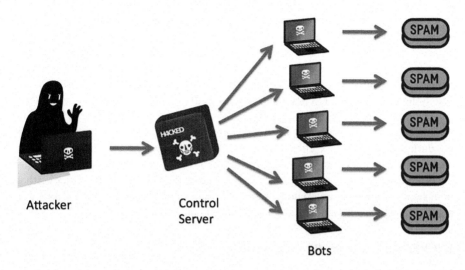

FIGURE 16.7   A botnet is depicted in a diagram.

BOTNETS FOR HIRE ARE INCREASINGLY POPULAR

Malicious software (DoS) attacks launched against organizations are causing more service interruptions, and the dark web is a contributing factor. Botnets are now being used as a new type of criminal activity. Distributed denial-of-service (DDoS) attacks are carried out using botnets and networks of infected zombie devices used to spread malware. As a result of the zombie devices, legitimate requests cannot be fulfilled. Other organizations' hacks are being distracted by DDoS attacks, it appears.

Meanwhile, cybercriminals conduct a second attack on the organization's systems while still dealing with the first. Due to the past success of this attack type, most cybercriminals are employing massive botnets to disrupt businesses. There have been numerous reports of botnets and botnet hiring on the dark web. Numerous attacks have been traced back to the Mirai botnet. Because of its Internet of Things (IoT) base, the Mirai botnet has amassed a sizable zombie device army. The security of IoT devices has been criticized, leaving them vulnerable to hackers. Thus, many botnets have emerged as a result of this. The Mirai botnet is believed to contain over 100,000 zombie devices capable of attacking their intended victims. They can take down a target by flooding it with 1 Tbps of traffic (Figure 16.7).

On the dark web, botnets sell for a surprisingly high price. It is possible to hire botnets for $10 per hour. For a full day, some vendors charge between $100 and $200. These botnets could harm numerous businesses. Botnets can be purchased on the dark web for use elsewhere. Though more expensive, the purchaser has unlimited access to the zombie devices when purchasing this option.

GROWTH OF HACKING-AS-A-SERVICE

Only those technically capable of coding used to hack in the old hacking scenario. People who did not know how to program were unable to cut because they lacked the necessary skills to bring down networks and systems.

However, on the dark web, a new pattern has emerged in which anyone can be a hacker. People are willing to pay for hacker services. As a result, businesses are exposed to significant risks. Dissatisfied employees, for example, should now be considered a threat because they can easily hire third parties to hack into their systems. By disclosing information about their employer, a hacker can simply bring down one system after another. They only need a small sum to pay the genuine hacker's fees. For experienced hackers, this criminal pattern pays off handsomely. They can no longer scour the area for new prey. They simply list the services they offer on the dark web and wait for clients to contact them. Hacking-as-a-service generates a respectable amount of revenue. As a result, their ability to monetize their skills has become easier. Expert hackers can simply charge by the hour for their services rather than steal money from companies, send it to money launderers, and take a cut. As a result, the cash is cleaner and does not require laundering.

INCREASED MALWARE FOR SALE LISTINGS

Dark web vendors now offer malicious codes, programs, and exploits, supporting the idea that today's hackers need not be expert programmers. The term "script child" refers to a new breed of hacker. Hackers who don't have any hacking skills against targets buy and use malicious codes and programs. They put their newly acquired hacking tools and codes to work against a wide range of organizations, which is why script kids have a bad rap. They pose a serious threat because they target one business after another simply for fun and to make a quick buck. Exploits are especially critical in this scenario. These are hacking tools that others can make use of. Security requires encryption code to bypass computer restrictions, such as those placed to prevent unauthorized file modification. A hacker can find dark web code and tools. Exploits are more expensive, and the cost varies based on how widely an attacker can use and exploit them. Older exploits lose their usefulness as time goes on because the target may have received a patch that prevents the exploit from working. A higher failure rate means that new exploits are more expensive. The dark web market for exploits raises the stakes for companies. A hacker's workload has been reduced. It's possible for a hacker to quickly put together a powerful hacking tool using code purchased on the dark web (Figure 16.8).

Organizations are impotent in the face of dark web operations. As a result, they've recruited third parties to monitor all malware markets on the dark web.

As a result, organizations will determine which countermeasures to implement and which patches to apply. The WannaCry ransomware, for example, was rendered ineffective against organizations that had installed the most recent Windows patch. The fix was built after a hacking organization named Shadow Brokers disclosed an exploit that could be used to bypass Windows security protections that prohibit file alteration. As a result, WannaCry's exploit to bypass security protections would fail if all companies were patched. Small crooks will have more attacks as malware for sale catches up.

THE BLACK MARKET FOR IVORY AND RHINO HORN

The ivory trade, according to Interpol, occurs on the dark web. No one has ever seen anything like this pattern before. Smugglers are now selling ivory on the dark web, benefiting from the anonymity of darkness and the secure architecture of cryptocurrencies. It has become more difficult to restrict the ivory trade on open markets since

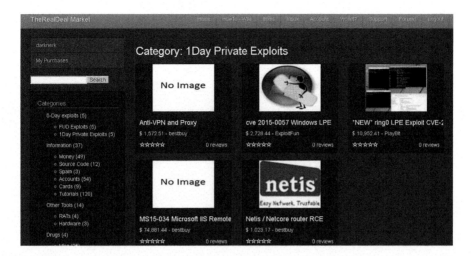

FIGURE 16.8   On the dark web, you can buy exploits.

so many agencies are tasked with doing so. The majority of these companies, on the other hand, concentrate on the physical and surface web markets. A small percentage of underground agents follow the same security protocols as their counterparts on the open internet. Ivory traders have turned to the dark web to communicate and transact because of this gap in the market. There are many anonymous shipping options available on the dark web, and these have proven to be effective for drug traffickers. Cryptocurrencies protect the payment portion.

The ease with which money can be laundered has made it very easy for authorities to go untraced by proceeds from the ivory trade. As a result, the dark web is catching up with the ivory trade (Figure 16.9).

PREFERRED CRYPTOCURRENCIES

Bitcoin was the preferred cryptocurrency for dark web transactions for a long time. Growing concerns over the coin's anonymity, on the other hand, are leading it to lose favor. It is not anonymous due to the blockchain and a distributed ledger. In terms of popularity, Monero appears to be overtaking Bitcoin. Monero is a cryptocurrency that is far more anonymous than Bitcoin. Monero's patented "mixing" algorithms make it more difficult to identify where money flows and who uses it. Only third parties can combine Bitcoin, and it is expensive, costing between 10% and 20% of the total amount mixed. Monero has also demonstrated that it is more reliable than Bitcoin. Bitcoin traded between $4,000 and $19,000 in August 2017 and January 2018 before settling at an average of $8,000 in 2017. These modifications will undoubtedly hamper business interactions.

STOLEN DATA LISTINGS FOR SALE

Since its inception, the dark web has transformed into a thriving black market economy. Some of the most common types of information thieves are hackers and money launderers. Cybercriminals today know how valuable stolen user data is, and they'll

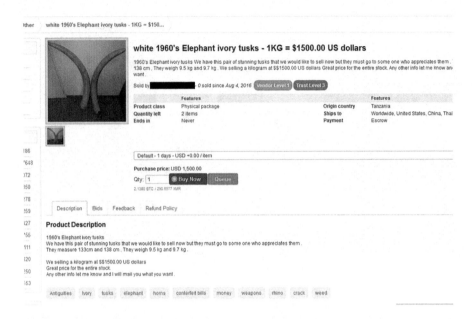

ther   white 1960's Elephant ivory tusks - 1KG = $150...

white 1960's Elephant ivory tusks - 1KG = $1500.00 US dollars

1960's Elephant ivory tusks We have this pair of stunning tusks that we would like to sell now but they must go to some one who appreciates them .
138 cm , They weigh 9.5 kg and 9.7 kg . We selling a kilogram at S$1500.00 US dollars Great price for the entire stock. Any other info let me know an
want .

Sold by [   ] - 0 sold since Aug 4, 2016   Vendor Level 1   Trust Level 3

Features			Features	
Product class	Physical package		Origin country	Tanzania
Quantity left	2 items		Ships to	Worldwide, United States, China, Thai
Ends in	Never		Payment	Escrow

Default - 1 days - USD +0.00 / item

Purchase price: USD 1,500.00

Qty: [1]   ● Buy Now   Queue

2.1380 BTC / 290.8977 XMR

Description   Bids   Feedback   Refund Policy

Product Description

1960's Elephant ivory tusks
We have this pair of stunning tusks that we would like to sell now but they must go to some one who appreciates them .
They measure 133cm and 138 cm . They weigh 9.5 kg and 9.7 kg .

We selling a kilogram at S$1500.00 US dollars
Great price for the entire stock.
Any other info let me know and I will mail you what you want .

Antiquities   ivory   tusks   elephant   horns   conterfeit bills   money   weapons   rhino   crack   weed

FIGURE 16.9   On the dark web, rhino horns are for sale.

do anything to get their hands on it. On the dark web, vendors sell stolen data, previously unheard of. Those who can profit from this data buy it from the vendors. Phishers, for example, could buy the data and use it against their victims. To socially engineer a hacker, buy a data dump with real people's names, addresses, and phone numbers. People may be tricked into sending money by someone pretending to be from a bank or government agency. Recipients will pay without hesitation because the email comes from a reliable source (Figure 16.10).

Because the dark web sells stolen data, organizations must pay third parties to check such listings. Companies may find their sensitive files sold on the dark web before knowing they've been hacked due to high demand and limited availability. As demand for user data grows, more hackers aim to steal it. As a result, consumers are paying more for goods and services.

THREAT MAPPING

A cyber threat map is a map that depicts current or previously recorded active threats from all over the world. Based on information from their security devices or reliable sources, cybersecurity companies regularly create threat maps for use by customers. They draw a picture of where the danger is coming from and where it will go. The maps in this section will be highlighted.

FORTINET

Like Norse, Fortinet provides a cyber attack map. Its threat map is thus a future replay of previously recorded threats. It displays threat statistics for users to crunch on their own in the lower portion of the screen. The threat map from Fortinet can be seen in Figure 16.11.

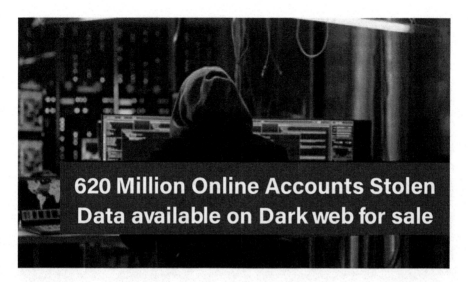

FIGURE 16.10 Selling stolen information on the dark web is commonplace these days.

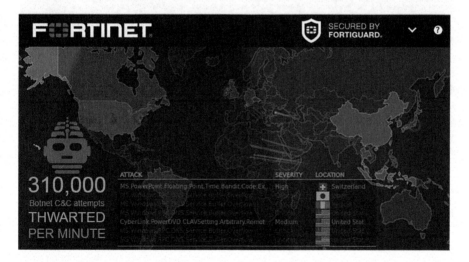

FIGURE 16.11 Fortinet threat map.

Norse

Norse's threat maps are based on historical data, not current threats and events. This threat data is derived from a subset of honeypots used to monitor new attack types and techniques. The screenshot below illustrates an example of a Norse threat map (Figure 16.12).

Checkpoint

Additionally, Checkpoint maintains a 24-hour cyber threat map that highlights possible threats. Each day at midnight, a new threat map is generated when the website

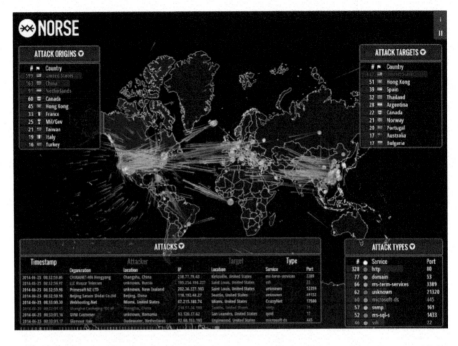

FIGURE 16.12   Map of the Norse threat.

resets itself to reflect the most recent detections. On the other hand, maps from companies such as Norse have a less appealing aesthetic than those from Checkpoint, and the map's overall structure is very similar to that of other threat maps. With Checkpoint, users can view historical data on the top attackers and targets over a month, week, or year, differentiating them from other security companies' threat maps. A threat map generated by Checkpoint security software is depicted in Figure 16.13.

FireEye

FireEye uses a straightforward approach to compiling a cyber threat map. Most of the data that other companies include in their threat maps is omitted by this program, and FireEye only keeps a subset of real-time data in its maps. Because the map data is segmented by industry, it reveals which countries have the most attackers. The below threat map was created by FireEye (Figure 16.14).

Arbor Networks

Arbor's threat intelligence system, ATLAS, produces a hybrid map. Arbor's threat intelligence system, ATLAS, produces a hybrid map. Arbor is a large company with many IP companies as clients, accounting for 300 customers. In total, these companies contribute 130 Tbps of global traffic. DDoS attacks are the most common type of threat that Arbor displays on its threat map, as they are the most common type of attack against ISPs. A screenshot of Arbor Networks' threat map is shown in Figure 16.15.

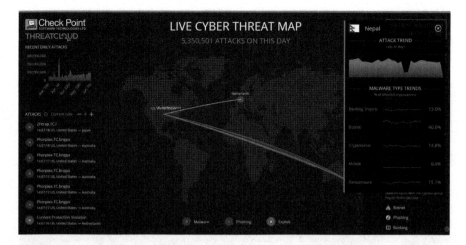

FIGURE 16.13 Threat map with checkpoints.

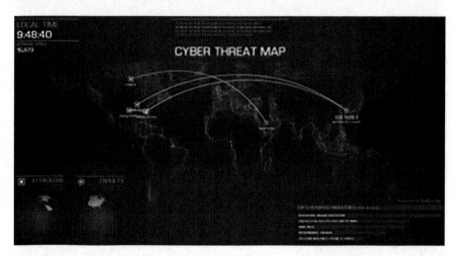

FIGURE 16.14 Threat map from FireEye.

THREAT MAP BY KASPERSKY

A well-known feature of Kaspersky's threat map is its ability to allow users to interact with it. It's made with its tools based on network, website, and email threats. The number of real-time threats increased in 2018 compared to 2017, and this is a warning sign that the dangers are multiplying. The map depicts the following dangers:

MAV—threat detections made by the mail antivirus

OAS—on-access scans or scans performed automatically by the tool when accessing a device.

ODS—On-Demand Scan is a scan carried out by the customer. Internet security software, such as WAV (web antivirus), scans the pages that people

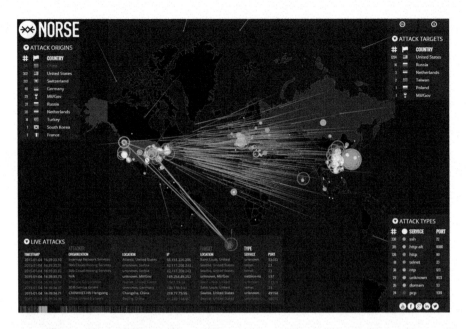

FIGURE 16.15   Threat map for the Arbor.

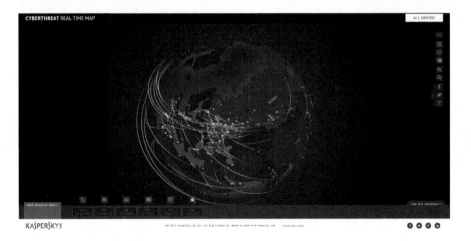

FIGURE 16.16   Threat map from Kaspersky Lab.

access online. The organization's intrusion detection systems. KAS scans emails for spam using Kaspersky Anti-Spam software. Scans for vulnerabilities are performed on computers running Kaspersky software. BAD stands for Botnet Detection Activity.

Figure 16.16 detected per second at the time this chapter was written.

ODS-6945897
OAS-4944569
WAV-7571041
MAV-79578

AKAMAI

As well as monitoring internet traffic, Akamai also has a very effective real-time threat monitor. When the map loads, the user is presented with two tabs. The first tab displays internet traffic worldwide, while the second tab displays the regions with the most attacks. A screenshot of an Akamai threat map is shown in Figure 16.17.

TREND MICRO

There is a small niche in which Trend Micro has created a threat map. There is a lot of useful information to be gleaned from this. Trend Micro's threat map is generated solely by botnet connections, and it reveals the locations of hacker hideouts. Command and control servers are used worldwide to keep tabs on botnets and other malicious software. Because mapping on these C&C servers takes time, the map data is typically 14 days old.

CUTTING-EDGE MITIGATION TECHNIQUES

Given the prevalent impression that cybercrime thrives on the dark web, law enforcement agencies may appear to be failing. Several times, the situation has arisen.

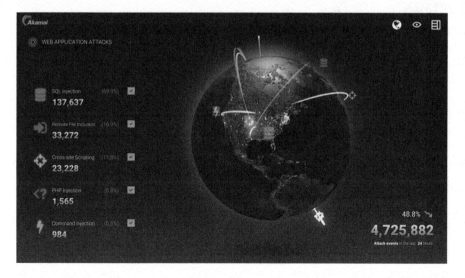

FIGURE 16.17   Threat map for Akamai.

The dark web's law enforcement has been compared to Whack-a-Mole. A smarter mole makes detection more difficult. Dark web threat actors and buyers of illegal items on the dark web are being arrested and prosecuted. Along with law enforcement, individuals and organizations have worked to reduce the threat posed by the dark web. If everyone works together, the dark web can be controlled much more effectively. Here is a list of current mitigation measures.

NETWORK INVESTIGATION TECHNIQUES

Unmasking the real IP addresses of 25 notorious dark web users who visited child pornographic websites was called "Operation Torpedo." The FBI's "network investigative technique" (NIT) to uncover the addresses made the operation a success. The Dutch investigation began. Authorities built a web crawler to look for Tor sites on the dark web. They then isolated the child pornographic websites. They started tracking users' IP addresses and unmasking their identities on darknet websites. They uncovered the IP addresses of Pedoboard, one of their monitored sites. Having this information enabled them to conduct investigations, so there are so few child pornographic websites on the dark web today. The FBI investigated Aaron McGrath after discovering he was hosting malicious websites. The FBI found McGrath and his servers after a year-long hunt. They have valid search warrants for all retrieved servers. The FBI used the warrant to change the code on the servers so their "NIT" could directly access them. This allowed for the identification of specific users. Proxy IP addresses normally protect users, but the NIT method could reveal real IP addresses. The FBI then served subpoenas on their ISPs for the users' home addresses.

MEMEX

Law enforcement agencies have difficulty tracking users and their activities on the darknet because of special browsers like Tor. When it comes to anonymity, law enforcement is doing what they do best: coming up with creative solutions. DARPA's Memex is a dark web search engine. As well as some dark web activity, Memex has aided anti-human trafficking efforts. There are millions of dark web pages that this algorithm can scrape. After scraping them for search queries, it adds them to an index. Compared to other dark web search engines like Tor, Memex delivers superior results (Figure 16.18).

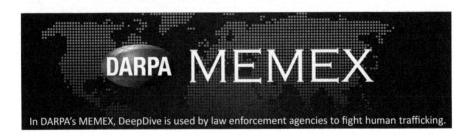

In DARPA's MEMEX, DeepDive is used by law enforcement agencies to fight human trafficking.

FIGURE 16.18   Memex by DARPA.

As a result, Memex cannot reveal the true IP addresses of Tor users because it cannot defeat the anonymity of Tor's users. The dark web can be analyzed by authorities to look for patterns that can be used to keep tabs on the people who use your services. Even if users are careful on the dark web, mistakes can reveal their true data, tracking their whereabouts or identifying them. Authorities attempt to keep dark web-related crime investigations within the legal framework with Memex. Criminal prosecutions employing illicit tactics to collect evidence against dark web criminal suspects have had certain complications.

The courts can throw out evidence that has been obtained illegally. Evidence can now be collected using completely legal methods, thanks to Memex.

SOME CONVENTIONAL TECHNIQUES

To combat some threats on the dark web, the use of high-tech tools by law enforcement is not always necessary. There have been instances where traditional techniques that have worked in the past have been used. These time-honored methods can be traced back to cases like the closure of Ross Ulbricht's arrest and the closure of the Silk Road. The following are the methods.

INFORMANTS

Law enforcement agencies continue to use informants despite their widespread use on the internet and in the real world. A small number of well-known darknet users enjoy the public's trust. They can be persuaded to help with investigations once they've been identified in exchange for a favor or the forgiveness of minor offenses. In addition to communicating with people who would never speak with the police, these informants have access to parts of the dark web that are not available to law enforcement agencies. Sources who know the shadowy dark web markets, such as informants, are invaluable. Cybercriminals and hacking groups that sell hacking tools and services on the dark web can also be identified with their assistance.

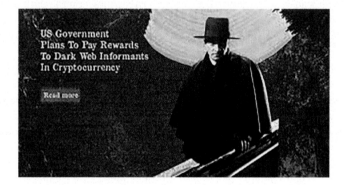

OPERATION UNDERCOVER

Prowlers use the dark web to approach their prey. Pose as a buyer or a seller to gain entry into the criminal supply chain. If they want to appear loyal, they can even

make repeated purchases from a well-known vendor. It's not uncommon for vendors to develop a soft spot for repeat customers, which they can use to learn more about the illegal goods' origins and distribution routes. While plans for Ulbricht's arrest were being hatched, he was supposed to be kept busy on the dark web by government spies. An undercover cop had flagged his Silk Road fake account, and he was in a library trying to resolve it. Other law enforcement agencies staged a brawl in the library, distracting Ulbricht long enough for him to be detained. An arrest made with the help of undercover operations is more effective.

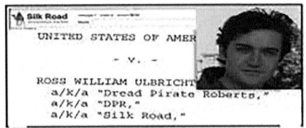

INDIVIDUALS' TRACKING

When people in the United States learned in 2017 that the National Security Agency (NSA) was spying on them and tracking their movements, they were outraged. This was the NSA's reaction to Edward Snowden's revelation that the agency had been secretly spying on Americans for a long time. Because the general public is now aware of this, dark web users will be more cautious in their actions in the future. When a dark web-related crime suspect is positively identified, the next step is to find the person who committed the crime. Law enforcement can easily mitigate threats to public safety because they can track a suspect's every move on the dark web.

POSTAL INTERCEPTION

Authorities can exploit a weak and vulnerable point in their infrastructure to combat illegal dark web purchases of physical goods. Every dark web product must be delivered to the customer's specified physical address. There was a peak in the dark web drug trade when sellers used covert methods to deliver their customers' drugs, which made them successful. Internet traffic can have its origins and destinations hidden, but not postal packages. Dark web drug sales are combated with postal interception. As parcel monitoring becomes more widespread, vendors, on the other hand, become more cunning. They smuggle drugs in with other items in packages. Even though the drugs are concealed inside, the package will appear normal when randomly inspected. Vendors also employ distractions to divert police attention away from the shipments themselves. Most drugs will go undetected because only a few packages can be inspected at a time. The success rate is low because only a few packages have

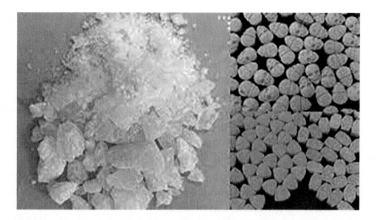

FIGURE 16.19   MDMA-laced package intercepted (type of drug, ecstasy).

been intercepted. Officers can find and arrest them if they are picked up by someone they don't know. Officers can track the drugs' origin and set up traps (Figure 16.19).

Cyber Patrols

Authorities keep a close eye on what's going on in the shadow web. A variety of topics interest them, including well-known suppliers on the darknet, listings on dark web stores, and the use of cryptocurrencies.

Regular monitoring has provided investigators with a wealth of information. Effective cyber patrols require a multidisciplinary team of experienced investigators. It has also aided law enforcement in adapting by identifying current dark web patterns and trends. Law enforcement has concentrated its efforts in six areas.

Memex, a DARPA-developed tool for mapping and indexing the dark web, was discussed previously in this section. Attempts are being made to raise public awareness about government dark web activity. By conducting regular searches to map out dark web services and websites, Illegal marketplaces can be crushed before they acquire popularity.

The dark web exists because willing users exist. Due to the unbreakable anonymity, customers have been led to believe that using the dark web is completely safe. However, there are some tried-and-true techniques that law enforcement can employ. For example, the dark web was cleansed of child pornographic websites, and the investigation focused on both the owners and users of child pornographic websites. Illegal purchases of products and services on the dark web must be discouraged. Due to law enforcement actions, users will be less likely to shop at dark web stores. If you purchase anything on the dark web, you will be arrested. Contrary to popular belief, law enforcement cannot identify dark web users.

Monitoring social media is an efficient way to collect data. This data can be used by law enforcement to stay informed about what is happening in the dark web's most remote corners. Both investigations and public awareness have benefited from social media posts. One of the most trusted sources of information on the dark web is Reddit. Redditors are often the first to know when a deep web market closes. Reddit

users are constantly updating a dark web archive. Anyone can access both new and old dark web services via the dark wiki.

Criminal investigators are now tracking secret services and websites. Immediately after they appear on the dark web, the police are notified, enabling them to formulate a strategy for combating the secret service. As a result, authorities will investigate any new covert service before its widespread dissemination. By employing this technique, you can protect your data from theft while browsing the dark web. Officials can act swiftly to remove a dark web listing selling stolen data and apprehend the seller as soon as it appears.

Utilizing market profiles is a time-tested strategy. Dark web marketplaces selling illegal weapons and drugs were largely shut down by authorities worldwide in 2017: the raid targeted site owners, workers, and customers. Authorities profile dark web merchants, buyers, and other agents. Authorities began by pursuing the owners of dark web marketplaces before shutting them down. Silk Road and AlphaBay, two popular online marketplaces, have been shut down. After removing the heads, the agents began harassing website staff and customers. Authorities in several countries have taken action against distributors and purchasers. For example, customers of Weapons Guy in the United States were detained in large numbers. After selling his wares on the black market, authorities apprehended WeaponsGuy and hacked his account to track his customers. To combat child pornography, the dark web used darknet marketplaces to profile actors. The FBI seized servers and profiled individuals who visited child pornographic websites using special codes. As a result, the visitors would be attacked and taken into custody. Historically, profiling market and website participants was a common practice.

DISRUPTIONS IN DARKNET TRADE

Today's world would be worse if the FBI hadn't shut down Silk Road. Without the shutdown of Hansa, AlphaBay, and other online marketplaces, the world would have descended into a drug crisis. Due to market disruptions, the world is safer, and a major social problem has been averted. Dark web market disruptions frequently target popular or emerging markets and specific individuals critical to their smooth operation.

Additionally, these snags aid law enforcement in assessing the dark web's illicit drug and item trade. Numerous operations have taken place.

That organization's mission was to eradicate the dark web market. Authorities carried out global sabotage in various countries and continents. Disruption is achieved through operations such as Onymous, Bayonet, and Graves. Their efforts were fruitful, as the largest dark web drug dealers were apprehended. Take a look at an intriguing disruption operation involving multiple countries (Figure 16.20).

Operation Onymous, which began in November 2014, targeted dark web markets that incorporated Tor software. Numerous marketplaces have been successfully shut down with the assistance of 16 EU and US agencies. Representatives from the FBI, Immigration and Customs Enforcement, and the Department of Homeland Security were present. We successfully ended the dark web drug and weapon trade and achieved other objectives. Additionally, 17 market employees and vendors were detained by police. This was a significant achievement because technology capable of defeating

anonymity had not matured to its full potential. Additionally, 600 onion addresses have been deactivated to thwart future drug and weapon trafficking (Figure 16.21).

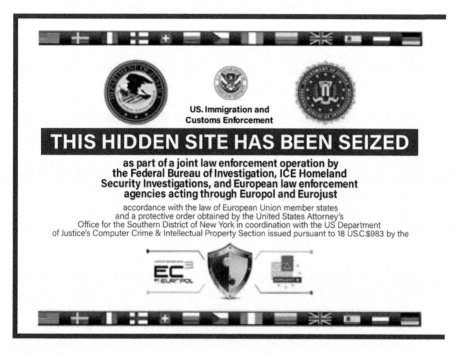

FIGURE 16.20 Onymous left a notice on shut-down websites.

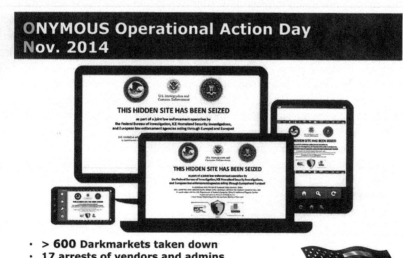

- > **600 Darkmarkets taken down**
- **17 arrests of vendors and admins**
- **13 search warrants**
- **$1 million in Bitcoins seized**
- **€180 000 seized in cash, drugs, gold, silver**

FIGURE 16.21 Accomplishments of operation onymous.

Additionally, 180,000 EU and $1 million in Bitcoin were discovered. Until recently, this project's success was felt globally due to the active dark web. Law enforcement agencies collaborated to disrupt the dark web's illegal item trade for the first time. As a result of this operation, we now understand the dark web's true resilience. Later, new ones appeared on the dark web in response to the originals, and vendors and buyers resumed business as usual in the new markets.

That is why, since then, several agencies have continued to conduct operations. In 2017, these operations ramped up the most, resulting in the near-complete eradication of unauthorized marketplaces. New markets may emerge in the future; these disruptions have helped slow the growth of illegal drug and other item trade.

SUMMARY

This chapter examined emerging dark web trends and countermeasures. It all began with a search for new developments on the dark web. The chapter asserts that the dark web's security, privacy, and usability have improved. They made it easier for newcomers to use while making it more difficult for law enforcement to hack. On the Tor network, the transition from C/C++ to Rust was explained. The upgrade was partly precipitated by complaints about how easily bugs could be used to profile users. Recent reports indicate that improved darknet and marketplace user interfaces are also rising. A trust-based market is discussed in response to law enforcement agents infiltrating the dark web. Both sellers and buyers have faith in one another in these markets. Because fewer markets permit covert operations, the total number of markets is limited. Lastly, the dark web has thrived despite being shattered by law enforcement. According to research, new markets have always emerged following historical takedowns.

This chapter discussed current dark web trends and their associated mitigation strategies. Researchers began by examining changes to the dark web. According to the research presented in this chapter, the dark web's security, privacy, and usability have all improved. Because they made the system easier for newcomers, law enforcement now has difficulty hacking it. The migration from C/C++ to Rust has been explained on Tor. The software was upgraded in response to complaints about how bugs could be used to profile users. Additionally, it has been mentioned that darknet and marketplace user interfaces are improving. A trust-based market is discussed in response to law enforcement agents' dark web use. Both vendors and buyers have confidence in the sellers they are dealing with in these markets. The total number of markets available is smaller due to the limited number of markets that permit covert operations. Lastly, the dark web has thrived despite law enforcement agencies' efforts to shut it down. Each historical takedown, according to research, resulted in the creation of new markets.

17 The Dark Web's Future

The technical aspects of accessing the Dark Web will be discussed in the following chapters.

When I first start using a new piece of technology, I try to imagine how it will evolve in the future. What will it be used for, how will it develop, and who will use it?

In this chapter, we'll try to answer these questions by focusing on the positive and practical aspects of the future, such as online markets and, more importantly, privacy, rather than the buzz you hear about, such as illegal activity, because the future of the Dark Web is inextricably linked to our collective privacy.

So let's travel back in time!

This chapter will cover the following topics:

- What does the Deep Web's future hold for us?
- The TOR Project.
- Dark Web markets.
- Public interest in the Dark Web.

WHAT DOES THE DEEP WEB'S FUTURE HOLD FOR US?

When discussing the future of the Dark Web, we must also evaluate the future of the Deep Web, as the two are intimately linked. As I mentioned in Chapter 1, understanding the Deep and Dark Web, the Dark Web is an extension. The future is almost always uncertain, especially regarding technology, which advances in leaps and bounds and is rarely linear.

Remember that the Deep Web differs from the Surface (World Wide Web) Web in that its sites and content aren't crawled or indexed, so they won't be found using standard search engines.

Organizational content and intranets are part of the Deep Web. Still, they're moving from on-premise solutions to cloud-based environments like Amazon Web Services, Azure, and Google Cloud. Users of these technologies are concerned that the vendors are collecting information about them.

Google, for example, has spoken about the continuous collection of data, both private and public. This is likely true of all search engines and hosting companies, so how businesses and individuals access the Deep Web will change.

Changes will be made to authenticate (biometrics, voice, 2FA, and more) and access the Deep Web.

However, many sites, services, and users will eventually change how they access Deep Web content.

And, you might wonder, what about the Dark Web?

According to predictions, the Dark Web will become more mainstream and difficult to penetrate.

DOI: 10.1201/9781003404330-17

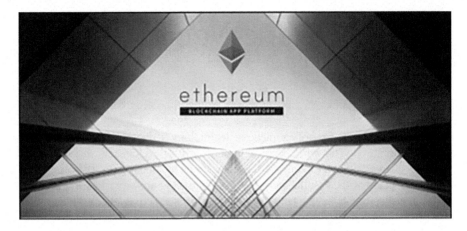

FIGURE 17.1 Ethereum.

The user interfaces of applications designed to access the Dark Web, such as Tor, are improving, assisting the mainstream trend.

DARK WEB CURRENCY

Dark Web currency (such as Bitcoin and other cryptocurrencies) will expand, with many more cryptocurrencies emerging as a result (or cause) of increased Dark Web access.

New, completely decentralized marketplaces based on Bitcoin's (or another cryptocurrency's) blockchain technology will emerge in the future. This technology will ostensibly ensure that buyers and sellers can trust each other and that transactions are safe.

The most popular cryptocurrencies include Ripple, Litecoin, Ethereum, Dash, Dogecoin, Banxshares, Stellar, BitShares, Bytecoin, and Nxt, with more on the way. The screenshots below were taken from various cryptocurrency websites. Ethereum is a decentralized platform that runs on a custom-built blockchain, a massively powerful global shared infrastructure that can move money and represent property ownership. You could think of it as a safe cryptocurrency exchange. Take a look at the following Figure 17.1.

Ripple is a company that offers RippleNet, a secure blockchain-based network for facilitating secure transactions. Take a look at the following image (Figure 17.2).

Litecoin is a peer-to-peer electronic cash system. It's a fully decentralized, open-source global payment network with no central authorities. Litecoin is a well-established alternative to Bitcoin as a means of exchange. Take a look at the following Figure 17.3.

THE TOR PROJECT

One of the ways to connect to the Dark Web is to use the Tor Browser, which we'll go over in detail in a later chapter. It allows users to connect to the Tor network, one of the most popular Darknets.

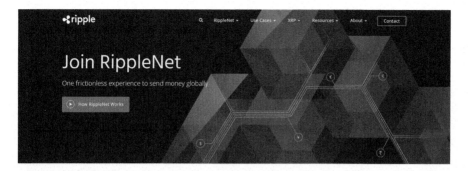

FIGURE 17.2   Ripple.

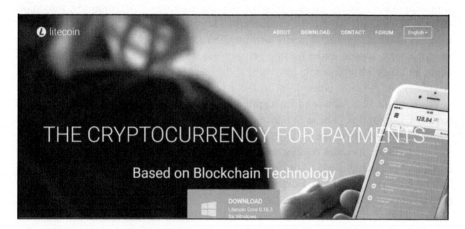

FIGURE 17.3   Litecoin (LTC) website.

The Tor Browser provides anonymity and privacy while surfing Surface Web websites, even if you aren't connected to the Tor network, as we'll see. The Tor Project is focusing even more on privacy and security due to the growing importance of privacy. One of the most significant enhancements is the ability for users to host websites anonymously and privately.

Tor's anonymity is based on relays and random computers (also known as routers or nodes) between which communication is bounced to obfuscate the communication route, effectively hiding the source and destination addresses and protecting their privacy.

The issue stems from Tor's inherent flaws (vulnerabilities), which can be found in any software or technology. For example, if an attacker has control of enough Tor nodes, they can see both the entry point and exit nodes. They will identify the request's origin and will not need to know what happens in the interim. They then change the headers of the packets in the entry nodes, and if those packets are found on the exit nodes they control, they can connect them to someone. Traffic confirmation attacks are the name for these types of attacks.

Tor's onion services feature has been upgraded to address these issues. Users can use onion services to hide their IP address and run a website, chat service, file

sharing, or video-calling platform. Users can use this feature to run onion services behind firewalls. The upgrade will fix several flaws in onion services since their inception.

For example, in the past, a Tor user could manually set up an onion service or use third-party programs like Onionshare. To make the services knew, which only the creator could do, he would have to do it manually. Because the services had to broadcast their existence to several Tor relays, one of the Tor vulnerabilities allows attackers to discover them. Suppose an attacker gained control of enough relays to identify new onion service registrations. They could compile an index of public and private onion sites, then replace onion service relays, effectively taking the sites offline.

Due to the upgrade, the network will randomly assign the relays that each onion service contacts. The relay message will be encrypted, rendering it unreadable by the human operator, but the relay will still obey the command. Additionally, the onion domain names will have more characters. They used to be made up of 16 characters generated at random. They'll now have 56 characters chosen at random. These enhancements should make finding private (hidden) onion services much more difficult, and they also require a password if they are discovered. In addition, the RSA cryptosystem is being phased out in favor of elliptic-curve cryptography, which is more efficient. The Advanced Encryption Standard's hash functions and secret keys have been upgraded. These enhancements aim to appeal to current Tor users and attract newnes users to the service.

Furthermore, as more regular users turn to Tor for ethical and legal reasons, the number of publicly broadcast onion services grows, providing more reliable services.

The following Figure 17.4 depicts the enhancements in Tor's most recent version (December 2018).

DARK WEB MARKETS

Since the operations leading to the closing of Dark Web markets and the ensuing trials are a matter of public record, hundreds of people think of new ways to work and create new markets that are more difficult to destabilize.

It's also worth remembering that many of these markets sell legal goods or services, with the illegal part usually being a lack of taxation on the sale of goods, a lack of vendor documentation, or other bureaucratic issues. Take, for example, Dr. X, who offers medical advice, drug testing, and support to recreational drug users. This is a legal and beneficial service in many countries around the world.

You can even buy and sell vegetables, electronics, and a variety of other items that are completely legal. The original goal of Dark Web markets was to create free, censorship-free marketplaces where prices are fair, there is no middleman between the vendor/seller and the buyer, and neither the market nor the vendor collects information about us.

Many traditional market sites encourage users to gather information to personalize the offered products.

I would rather search independently rather than receive offers or product advertisements, but marketing works nowadays.

Unless we allow it, the Dark Web markets of the future (and even today) will not collect information about us. That's how the Dark Web operates.

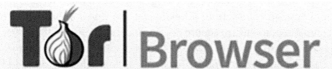

New Release: Tor Browser 8.0.4

by gk | December 11, 2018

Tor Browser 8.0.4 is now available from the Tor Browser Project page and also from our distribution directory.

Tor Browser 8.0.4 contains updates to Tor (0.3.4.9), OpenSSL (1.0.2q) and other bundle components. Additionally, we backported a number of patches from our alpha series where they got some baking time. The most important ones are

- a defense against protocol handler enumeration which should enhance our fingerprinting resistance,
- enabling Stylo for macOS users by bypassing a reproducibility issue caused by Rust compilation and
- setting back the sandboxing level to 5 on Windows (the Firefox default), after working around some Tor Launcher interference causing a broken Tor Browser experience.

Moreover, we ship an updated donation banner for our year-end donation campaign.

The full changelog since Tor Browser 8.0.3 is:

- All platforms
  - Update Firefox to 60.4.0esr
  - Update Tor to 0.3.4.9
  - Update OpenSSL to 1.0.2q
  - Update Torbutton to 2.0.9
    - Bug 28540: Use new text for 2018 donation banner
    - Bug 28515: Use en-US for english Torbutton strings
    - Translations update
  - Update HTTPS Everywhere to 2018.10.31
  - Update NoScript to 10.2.0
  - Bug 1623: Block protocol handler enumeration (backport of fix for #680300)
  - Bug 25794: Disable pointer events
  - Bug 28608: Disable background HTTP response throttling
  - Bug 28185: Add smallerRichard to Tor Browser
- Windows
  - Bug 26381: about:tor page does not load on first start on Windows
  - Bug 28657: Remove broken FTE bridge from Tor Browser
- OS X
  - Bug 26475: Fix Stylo related reproducibility issue
  - Bug 26263: App icon positioned incorrectly in macOS DMG installer window

FIGURE 17.4   Enhancements in Tor's most recent version.

Consider this scenario: you go to a market site and search for something you want, but you don't get any suggestions or offers based on your previous purchases because the market doesn't collect any information about you. That is something I am sure I would enjoy.

Dark Web markets came and went until recently. Usually, they were shut down by law enforcement, but occasionally, they were taken down by hackers.

For example, Agora, one of the most popular markets in 2015, was forced to close due to security breaches (it is unknown if they shut down themselves or were forced to shut down).

Other markets, such as Hansa and Silk Road Reloaded, have expanded their trading to Invisible Internet Project (I2P) channels. They compete with more traditional

marketplaces, such as OpenBazaar, a Bitcoin-based market on the Surface Web that offers an inventory of goods and services. Their framework enables direct trading with customers via the I2P network, multisig addresses (which require multiple keys to authorize a Bitcoin transaction, allowing for the division of bitcoin ownership), and digital signatures to ensure secure communication between the buyer and seller.

After the Hansa site was shut down, this was displayed as shown in Figure 17.5.

In May 2017, OpenBazaar added a Tor mode option, allowing users to join the Tor network as a relay. The homepage is shown in Figure 17.6. This effectively hides and protects their identity, transforming OpenBazaar into a Dark website. Because the creators of OpenBazaar see their market as anonymous, illegal goods may be sold there, but only time will tell if this has or will happen.

OpenBazaar added a Tor mode option in May 2017, allowing users to join a Tor network and become a relay. As a result, OpenBazaar will effectively conceal and protect its identity, making it a Darknet site. Because the creators of OpenBazaar see their market as anonymous, illegal goods may be sold there; however, only time will tell if this has happened.

The following Figure 17.7 shows the OpenBazaar site's FAQs, which explain the concept.

Decentralization has been proposed as a solution for these Dark Web markets, and it may be useful in resolving issues of market operator trust. It offers peer-to-peer sites written in open-source code (which makes them more secure), has a high level of encryption, and is private.

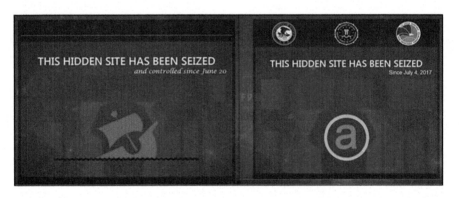

FIGURE 17.5   Seized site.

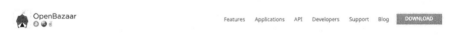

FIGURE 17.6   Homepage of OpenBazaar.

Frequently Asked Questions

What is OpenBazaar?

OpenBazaar is a different way to do online commerce. It's a peer to peer application that doesn't require middlemen, which means no fees & no restrictions.

How does OpenBazaar work?

OpenBazaar connects people directly via a peer to peer network. Data is distributed across the network instead of storing it in a central database.

How are there no fees and restrictions?

OpenBazaar isn't a company nor an organization; it's free open source software. It was built to provide everyone with the ability to buy and sell freely

Who controls the OpenBazaar network?

Nobody has control over OpenBazaar. Each user contributes to the network equally and is in control of their own store and private data

Is Bitcoin the only supported payment method?

Pay with 50+ cryptocurrencies on OpenBazaar: Bitcoin, Ethereum, Litecoin, Zcash, Dash, etc. Seller receives payment in Bitcoin, Bitcoin Cash or Zcash. Their choice.

FIGURE 17.7   FAQs OpenBazaar.

On the Surface Web, centralization is a problem. Large corporations control a significant portion of the internet's real estate. Take, for example, Google, Amazon, and Microsoft. Can we trust them when it comes to our personal information? Let's hope that's the case.

In the future, these marketplaces should incorporate blockchain behavior.

The Pirate Bay was one of the first places where decentralization was attempted. They planned to implement a decentralized version of their site in 2014, which would use the user's machine's resources (buyer or seller). This would ensure that the site would remain up and running as long as users continued to visit it.

Although this did not happen, the concept was sound and could be implemented in the future.

ZERONET

ZeroNet has created a peer-to-peer system that prevents censorship and hosting costs without a single point of failure. Webpage is shown in Figure 17.8.

ZeroNet removes IP addresses and assigns cryptographic keys to websites, like a cryptocurrency wallet address. The site address is the public key, and the private key allows the key holder to create and maintain the site. As peers, users provide the sites to one another.

This is a screenshot of what ZeroNet has to say about itself on its website (Figure 17.9).

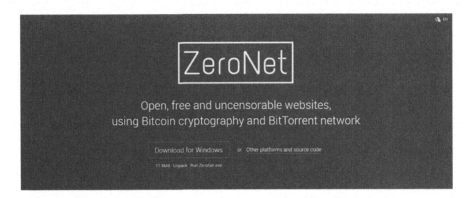

FIGURE 17.8   ZeroNet webpage.

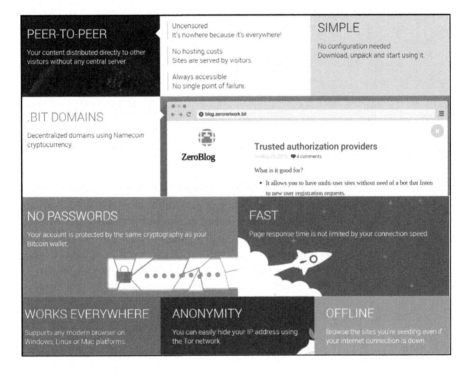

FIGURE 17.9   ZeroBazaar.

ZeroBazaar is an example of a new project that combines ZeroNet and OpenBazaar to provide a truly free and private online market, combining the best of both technologies.

PUBLIC INTEREST IN THE DARK WEB

The Dark Web is gaining popularity, particularly among regular users. These include regular people like you and me, who aren't criminals but are fascinated by the Dark Web due to the media's overabundance of content.

In recent years, television shows (Mr. Robot, CSI: Cyber, and Black Mirror, to name a few), as well as movies, books, documentaries, and other forms of media, have covered the Dark Web, and it appears that this trend will continue.

Massive hacks (Facebook, British Airways, Ashley Madison, and others) are reported in the news, with the theft of personal information and the sale of it on the dark web to the highest bidder.

Following their hack, British Airways displayed Figure 17.10.

All of this has piqued the interest of even the most averse technophiles in visiting the Dark Web just to see what they've heard about.

As we progress through this book, you'll notice that there isn't much of a difference between the Surface Web and the Dark Web, aside from two main factors: the technological one, which requires the use of specific software to access the content there, and the philosophical one, which abounds in anonymity and privacy, making it easier for criminal elements to carry out their activities.

That is why illicit activities are more visible or easily accessible on the Dark Web.

However, as we've discussed and will continue to discuss, taking the necessary precautions to protect your anonymity and security will result in a user experience that is very similar to what you'd get on the Surface Web.

Private delivery services will provide untraceable, secure, and anonymous delivery.

The way most regular delivery services invade people's privacy is one of the things that many people dislike. The goal of these delivery companies will be to provide autonomous and anonymous drones that are invisible to street cameras, radar, and infrared scanners and that deliver packages for a fee paid in cryptocurrency with no delivery logs.

Yes, this could be used to deliver illegal goods. Still, one proposed safety feature would be to detect bombs or other weapons of mass destruction and only deliver items that aren't dangerous to the public. I expect this to be a hot topic, as sending such objects, which could cause harm to others, would be a liability for these delivery services, tarnishing their reputation and reducing their non-criminal market revenue. But since we're talking about the future, we'll just have to wait and see.

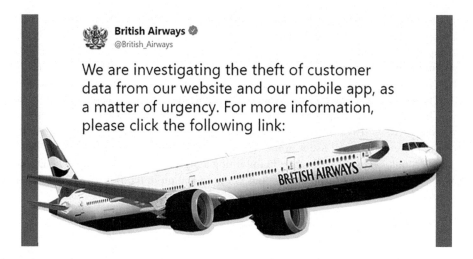

FIGURE 17.10 Darkweb impact.

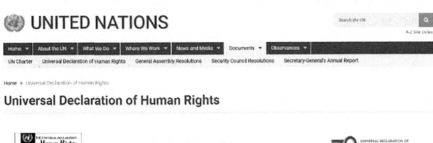

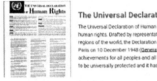

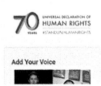

The Universal Declaration of Human Rights

The Universal Declaration of Human Rights (UDHR) is a milestone document in the history of human rights. Drafted by representatives with different legal and cultural backgrounds from all regions of the world, the Declaration was proclaimed by the United Nations General Assembly in Paris on 10 December 1948 (General Assembly resolution 217 A) as a common standard of achievements for all peoples and all nations. It sets out, for the first time, fundamental human rights to be universally protected and it has been translated into over 500 languages.

FIGURE 17.11 UN declaration.

The lack of a legal system on the Dark Web is one of the issues. No organization is supposed to moderate or prevent wrongdoing. Of course, there's a fine line between what's wrong and right on the Dark Web, but it's generally agreed that its original purpose was to increase anonymity and privacy, not encourage crime. Many experts agree that, in addition to scams and theft, actions that harm an individual's or a business entity's privacy and anonymity should be avoided, as should honest trading (buy/sell anonymously and don't cheat the other side). Unfortunately, the reality is a little different, and people with a bad reputation will always try to take advantage of others and do whatever they want without regard for morality.

Thankfully, a Dark Web justice system is evolving. Based on early indications, there will be a peer justice system, with most users deciding how to resolve conflicts and punish wrongdoers.

SUMMARY

As there are nearly limitless ways in which information about us is collected, privacy is becoming increasingly important. In some areas, it is regulated in some way (for example, the General Data Protection Regulation in the EU), while in others, it is completely unregulated.

Human rights, including the right to privacy, have attempted to be standardized by the United Nations (Article 12 of the Universal Declaration of Human Rights).

The UN site with the declaration is shown in Figure 17.11.

The Dark Web acts as a great leveler. A way to use the internet without sacrificing our privacy. It is the start of a revolution that will prioritize our privacy. As a result, more people will use it in the future to communicate, consume content, buy or sell goods, and so on, all while maintaining a high level of anonymity. The Dark Web will be the medium of anonymous communication in the future. Keep an eye out for it.

18 Your Business on the Dark Web

We listed Dark Web case studies and used cases in the previous chapter. As you can see, people use the Dark Web in various ways.

You can search for information, consume content (music, audio, video, written content, and more), participate in social networks, post content, and communicate on the Dark Web. The main difference is which browser you use to access the sites.

Furthermore, suppose you use the Dark Web correctly. In that case, you will be anonymous and able to protect your privacy, which is much more difficult on the Surface Web due to its design and architecture (and use – consider targeted ads, for example).

In this chapter, I'll focus on business applications of the Dark Web, with the hope of providing readers with tips on how to use the Dark Web for their businesses. Based on common and personal experience, my goal in this chapter is to provide ideas and use cases that can benefit businesses.

Businesses can use Tor or any other Dark Web browser to gain anonymity and privacy, which allows them to take actions that would otherwise expose them and the information they're looking for, potentially causing financial or reputational harm.

In this chapter, we'll look at the different types of users who use the Dark Web for various reasons:

- Business companies
- IT professionals
- Law enforcement agencies
- Cybersecurity professionals
- Military organizations

BUSINESS COMPANIES

Many companies set up security-breach information repositories (clearinghouses) to collect data on breaches and attempted breaches. Then they correlate the data and try to spot patterns or definitive information, allowing them to protect themselves better, mitigate risk, and alert internal security teams or even similar businesses to these attacks.

Furthermore, because these repositories are prime targets for attackers, managing them on the Dark Web protects the information and its source Ips from detection and exfiltration.

Employee-focused organizations use the Dark Web as a haven for employees to report irresponsible or illegal activity occurring within the organization without fear of retaliation.

Many businesses also employ analysts who scour the internet for information to assist them. They use Tor to prevent their competitors from detecting what they're watching (to prevent industrial espionage) and compiling patterns or information about them.

We've been focusing on the Dark Web. Still, it's important to remember that there's a wealth of information on the Deep Web, hidden away in organizational databases and systems that aren't indexed by search engines and can only be accessed via a dedicated search system or by signing up and logging into the organizational systems.

The following are a few examples:

- **Sciencegov:** A site that collects scientific articles from US government agencies (Figure 18.1).
- **Academic Index:** A site that provides access to Deep Web academic sites (Figure 18.2).
- **DeepDyve:** A site with millions of scholarly articles that you can only access if you sign up (Figure 18.3).
- **Law Library of Congress:** With over 2,000,000 volumes available, it claims to be the world's largest collection of legal materials, as shown in Figure 18.4.
- **PubMed:** Database of the US National Library of Medicine is as follows, as shown in Figure 18.5.
- **JSTOR:** One of the first and most well-known online libraries. Members have access to over 12,000,000 academic journal articles, books, and primary sources from 75 disciplines (Figure 18.6).

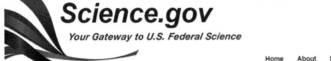

Science.gov
Your Gateway to U.S. Federal Science

Home   About   STEM Opportunities   Translate

Science.gov searches over 60 databases and over 2,200 scientific websites to provide users with access to more than 200 million pages of authoritative federal science information including research and development results.

New:

Find federal research on Coronavirus (COVID-19)

Find out how the COVID-19 search works ❯
For the latest public health information about COVID-19, visit the CDC ❯
For information about the U.S. Government's response, visit USA.gov ❯

Enter Search Terms   🔍

Advanced Search

U.S. Federal Science Agencies' Public Access Plans

How To Submit Research Papers to Funding Agencies

Inventory of Agency APIs and Other Services for Public Access Collections

FIGURE 18.1   Science.gov.

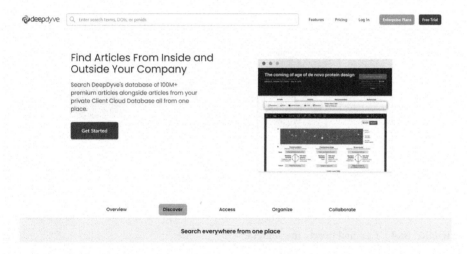

FIGURE 18.2   Academicindex.net.

FIGURE 18.3   DeepDyve.

IT PROFESSIONALS

I'll start with IT specialists. They are usually the closest to the Dark Web and feel most at ease using it, whether because of their profession or simply out of curiosity.

They know how to use VPNs and Tor, among other tools, to gain safe access to the Dark Web.

Many IT professionals require internet access for their jobs, violating company policies such as not using organizational browsers to access site X. This is difficult because they can't do their job without breaking the procedure or policy. To resolve

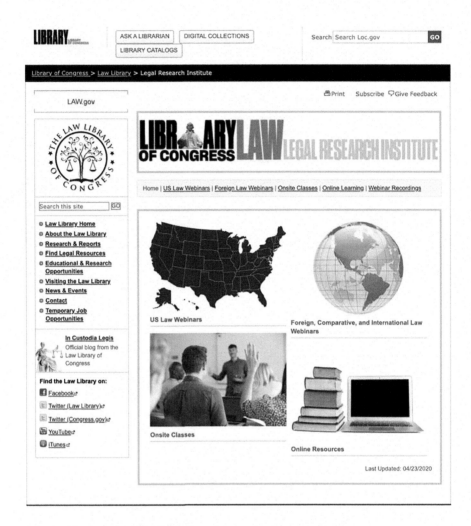

FIGURE 18.4 Law and liberty in congress.

this, IT professionals can use the Tor Browser (or other Dark Web browsers), which will not alert the organization's security systems of this action due to the way Tor works.

Furthermore, suppose IT professionals do this regularly. In that case, they usually have a dedicated machine ready for Dark Web access, which reduces their risk of exposing the organization (monitoring search terms aids attackers' information gathering, so if they can't monitor the searches, this reduces the attack surface), which would naturally conflict with the original intent – preventing the organization from being exposed. These dedicated machines would be equipped with a secure operating system, similar to those discussed in previous chapters, and a VPN, and all traffic would be routed through Tor.

They can also use Tor to test rules that allow or block specific IP addresses or ranges and verify their IP-based firewall rules. Because Tor does not use an IP from

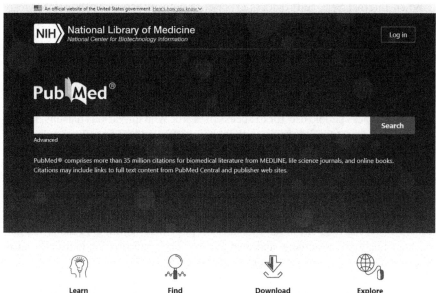

FIGURE 18.5   PubMed.

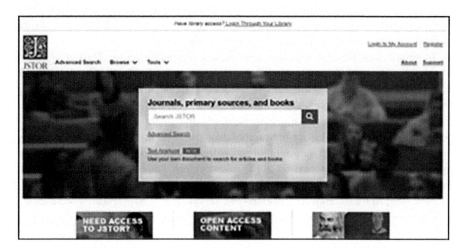

FIGURE 18.6   JSTOR website.

the organizational ranges, IT professionals can verify that the rules are working. Checking whether external IPs have access to internal resources, checking whether organizational Network Access Control systems are working effectively by preventing access to organizational resources from IP ranges that aren't in the organizational pool, and even preventing access from MAC addresses that the organization doesn't recognize are all examples of how this can be done.

When Internet Service Providers experience network issues, such as DNS resolution or routing issues, IT professionals can use Tor to access internet resources, ensuring business continuity.

Similarly, an IT professional can connect to services without requiring a third-party machine or account. Of course, this is dependent on the nature of the network problem. Tor can't solve all of these problems, but it can help with a lot of them, so be aware and always assess the situation.

Many business people use Tor to access the Dark Web for various reasons, including viewing competitors' websites without being affected by any website rules, such as displaying misinformation to machines accessing it from specific IP ranges or sources. Tor obfuscates the source machine's IP address, preventing detection and allowing the user to access resources on the Dark Web and the Surface Web with a very low chance of being detected (if precautions are taken, of course).

The Dark Web is a gold mine of hidden or unprocessed information. As a result, businesses research scientific and business topics there, gaining valuable insights into their business, customers, and competitors. Their information is usually unfiltered and unbiased, allowing them to make better decisions.

LAW ENFORCEMENT AGENCIES

As I previously stated, law enforcement agencies are well represented on the Dark Web. These agencies' officers can conduct undercover sting operations to apprehend criminals and others involved in illegal activity. Tor provides anonymity and hides the officers' computers' source IPs, which would otherwise have blown their cover.

Similarly, law enforcement agencies use Tor to conduct covert online surveillance of services and websites without revealing their identities.

To better understand how law enforcement can operate on the Dark Web, we'd like to tell you about Operation Bayonet, a sting operation led by the Dutch that took down Hansa. A Dark Web market site with 3,600 dealers selling over 24,000 drug product listings, fraud tools, and counterfeit documents. They were able to monitor Hansa's buyers and sellers using various tools and methods and modify Hansa's code to obtain additional information that assisted in identifying those users. They even tricked many of Hansa's anonymous sellers into opening a file on their computers that revealed their location to the investigators. During the investigation, the investigators used both Surface and Dark Web capabilities, leveraging the anonymity provided, to locate Hansa's development server, where new features were tested before being deployed to the live site, seize control of it, and use it to locate the live site servers.

They copied the server's hard drives, including records of every transaction and communication, through its anonymized messaging system. This led them to the founders' IRC chat logs, which revealed the administrators' names and even their home addresses, which was surprising.

Even if you think the operation is over, there is more to come. Instead of arresting the site administrators right away, the Dutch investigators waited to see if they could catch vendors selling illegal goods through Hansa. The operation suffered a setback as the Hansa servers they had discovered vanished, but the site continued to function.

They realized the site administrators had discovered them. Rather than admit defeat, the investigators spent months going over all of the evidence they'd gathered so far, and in April 2017, they got a lucky break: a bitcoin payment had been made from an address found in the IRC chat logs. The bitcoin payment provider discovered an office in the Netherlands using blockchain-analysis software.

When the police contacted a bitcoin payment company, they learned about a Lithuanian payment recipient.

The investigators paused before shutting down AlphaBay after meeting with the FBI, who informed them that they would be shutting down one of the most popular drug markets on the Dark Web at the time.

Vendors and buyers would then look for a new market, which would most likely be Hansa. The Dutch police realized that if Hansa were shut down, they would apprehend more drug dealers and people selling illegal goods. They'd also be able to raise doubts about the security of Dark Web markets and that law enforcement could track them down anywhere, including on the Dark Web.

German police arrested two people suspected of being Hansa's administrators in a joint operation and seized their hard drives. The data from the Hansa server was then transferred to the Dutch police's servers, effectively seizing control of the website.

They then rewrote the site's code, logged users' passwords, and unencrypted the site's messages, revealing many of the buyers' home addresses.

They also disabled a feature that anonymized photos, allowing them to track down more than 50 drug dealers by leaving user metadata embedded in the files.

Files that acted as homing beacons disguised as backup keys for bitcoin received on the website were sent to sellers. The sellers' devices were connected to a specific URL when the file was opened, revealing their IP addresses.

Over 30,000 drug buyers registered on Hansa after AlphaBay was shut down in July 2017, putting them under police surveillance. The number of newly registered users grew to the point where the police had to halt registration for nearly two weeks.

The Dutch police shut down Hansa after 27 days of collecting information about people buying and selling on the site, leaving a notice for anyone who might try to access it.

The site stated, "We trace active people at Dark Markets and offer illicit goods or services." "Is it possible that you're one of them? Then you've got our full attention."

Hundreds of arrests were made, and over $12 million in bitcoin was seized, not to mention the impact on the Dark Web criminal element.

Additionally, in a massive sting operation in the United States, law enforcement agents from multiple state departments – in addition to law enforcement agencies like the Department of Justice, Homeland Security, the US Secret Service, and the Postal Inspection Service (PIS) – apprehended and arrested over 35 dark web traders across the country by posing as traders and vendors.

Furthermore, posting anonymous tips on the Dark Web or using Tor will keep the reporters anonymous.

Of course, there are many, many more.

CYBERSECURITY PROFESSIONALS

Cybersecurity professionals also use the Dark Web. They monitor websites, forums, and blogs where hackers discuss new exploits and hacks and the companies and individuals they've targeted. Threat intelligence and new insights into emerging threats are provided, allowing them to protect their businesses better.

Many systems, including Silobreaker, Webhose, RepKnight, Terbium Labs, Massive, Recorded Future, Sixgill, Hold Security, and AlienVault, collect threat intelligence, some from the Dark Web, and provide information about new malware and exploits, as well as allowing users to detect whether there is jabber about a person or company by searching for a credit card. This enables them to detect new vulnerabilities and exploits and determine whether businesses are being targeted or if their data has been compromised due to a hack.

If you recall, I mentioned that Facebook and other websites have a presence on the Dark Web. The business advantage is that citizens in countries where these sites are blocked can access their services and businesses, thereby expanding their customer base (and ultimately making more money).

MILITARY ORGANIZATIONS

Military organizations use the Dark Web for covert communications, to protect military actions and operations, and to adhere to military data security procedures (such as nondisclosure).

It also allows military, government, and civilian intelligence and counterintelligence units to collect data without disclosing their identities to the people they're investigating.

As you may know, DARPA created and launched the internet to ensure continued communication in the event of a US attack and conceal the physical location of communicating objects. Tor was created due to this, and it further ensures those above.

To combat the use of the Dark Web for sex trafficking, DARPA created Memex, a search engine that tries to find information and leads on the Dark Web.

It has been used by over 33 law enforcement agencies since 2014, costing $67 million to DARPA. It looks for online behavioral signals in advertisements to see if a person is being trafficked.

Despite the difficulty of gathering information about a person on the Dark Web, signals can be found in data, online photos, and even ad text.

To better understand the human trafficking footprint in cyberspace, intelligence capabilities compare collected data to trafficking-related behaviors.

"Our goal is to learn more about human trafficking's online footprint, whether on the dark web or the open web." Wade Shen works for DARPA's Information Technology Division as a program manager.

SUMMARY

Cybersecurity professionals also use the Dark Web. They monitor websites, forums, and blogs where hackers discuss new exploits, hacks, and companies and individuals they've targeted. Threat intelligence and new insights into emerging threats are provided, allowing them to protect their businesses better.

Many systems, including Silobreaker, Terbium laboratories, Massive, Recorded Future, and AlienVault, as well as Webhose and RepKnight, collect threat intelligence, some from the Dark Web, and provide information about new malware and exploits. They also allow users to detect whether there is jabber about a person or company by searching for a credit card. This enables them to detect new vulnerabilities and exploits and determine whether businesses are being targeted or if their data has been compromised due to a hack.

If you recall, I mentioned that Facebook and other websites have a presence on the Dark Web. The business advantage is that citizens in countries where these sites are blocked can access their services and businesses, thereby expanding their customer base (and ultimately making more money).

Glossary

ACSC	Australian Cyber Security Centre
AI	Artificial Intelligence
AM	Anti-Malware
AOL	An American Web Portal
API	Application Programming Interfaces
ASIC	Australian Securities and Investments Commission
ATLAS	Arbor's Threat Intelligence System
ATM	Automated Teller Machines

"B"

BAD	Botnet Detection Activity
BTC	Bitcoin

"C"

CIA	Code Injection Attacks
CIA	Confidentiality, Integrity, Authenticity
CMS	Content Management System
CPU	Central Processing Unit
CSI	Crime Scene Investigation
CTA	Cumulative Timeline Analysis

"D"

DARPA	Defense Advanced Research Projects Agency
DDoS	Distributed Denial of Service
DEA	Drug Enforcement Administration
DFRWS	Digital Forensics Framework
DHL Courier	Dalsey, Hillblom, and Lynn (International Courier)
DNS	Domain Name System
DOJ	Department of Justice
DoS	Denial of Service
DSS	Decision Support System
DW	Dark Web

"E"

EEA	European Economic Area
ERP	Enterprise Resource Planning
Eth	Ethereum
EU IRU	Europol's European Union Internet Referral Unit

"F"

FBI	Federal Bureau of Investigation
FTK	Forensic Toolkit

"G"

GDPR	General Data Protection Regulation
GPU	Graphics Processing Unit

"H"

HDFS	Hadoop's Distributed File System
HS	Homeland Security
HTML	HyperText Markup Language

"I"

I2P	Invisible Internet Project
IDS	Intrusion Detection Systems
IoT	Internet of Things
IP	Internet Protocol
IRC	International Rescue Committee
ISIS	Islamic State of Iraq and the Levant
ISPs	Internet Service Providers
ITU	International Telecommunications Union

"K"

KAS	Kaspersky Anti-Spam

"L"

LEA	Law Enforcement Agents/Agencies
LTC	Litcoin

"M"

MAV	Mail Antivirus
WEKA	Machine Learning Software in Java
MDMA	Methylenedioxy-N-Methamphetamine
MPAA	Motion Picture Association of America
XMR	Monero Crypto Coin

"N"

NAC	Network Access Control
NATO	North Atlantic Treaty Organization
NCA	National Crime Agency
NIT	Network Investigative Technique
NLP	Natural Language Processing
NSA	National Security Agency
NVD	National Vulnerability Database
IT	New Information Technology

"O"

ODS	On-Demand Scan
OSINT	Open-Source Intelligence
OTR	Off-the-Record

"P"

PII	Personally Identifiable Information
PIS	Postal Inspection Service

"R"

RaaS	Ransomware as a Service
RAT	Remote Access Trojans
ROI	Return on Investment

RSA	Ron Rivest, Adi Shamir and Leonard Adleman – RSA is a public-key cryptosystem
XRP	Ripple

"S"

SN	Social Network
SQL	Structured Quarry Language

"T"

TB	Tera Bite
2FA	Two Factor authentication

"U"

URL	Uniform Resource Locator
USSS	US Secret Service

"V"

VM	Virtual Machine
VNC	Virtual Network Computing
VPN	Virtual Private Network

"W"

WAV	Web Antivirus
WWW	World Wide Web

Bibliography

[1] Global Communication in the Cyberworld. (2019). *Movement and Time in the Cyberworld* (pp. 126–137). https://doi.org/10.1515/9783110661033-007

[2] Huber, E. (2019). Cybercrime. *Cybercrime*, 21–29. https://doi.org/10.1007/978-3-658-26150-4_3

[3] Ali, A., Jadoon, Y. K., Dilawar, M. U., Qasim, M., Rehman, S. U., & Nazir, M. U. (2021, April). Robotics: Biological Hypercomputation and Bio-Inspired Swarms Intelligence. In *2021 1st International Conference on Artificial Intelligence and Data Analytics (CAIDA)* (pp. 158–163). IEEE.

[4] Dolliver, D. S., & Kenney, J. L. (2016). Characteristics of drug vendors on the tor network: A crypto market comparison. *Victims Offenders*, *11*(4), 600–620.

[5] Wasielewski, A. (2021). *From City Space to Cyberspace: Art Squatting, and Internet Culture in the Netherlands.* Amsterdam, the Netherlands: Amsterdam University Press. https://doi.org/10.5117/9789463725453

[6] Mohsin, K. (2021). The internet and its opportunities for cybercrime - Interpersonal cybercrime. *SSRN Electronic Journal.* https://doi.org/10.2139/ssrn.3815973

[7] Akhgar, B., Gercke, M., Vrochidis, S., Gibson, H., & SpringerLink (Online service). (2021). *Dark Web Investigation.* Springer Nature eBook.

[8] DNStats. (2019). Dark Net Stats [Online]. Available at: https://dnstats.net/

[9] Defining the workforce and training array for the cyber risk management and cyber resilience methodology of an army. (2020). *Proceedings of the 19th European Conference on Cyber Warfare.* https://doi.org/10.34190/ews.20.114

[10] Dingledine, R., Mathewson, N., & Syverson, P. (2004). *Tor: The Second-Generation Onion Router.* Washington, DC: Naval Research Lab.

[11] Jones, sir Kenneth Lloyd, (Sir Ken), (born 13 June 1952) (2009). Global counter-terrorism, policing and cybersecurity consultant since 2015; Defence and security adviser, British Embassy, Washington, DC, 2013–14. Who's Who. https://doi.org/10.1093/ww/9780199540884.013.250305

[12] Weimann, G. (2004). *Cyberterrorism: How Real Is the Threat?* (Vol. 31). Washington, DC: United States Institute of Peace.

[13] Ahmed, K. (2021). Canada's Cybersecurity in a Globalized Environment. In *Routledge Companion to Global Cyber Security Strategy* (pp. 451–462). https://doi.org/10.4324/9780429399718-38

[14] Fishwick, M. W. (2021). Cyberspace. *Popular Culture*, 140–143. https://doi.org/10.4324/9781315865355-30

[15] Bhatele, K. R., Shrivastava, H., & Kumari, N. (2021). The Role of Artificial Intelligence in Cybersecurity. In *Research Anthology on Artificial Intelligence Applications in Security* (pp. 1806–1823). https://doi.org/10.4018/978-1-7998-7705-9.ch079

[16] Sandler, T. (2018). Role of terrorist groups. *Terrorism.* https://doi.org/10.1093/wentk/9780190845841.003.0003

[17] Zhao, H. (2021). Cyberspace & Sovereignty. https://doi.org/10.1142/12027

[19] Owen, T. (2020). CyberTerrorism: Some insights from Owen's genetic-social framework. In: Owen, T., & Marshall, J. (eds) *Rethinking Cybercrime.* Cham, Switzerland: Palgrave Macmillan (pp. 3–22). https://doi.org/10.1007/978-3-030-55841-3_1

[20] Mitră, S. (2020). The structure of cyberattacks. *International Journal of Information Security and Cybercrime*, *9*(1), 43–52. https://doi.org/10.19107/ijisc.2020.01.06

[21] Brennan, A. M. (2018). The network-based structure of transnational terrorist groups: An analysis of their effectiveness in perpetrating terrorist attacks. *Transnational Terrorist Groups and International Criminal Law*, 21–32. https://doi.org/10.4324/9781315264981-2

[22] Amores, R., & Paganini, P. *The Deep Dark Web: The Hidden World* (Vol. 1). Seattle, WA.

[23] CreateSpace Independent Publishing Platform (2014).

[24] Bartlett, J. (2016). *The Dark Net: Inside the Digital Underworld*. Brooklyn, NY: Melville House.

[25] Bishop, M. (2004). *Introduction to Computer Security*. Boston, MA: Addison Wesley Professional.

[26] Chen, H. (2012). *Dark Web: Exploring the Data Mining the Dark Side of the Web*. New York: Springer.

[27] Eric, A. F. (2016). Cybersecurity Issues, and Challenges. In *Brief, Congressional Research Service (CRS) Report- R43831*, August 12, 2016. Available at: https://crs.gov

[28] Henderson, L. (2013). *Darknet: A Beginner's Guide to Staying Anonymous Online*. Seattle, WA: CreateSpace Independent Publishing Platform. Available at: https://turbofuture.com/internet/A-Beginners-Guide-to-Exploring-the-Darknet

[29] https://theguardian.com/technology/2009/nov/26/dark-side-internet-freenet

[30] https://deepweb-sites.com/

[31] ITU Publication (2012). Understanding cybercrime: phenomena, challenges, and legal response, September 2012. Available at: www.itu.int/ITU-D/cyb/cybersecurity/legislation.html

[33] Kim, P. (2014). *The Hacker Playbook: Practical Guide to Penetration Testing*. Seattle, WA: CreateSpace Independent Publishing Platform.

[34] Lee, N. (2015). *Counterterrorism and Cybersecurity: Total Information Awareness* (2nd ed). New York: Springer.

[35] Nikola, Z. (2015). *Computer Security and Mobile Security Challenges*. ResearchGate. Available at: https://researchgate.net/publication/298807979

[36] Rogers, D. (2013). *Mobile Security: A Guide for Users*. Copper Horse Solutions Limited.

[37] Singer, P. W., & Friedman, A. (2014). *Cybersecurity and Cyberwar: What Everyone Needs to Know*. New York: Oxford University Press.

[38] State of Alabama Information Services Division, Why Cyber Security Is Important. Available at: www.cybersecurity.alabama.gov. Retrieved on November 20, 2016.

[39] Wu, C. H., & Irwin, J. D. (2013). *Introduction to Computer Networks and Cybersecurity*. Boca Raton, MA: CRC Press.

[40] Ali, A., Shehzad, K, Farid, Z., & Farooq, M. U. (2021, June). Artificial intelligence potential trends in mMilitary. In *Foundation University Journal of Engineering and Applied Sciences* (Vol 2, No 1, pp. 20–30).

[41] Ali, D. (2021). Artificial intelligence and criminal liability: Challenges in articulation of legal aspects for counter-productive actions of machine learning. *International Journal of Instructional Technology and Educational Studies*, 2(3), 13–20. https://doi.org/10.21608/ihites.2021.90657.1049

[42] Khan, K. F., Ali, A., Khan, Z. F., & Siddiqua, H. (2021, November). Artificial Intelligence and Criminal Culpability. In *2021 International Conference on Innovative Computing (ICIC)* (pp. 1–7). IEEE.

[43] Alkhatib, B., & S. Basheer, R. (2019a). Mining the dark web: A novel approach for placing a dark website under investigation. *International Journal of Modern Education and Computer Science*, *11*(10), 1–13. https://doi.org/10.5815/ijmecs.2019.10.01

[44] Al-Nabki, M. W., Fidalgo, E., Alegre, E., & Fernández-Robles, L. (2019). ToRank: Identifying the most influential suspicious domains in the Tor network. *Expert Systems With Applications*, *123*, 212–226. https://doi.org/10.1016/j.eswa.2019.01.029

[45] Broadhurst, R., Ball, M., & Trivedi, H. (2020). Fentanyl availability on darknet markets. *Trends and Issues in Criminal Justice, No. 590.* Canberra, Australia: Australian Institute of Criminology. Available at: https://www.aic.gov.au/publications/tandi/tandi590

[46] Cimpanu, C. (2019, April 30). *Dark Web Crime Markets Targeted by Recurring DDoS Attacks.* ZDNet. Available at: https://www.zdnet.com/article/dark-web-crime-markets-targeted-by-recurring-ddos-attacks/

[47] Martin, J., Munksgaard, R., Coomber, R., Demant, J., & Barratt, M. J. (2020). Selling drugs on darkweb cryptomarkets: Differentiated pathways, risks and rewards. *The British Journal of Criminology, 60*(3), 559–578.

[48] Owenson, G., Cortes, S., & Lewman, A. (2018). The darknet's smaller than we thought: The life cycle of Tor hidden services. *Digital Investigation, 27,* 17–22. https://doi.org/10.1016/j.diin.2018.09.005

[49] Maimon, D., Ouellet, M., Swahn, M. H., Strasser, S. M., Feizollahi, M. J., Zhang, Y., & Sekhon, G. (2019, July). Python Scrapers for Scraping Cryptomarkets on Tor. In *Security, Privacy, and Anonymity in Computation, Communication, and Storage: 12th International Conference, SpaCCS 2019, Atlanta, GA, July 14–17, 2019, Proceedings* (Vol. 11611, p. 244). Springer.

[50] Kamphausen, G., & Werse, B. (2019). Digital figurations in the online trade of illicit drugs: A qualitative content analysis of darknet forums. *International Journal of Drug Policy, 73,* 281–287. https://doi.org/10.1016/j.drugpo.2019.04.011

[51] Adewopo, V., Gonen, B., Varlioglu, S., & Ozer, M. (2019). Plunge into the Underworld: A Survey on Emergence of Darknet. In: *2019 International Conference on Computational Science and Computational Intelligence (CSCI)* (pp. 155–159). IEEE.

[52] Arora, T., Sharma, M., & Khatri, S. K. (2019). Detection of Cyber Crime on Social Media Using Random Forest Algorithm. In: *2019 2nd International Conference on Power Energy, Environment and Intelligent Control (PEEIC)* (pp. 47–51). IEEE.

[53] Ozer, M., Varlioglu, S., Gonen, B., & Bastug, M. (2019). A Prevention and a Traction System for Ransomware Attacks. In: *2019 International Conference on Computational Science and Computational Intelligence (CSCI)* (pp. 150–154). IEEE. Available at: https://arxiv.org/pdf/2001.02282.pdf

[54] Zenebe, A., Shumba, M., Carillo, A., Cuenca, S. (2019). Cyber Threat Discovery From Dark Web. In: *EPiC Series in Computing* (Vol. 64, pp. 174–183). EasyChair. Available at: https://doi.org/10.29007/nkfk

[55] Ali, A., Septyanto, A. W., Chaudhary, I., Al Hamadi, H., Alzoubi, H. M., & Khan, Z. F. (2022, February). Applied Artificial Intelligence as Event Horizon of Cyber Security. In *2022 International Conference on Business Analytics for Technology and Security (ICBATS)* (pp. 1–7). IEEE.

Index